Mega-events and Urban Image Construction

T0298897

While societies shape the way their cities look and are represented, urban images, in turn, nurture and structure social relations in multiple ways. Nowhere is this dialectical relationship between social processes and urban representations more visible than in the hosting of global spectacles such as the FIFA World Cup and the Olympic Games, which both embody some of society's deepest dreams and desires.

The focus of this book is the image of cities. It is not only interested in the mechanisms of urban image construction but also in the politics of such a phenomenon, especially its social impacts in terms of representation and right to the city. The book investigates the complex power relationships that underscore the production of the urban landscape and the construction and diffusion of urban images, especially in the context of urban mega-events. It uses the notion of urban image construction as a lens through which to examine the mega-event spectacle, with chapters exploring the physical, social and political dimensions of the imagineering process as well as emerging resistance to controversial initiatives. Through an analysis of event-related urban construction efforts in Rio de Janeiro and Beijing, this book examines the effects of mega-events upon the construction of an exclusive vision of urbanity. It demonstrates how mega-events are increasingly utilized by local political and economic elites to reconfigure power relations, strengthen their hold upon the urban territory and exclude vulnerable population groups.

The book thus offers a critical analysis of the practice of urban image construction, and will be of interest to those working in geography, urban studies, tourism, sport studies, development studies and politics.

Anne-Marie Broudehoux is Associate Professor at the School of Design of the University of Quebec at Montreal, Canada. She received her doctoral degree in architecture from the University of California at Berkeley in 2002. She is the author of *The Making and Selling of Post-Mao Beijing* (2004), which was awarded the 2004–2005 International Planning History Society (IPHS) book prize in 2006. She has published several book chapters and articles on processes related to urban image construction in the context of mega-event preparation, on aspects ranging across tourism development, planning, architecture and social reforms, especially regarding Beijing and Rio de Janeiro.

Routledge Studies in Urbanism and the City

This series offers a forum for original and innovative research that engages with key debates and concepts in the field. Titles within the series range from empirical investigations to theoretical engagements, offering international perspectives and multidisciplinary dialogues across the social sciences and humanities, from urban studies, planning, geography, geohumanities, sociology, politics, the arts, cultural studies, philosophy and literature.

For a full list of titles in this series, please visit www.routledge.com/series/RSUC

Mega-Urbanization in the Global South
Fast cities and new urban utopias of the postcolonial state
Edited by Ayona Datta and Abdul Shaban

Green Belts
Past; present; future?
John Sturzaker and Ian Mell

Spiritualizing the City
Agency and resilience of the urban and urbanesque habitat
Edited by Victoria Hegner and Peter Jan Margry

The Latino City
Urban planning, politics, and the grassroots
Erualdo R. Gonzalez

Rebel Streets and the Informal Economy
Street trade and the law
Edited by Alison Brown

Mega-events and Urban Image Construction
Beijing and Rio de Janeiro
Anne-Marie Broudehoux

Mega-events and Urban Image Construction

Beijing and Rio de Janeiro

Anne-Marie Broudehoux

Routledge
Taylor & Francis Group

LONDON AND NEW YORK

First published 2017
by Routledge
2 Park Square, Milton Park, Abingdon, Oxon OX14 4RN

and by Routledge
52 Vanderbilt Avenue, New York, NY 10017

First issued in paperback 2020

Routledge is an imprint of the Taylor & Francis Group, an informa business

British Library Cataloguing in Publication Data
A catalogue record for this book is available from the British Library

Library of Congress Cataloging in Publication Data
A catalog record for this book has been requested

ISBN 13: 978-0-367-66794-8 (pbk)
ISBN 13: 978-1-138-22817-7 (hbk)

Typeset in Times New Roman
by Saxon Graphics Ltd, Derby

I dedicate this book to the two most important people in my life, Thomas and Gabriella.

Contents

Figures

Preface

There is much to be learned from studying how societies shape and transform their cities. As our principal habitat and the site of most human activity, cities are complex social, territorial, and economic entities produced by human genius, creativity and enterprise. While societies shape the way urban environments are built, organized, and represented, urban environments, in turn, nurture and structure social relations. The way cities are envisioned, imagined and represented thus allows rich insights into the values, priorities and ideals that inspire their society as well as the biases, prejudices and ideologies that govern it.

This book is concerned with the image of cities. It is not only interested in the mechanisms of urban image construction and the various instruments and strategies used in the production and diffusion of urban representations, but its also concerned with the politics of such imaging endeavours. The book investigates the complex power struggles that underscore the transformation of the urban landscape as well as the multiple social impacts that result from these alterations. Nowhere is the dialectical relationship between cities, as social, material and spatial objects, and their representation more visible than in the hosting of global spectacles such as the FIFA World Cup and the Olympic Games. As exacerbated embodiments of society's deepest ambitions, dreams, and aspirations, large-scale media events like World Exhibitions, international conferences and major sporting competitions represent unique occasions to study the production and consumption urban images.

With their vast media coverage and unrivalled branding power, mega-events constitute rare promotional opportunities for their host cities and the chance to launch large-scale urban regeneration programmes. This book sustains that mega-events are increasingly instrumentalized by local political and economic elites to reconfigure power relations, strengthen their hold upon the urban territory and exclude certain population groups from the decision-making process. Through an analysis of event-related urban construction efforts in Rio de Janeiro and Beijing, two recent Olympic host cities marked by sharp social inequalities, it examines the effects of mega-events upon the construction of an exclusive and increasingly revanchist vision of urbanity. It suggests that these events facilitate the state-assisted privatization and commodification of the urban realm in ways that serve the needs of capital while exacerbating socio-spatial segregation, power imbalance and conflicts.

Acknowledgements

This book is the result of years of research, much of it financed by a grant for new researching professors from Quebec's Society and Culture Research Fund (FRSCQ) (2008–2011) as well as by a research group grant from the same organisation for the *Groupe interuniversitaire de recherche sur les paysages de la représentation, la ville et les identités urbaines*, (2009–2013) headed by Lucie K. Morisset. A more recent grant from the Social Sciences and Humanities Research Council of Canada (2015–2019) has also helped finance several research trips to Rio de Janeiro to conduct fieldwork in the months leading to the Olympic Games. I also received logistical support from my home institution, the School of Design at the University of Quebec at Montreal, as well as from the Faculty of Arts. I would also like to thank the University of Quebec for the sabbatical year that allowed me to put together and write this book.

This research would not have been possible without the collaboration of many Brazilian academics, who have been very generous in including me in their research groups, and have become dear friends. These include Carlos Vainer, at the Federal University of Rio de Janeiro, Fernanda Sánchez at the Fluminense Federal University in Niteroi and Gilmar Mascarenhas at the State University of Rio de Janeiro. Three close collaborators, Nelma Gusmão de Oliveira, João Monteiro and Helena Galiza, deserve special gratitude for their help, friendship and constant encouragement, especially regarding my slowly improving Portuguese language skills.

I would also like to thank several scholars, many of whom have become good friends, and who have helped me along the way, inviting me to present my work, collaborating on projects and encouraging me to submit articles to collective book projects. These include John Horne, Chris Gaffney, Lucia Capanema, Nezar AlSayyad, Hyun Bang Shin, Sofia Shwayri, Clara Irazabal, Heba Farouk, Garrett Jones, Jim Freeman and many more. I would also like to express my gratitude to several of my students at UQAM for their interest, their hard work and their collaboration.

Finally, I would like to thank my children, my parents, my partner, for their unfaltering patience, support and affection throughout the process of writing this book. Merci mes chéris.

Introduction

The dark side of place image production – between Faust and Dorian Gray

We live in an image society. Never in history have people been so influenced and preoccupied by images and representations. In the age of the ubiquitous 'selfie', we consume, produce and share images at a rate and in quantities unimaginable just a few decades ago. Images are everywhere, they define and engross us, and, as this book suggests, they have an increasingly large impact upon our lives, conditioning our behaviour, determining our life choices, motivating our actions and shaping our identities.

We also live in what has largely become an urban society. Cities have become our principal habitat, and the site of most human activity. As complex, man-made environments, cities are the product of human genius and creativity, shaped by social relations and enterprise. As the concretization of human ambitions, they are also contested terrains, and the site of political strife and power struggles over the control of resources and territories. Over the centuries, these conflicts and trials have shaped urban agglomerations and left their mark on their representations.

This book is concerned with the image of cities. It investigates the complex, dialectical relationship that exists between cities, as social, material and spatial objects, and their representations. While societies shape the way their cities look and are represented, urban images, in turn, nurture and structure social relations in multiple ways (Lefebvre 1991; Massey 2005). This book examines how images are constructed, transformed and manipulated, and the impact these representations have upon different population groups. It is particularly concerned with one major driver in the contemporary production of urban images: mega-events, especially global-scale sporting spectacles. As exacerbated representations of society's dreams and desires, in their most extravagant and superlative dimensions, spectacles themselves largely rest upon the production of images.

This book is based on the premise that there is much to learn about how societies transform the image of their cities in preparation to host mega-events, whether major international conferences, commercial exhibitions or global sporting competitions. It investigates the production of the 'event-city' as a complex image-construction endeavour that mobilizes multiple agents and requires important social, spatial and political reconfigurations. The book thus offers a critical analysis of the practice of urban image construction, and examines the role of sporting mega-events like the FIFA World Cup and the Olympics in transforming the urban landscape, in its visual, social and material dimensions. The book is not only interested in the mechanisms of urban image construction, but also in their politics, especially their impacts on the city's inhabitants in terms of representation and right to the city.

The book rests upon the hypothesis that mega-events are increasingly instrumentalized by local political and economic elites to reconfigure power relations, strengthen their hold upon the urban territory and increasingly exclude certain population groups from the decision-making process. Through an analysis of event-related urban construction efforts in Rio de Janeiro and Beijing, two recent Olympic host cities marked by sharp social inequalities, the book examines the effects of mega-events upon the construction of an exclusive vision of urbanity. Based on the accelerated implementation of large urban projects and on the projection of an illusory image of successful urbanity, these image construction initiatives often result in radical territorial transformations and in socio-spatial exclusions that have lasting impacts upon vulnerable populations affected by these interventions. Findings suggest that such urban vision can open the way for the state-assisted privatization and commodification of the urban realm and serve the needs of capital while exacerbating socio-spatial inequality, power imbalance and social conflicts.

Implicit to this hypothesis is the notion that an inquiry into the ways cities build, control and use their image can provide rich insights into the inner workings of urban society. How power holders, decision-makers and other influential agents chose to portray their city, what they push to the fore and what they brush aside and conceal can shed light upon the social biases, prejudices and ideologies that govern society. Without claiming that the image of the city is a mirror of its society, I contend that a study of the diverse mechanisms, strategies and instruments used in the construction of this image can provide a rare access into the complex, unspoken rules that underlie social relationships and enrich our understandings of the power struggles that shape and define society, especially in highly unequal countries.

This book thus explores the dark underside of the process of urban image construction. In their attempt to build an attractive place image that will seduce the rich and the powerful, host cities make huge sacrifices, going as far as selling their soul and destroying, in the process, the essence of their unique characters. They strike a sort of Faustian bargain in exchange for power, wealth and recognition, with lasting consequences for those who have, through their hard work, given the place its culture, identity, and very essence. Faustian references in the urban literature are not new. In his 2008 introduction to *The Spaces of the Modern City*, Gyan Prakash states that 'if modernity is a Faustian bargain to unleash human potential and subdue nature to culture, then modern cities are its most enduring and forceful expressions' (Prakash and Kruse 2008 : 1). Marshal Berman (1983: 74) also talks about a 'Faustian model of development' in his detailed discussion of the modernization process, suggesting that an unshakable belief in progress and insatiable development can bring spectacular devastation. Stavrides (2014) denounces the Olympic Games as fostering a 'Faustian imaginary of development', whose demands for the production of marketable urban images can have genuinely tragic consequences.

If the Faustian legend aptly epitomizes the processes described in this book, it is one of its reinterpretation, found in Oscar Wilde's novel *The Picture of Dorian Gray*, that best reflects the phenomenon under study. Such a parallel between the vain and self-indulgent transformation of ambitious cities and Wilde's modern retelling of the myth of Narcissus was first drawn by Brazilian sociologist Carlos Vainer in a personal conversation in 2015. The narrative of a carefully constructed façade of youth and beauty, which conceals the dark, twisted picture of its corrupted soul, echoes the processes by which cities engage in costly beautification projects while concealing the hardship, injustice and corruption upon which this superficial image is built. The motifs of aestheticism and moral duplicity pursued in Wilde's novel, and the destructive self-indulgence demonstrated by the main character quite finely mirror the aspirations of local political and economic elites in their quest to make their city both prestigious and remarkable. The dark motives that drive their interventions, coupled with their elitist hyper-aestheticism, are literally destroying the lives of those unfortunate enough to stand in the way of their ambitions.

The nature and visual appeal of place images

The notion of image is not a simple one. The word *image* has its roots in the Latin word *imitari*, which signifies 'to copy or imitate'. This definition implies that images are tied to a referent that they seek to emulate or to reproduce, and are appraised by their capacity to capture or to replicate the original. Most definitions of the word 'image' tie the concept to a representation, which can be mental or more tangible, with a strong iconic or visual component. This representation is sometimes said to be superficial, as in Jungian philosophy, where the image is conceived as a façade that one presents to the world, or it can be a general impression that is projected outwardly, but which may or may not reflect reality. The image can also be a conception, a notion or an opinion of someone or something, often idealized in a paradigmatic way, as found in the realm of psychoanalysis, or in popular mass culture. An image is also a rhetorical device, a figurative use of language to create an effect, often without regard for literal significance.[1] An image can thus be a physical likeness, a mental representation, even a symbolic and metaphorical embodiment.

But images remain first and foremost visual representations. This is due, in great part, to Western society's historical conditioning to value vision over all other senses. Many scholars have historicized the importance of the visual and demonstrated the increasing saturation of modern societies by visual images (Rose 2001). They claim that since Ancient Greece, Western culture has been dominated by an ocular-centric paradigm (Jay 1993), and that our interpretation of knowledge, truth and reality has largely been based on visuality (Levin 1993).

The twentieth century has witnessed an explosion of images and visual technologies, which have revolutionized the way we see, understand and experience the world and its globalized society. Debord (1967: 18) saw sight, the most abstract and mystifying of all the senses, as embodying the generalized abstraction of late twentieth-century society. Hawkes (1996: 3), for his part, describes the era as being overdetermined by the visual, marked by 'an unprecedented explosion in number of kinds of images to which people are exposed every day', while Nicholas Mirzoeff (2002) sees contemporary human experience as more visual and visualized than it has even been.

Some historians go as far as suggesting the coming of an era when the image would replace both speech and the written word as the dominant cultural form and privileged channel of communication (Gombrich 1996; Lasch 1991). In W.J.T. Mitchell's words, the world as text is being eclipsed by the world as image (Mitchell 1986). It is true that much of the organizational principles of modern social formation are already founded on visual language (Emmison *et al.* 2000). As immersion in the visual comes to dominate everyday life, our contemporary world is increasingly conceptualized as a 'seen phenomenon' (Jenks 1995: 2). In our 'now' society, obsessed with the immediate and instantaneous, an image is indeed worth a thousand words. And it is certainly worth 140 characters, as Instagram now surpasses Twitter.

Scholars claim that the centrality of the visual has reached unprecedented levels in contemporary life, so that we now interact with the world mainly through how we see it. Today, a seemingly uninterrupted flow of images fills our lives. From the clothes we wear to our body language, all public interaction is based on visual communication (Goffman 1976). The objects that surround us, the buildings we inhabit, the cities where we live, project a host of images that are vehicles for endless visual meanings.

Mirzoeff (2002) suggests that the 'oculocentric' character of postmodern society is not simply due to the ever growing quantity of images that circulates, nor to the fact that knowledge is increasingly articulated visually, but it is because individuals interact more and more with totally constructed visual experiences. Debord (1967) rightly foresaw how social relations would increasingly be mediated by images, which would play a central role in the construction of social life. Advertising, entertainment, television and mass media and other culture industries increasingly define and shape urban life while obscuring the alienating effects of capitalism. But visual cultural studies specialists warn us that images are neither reality, not even representations of reality, but that they are mere constructions and interpretations of reality (Mirzoeff 2002).[2] This means that they are filtered by our own biases, ideologies and limitations, and should always be approached critically.

Visual attractivity plays a central role in the development of a strong mental picture of places, and it is often in terms of visual images that places are consumed. In his seminal work on *The Image of the City* (1965), Kevin Lynch measures urban imageability by a city's capacity to create a vivid and memorable mental picture. If all the senses are solicited in conjuring such mental representation, vision clearly dominates all other senses. As suggested by the 'method of loci' or 'mind palace' mnemonic technique, memories are often rooted in evocations of visual elements of the urban landscape.[3]

As a practice, tourism demonstrates how the allure and attractivity of place is largely based on visual appeal and depends upon the photogenic qualities of destinations. Any postcard stand provides a quick survey of a city's main attractions. Tourist attractions, incidentally, are called sights, not sites, which suggests that views, not places, predominate in their appreciation. In describing the dynamics of the tourist experience, sociologist John Urry (2002) wrote of the 'tourist gaze' as the organizing principle that structures encounters between tourists, local residents and places, suggesting that this experience is based on a particular way of seeing.

For Holcomb (2001), the promotion of places has more to do with the manipulation of consumer desires and tastes than with the actual place that is being sold. The image of the city thus includes an important symbolic dimension, based on mental representations of the city as it is imagined in the collective consciousness, constructed organically through story-telling, travelogues, films, novels and other elements of popular culture. Such mental representations can be purposely transformed and manipulated through active promotional activities or official rhetoric, and alternative images can be imposed. But the image of the city is also construed through the direct experience of the city's objective reality, as both a social entity and a concrete, man-made object, and through the memories and affective associations born from such experience. This explains why Dell Upton (1991: 197) defined the image of the city as a 'fusion of the physical and imaginative structures that all inhabitants use in constructing and construing it'. The city's image is thus simultaneously based on fiction and reality.

In our image-saturated society, dominated by an all-pervasive sign economy and visual mass media of communication, images and representations have come to play a ubiquitous role in urban development strategies. In recent decades, the image of the city has taken centre stage in urban public policy, as the economic survival of cities increasingly depends on their capacity to attract capital, high-paying visitors and wealthy residents (Palmer and Richards 2010). In this context, the visual control of the city's image has gained a strategic importance for policy-makers who seek to enhance the attractiveness of their locality and increasingly base their decisions on aesthetic considerations (Hannigan 1998).

The late capitalist city has thus witnessed the emergence of new, especially visual, forms of urbanism, which rest upon imaging strategies as primary generators of symbolic capital. Visuality permeates urban image construction practices, and urban policy decisions are increasingly made on visual terms. Demands for a competitive urban image have turned urban development into a normative process, as civic leaders attempt to determine, control and regulate their city's identity, which they submit to what amounts to a 'dictatorship of the visual' (Broudehoux 2015).

The making and selling of urban place images in historical context

Kotler *et al.* (1993: 3) define the image of a place as 'the sum of beliefs, ideals, and impressions people have toward a certain place'. The general goal of urban image construction is to forge and project a desirable representation of the city that will be attractive to a target audience of potential visitors, investors and residents. It generally seeks to alter an undesirable image or enhance a favourable image by emphasizing distinctiveness, through orchestrated activities designed to reframe perceptions of the city (Gotham 2005). City imaging, in this sense, is the process of constructing visually based narratives about the potential of places. Image-building efforts encompass not only changes to the built environment but also encode broad conceptual orientations as well as social experiences (Vale and Bass Warner 2001).

Cities have always been concerned with their image. Throughout history, the deliberate projection of favourable place images through concerted place promotion, a process referred to as boosterism, was central to the successful development of human settlements, from the Viking colonization of Greenland to the rapid growth of medieval Italian city-states (Ward 1998; Ashworth and Voogd 1990). Civic boosterism was key to North America's westward expansion, and the idea of place selling an integral part of the American dream (Ward 1998). Private business owners and civic leaders alike actively pursued advertising campaigns to lure potential customers and economic agents to a particular place, as exemplified by the great railway publicity operations of the nineteenth and early twentieth centuries.

Mega-events also played an active role in place promotion. After the great fire of 1906, San Francisco hosted the Panama-Pacific exhibition in 1915 to celebrate its reconstruction and advertise to the world that it was open for business (Benedict 1983). Other world exhibitions had a great impact on the image of cities, establishing London in 1850 as the world's greatest imperial power, while the 1893 Columbian exposition placed Chicago at the forefront of the City Beautiful movement, a vast urban beautification vision that remains influential today. Mega-events have thus played an important role in urban image construction, attracting visitors to participate in the event and stimulating urban beautification efforts. Practices of place promotion have enjoyed a great resurgence in the post-industrial era, as declining cities sought to correct perceptual problems associated with their derelict image. The recent recrudescence of such practices is a direct result of the urban crisis that marked the late twentieth century, linked to de-industrialization, a falling tax-base and declining public expenditures (Hannigan 2003).

Today, aspiring global cities engage in image construction practices in their effort to adapt to the new information age and to compete on the world stage. Place selling has become an essential part of the broad 'entrepreneurial ethos' (Ward 1998) that now dominates neoliberal public policy. With the growing mobility of capital investment, the footloose quality of enterprises and increased global connectivity, cities have had to become proactive in capturing mobile investment, attracting prospective firms and their workforce, enticing up-market tourists and conference organizers and convincing high-tax payers to settle there permanently (Hannigan 2003; Ashworth and Voogd 1990; Keans and Philo 1993). Cities have thus taken an entrepreneurial approach to urban territorial management in order to efficiently compete on the global market (Harvey 1989).

City marketing has become one of the defining features of the new entrepreneurial approach to urban management in the post-Fordist city (Holcomb 2001). The object of city marketing is not the city itself, but its image and representation. Initially, most marketing initiatives were based on a city branding approach that applied concepts borrowed from corporate branding to the urban environment (Karavatzis and Ashworth 2005). They relied upon promotional campaigns and visual identity tactics, with the use of slogans and advertising operations designed around strong visual components that included a logo and key iconic features. More recently, city marketing began transcending advertising to include hallmark events and high-profile flagship projects in a more complex and holistic approach (Karavatzis 2007).

Today, these practices are not restrained to derelict post-industrial cities but prestigious national capitals and world-class tourism destinations like London, Paris and Amsterdam also carry out concerted urban image construction programmes. They are driven by the fear of being upstaged by rivals, both national and international, and by a desire to redynamize their image, update ossified representations and maintain their competitive advantage. This phenomenon is exemplified by the case of Mitterand's Grands Projets in 1980s Paris, or more recently by Amsterdam's very successful *I am sterdam* strategic re-branding campaign of 2004 by Kessels Kramer. This drive to remain relevant in a constantly evolving world explains why two successful global cities like Paris and London, which both enjoy an unquestionable global visibility, so bitterly competed to host the 2012 Olympic Games.

The politics of urban image construction

There are multiple reasons to want to alter, or at least control, the image of a city. Apart from the more obvious economic motivations, which assume that a positive image will attract new residents, investors and consumers and thus stimulate the local economy, there are other, less quantifiable reasons for improving a city's image. Recent research suggests that the realm of influence of image construction is increasingly locally oriented, as image construction efforts target internal audiences more than external actors (Karavatzis 2007).

Studies also suggest that image construction initiatives can have positive, yet often intangible, benefits for local communities, for example by boosting self-confidence and developing civic consciousness. A positive identification with their city can foster civic pride among citizens, promote a harmonious social climate and encourage active involvement in the betterment of the urban environment. It can also help promote community development and activate social forces to avoid conflicts, thereby improving local quality of life. For local authorities, these multiple intangible benefits can be translated into political capital. By fostering local pride and promoting unity through a shared sense of identity, city leaders can help engineer consensus, promote political stability and use image construction as an instrument of legitimization to consolidate their position. Similarly, a positive urban image can yield a certain amount of symbolic capital, testifying to grandeur and genius of a leader, and helping improve the city's position in the national and global hierarchy. These symbolic motives for undertaking image construction initiatives can also generate quantifiable monetary gains, as quality of life, political stability and satisfaction about one's living environment improve the attractivity of place.

But the fact that notions of the good life and definitions of successful urbanity differ from one population group to the next means that competing visions of what is a positive urban image necessarily coexist. The way global cosmopolitan elites and members of the middle and upper classes envision the city is often associated with images of the futuristic metropolis, with sleek skyscrapers and fleets of fancy cars rolling down elevated freeways. For less affluent residents, the ideal city may simply be a place where basic needs are met and where all are treated fairly, as equal members of society, without exploitation and discrimination.

Urban image construction is therefore a highly contested practice. Because of its selective and potentially exclusive nature, it is also highly political. The construction of an attractive place image is generally achieved by altering the city's physical and social landscapes, and by discursively reframing its symbolic representations. Such alterations entail certain omissions, manipulations and skewing of reality, especially when serving the particular needs and interests of one group to the detriment of others. Carter (2006: 156) views city image formation as a 'highly contentious and problematic process that is rife with social divisions of all sorts'. Similarly, for Vale and Bass Warner (2001) city images are not static. They are subject to constant revision and manipulation, and it always matters who builds these images, for whom and with what motives. Representations of place are thus inherently restrictive, both in their content and frame of reference, and often say less about the reality they portray than about image producers, whose intent, values and selective point of view they communicate (Gaffney 2016).

This explains why so many social scientists regard city marketing with scepticism (Harvey 2001; Smith 2005; Healey 2002; Colomb 2012). They find the practice to be socially regressive, instrumentalized for economic purposes, and view the mind-set that drives city marketing initiatives as incompatible with the welfare objectives of public policy (Healey 2002). Seeking brand consistency for place identity is a top-down intervention that is deeply problematic from an ethical point of view. For Rosalynd Deutsche (1996), the construction of a unified, coherent and cohesive urban image is a highly exclusive process that can only be achieved by expelling differences and conflicts within. It entails the reduction of a rich, complex, heterogeneous urban reality into a simplified, homogenous, one-dimensional marketable commodity (Deutsche 1996). More critically, Healey (2002) likens urban image construction to the creative projection of a fictional yet totalizing image of society, which undermines more plural, multidimensional and progressive visions.

Power is a determining factor deciding who and what are to be included in official urban representations (Powell and Marrero-Guillamón 2012). The resulting image embodies the desires and aspirations of those who have the power to shape the urban environment, and becomes the concretization of their cultural imaginings and visual fantasies (Smith 2005). Based on elitist conceptualizations of what is deemed desirable, respectable or attractive, cities are expected to be at once vibrant, exciting and reassuringly safe, while providing a complete package of assets linked to status, quality of life and business opportunities (McCann 2009). For Healey (2002), the process of giving a city what elites believe is a 'modern' face depends upon silencing the politically weak and making poverty – and the poor – purposely invisible. Usually left out from representations are the ordinary landscapes of the poor, the black, the homeless and the 'unmodern', considered to be 'out of place' in the city's public space by local political and economic leaders (Wright 1997). The process of urban image construction is therefore deeply rooted in a politics of visibility, as selective visualizations of place and space increasingly shape urban policy interventions (Raco and Tunney 2010). Deutsche (1996: 173) talks of a 'politics of erasure', where undesirable groups are physically expelled from physical space while their absence is discursively inscribed in representations of the city.

Patrizia Faccioli (2007) describes the production of visual images as both expressing and embodying power relations. It is a social construction, which aims to define reality, convey meaning and produce a specific vision of the world. Yet, she reminds us that images are not reality, nor even its representation, but a construction and an interpretation of reality. And this interpretation is necessarily filtered by one's point of view, however biased or interested. It is in this point of view that power lies, writes Faccioli (2007), the power to state one's view point.

The three-dimensional production of the city's image

This book largely rests upon the analysis of three dimensions of the city's image, which are acted upon in the practice of urban image construction: the conceived, the built and the lived image of the city. They are based on Henri Lefebvre's distinction, in *The Production of Space* (1991), between conceived space (or the *representation of space*) and lived space (*spaces of representation*). Conceived space corresponds to a theoretical representation of the city, as imagined by city officials, planners and urban imagineers. Lived space is understood as the actual physical city, as it is experienced at street level on a daily basis, and used by diverse groups for self-representation. I envision lived space as having both a social and a material dimension, thus resulting in a tripartite conceptualization of the city's image: the conceived (discursive or imagined) image of the city, the built (physical, material or concrete) image of the city and the lived (experienced or social) image of the city.

In this typology, the discursive image of the city refers to abstract, mental place images promoted through media-based advertising and city marketing campaigns for both internal and external consumption. This first spatial dimension of the city's image encompasses intangible or rhetorical representations of the city, projected upon collective consciousness. This is the city found on glossy magazine covers, tourism brochures and boosterist discourse. The second aspect of the city's image focuses on the more material, concrete image of the city, built through architecture and landscape interventions. It is concerned with the city's actual physical landscape, composed of the city's existing assets, inherited from the past, as well as newly built edifices and spaces, created as image-building improvements.

The third level of intervention analysed in this book is the social image of the city, shaped through initiatives that seek to transform both the bodies and the minds of the local population. It corresponds to the city's human landscape in its various expressions. Each of these three levels of intervention in the practice of urban image construction is the object of an individual chapter, illustrated with multiple empirical examples.

Scope of the study

This book understands the image of the city as a complex amalgam of the combined actions of thousands of city dwellers, city builders and multiple other public and private actors superimposed over time. Processes of mental image formation and individual receptivity to place images have been the object of much research in the field of city marketing, place promotion and tourism studies, leading to the elaboration of several conceptualizations of the way places images are decoded (Karavatzis and Ashworth 2015; Karavatzis 2007; Smith 2006; Hudson *et al.* 2011). Place images function in a host of different ways, and act upon image consumers at both the perceptual and affective levels. The reception and interpretation of place images depends upon the subjectivity and unique experience of distinct individual observers. Ashworth and Graham (2005) view place images as polysemic, unstable and largely user-determined. For them, individuals create place identities, and develop different narratives of belonging at different times and for different reasons. The ambiguous nature of images and their weak iconic code makes studying the reception of images a highly complex and contingent issue.

But enquiry into the way discrete individuals perceive places and read urban images is beyond the focus of this book, which centres on the production of images rather than on their reception. The present study is therefore more concerned with the politics of urban image construction than with its phenomenology. Based on a close analysis of the processes, mechanisms and strategies used to build and project urban representations and to convey particular meanings, this book interprets the intent of image producers and power coalitions, which are less dependent upon individual subjectivity. While recognizing that the image of the city cannot be the sole product of an organized, top-down process, the book takes a structuralist approach and concentrates its focus on the concerted actions of those who seek to control, impose or consolidate a particular image of the city, based on their own worldview, biases and interests. It thus centres on the production side of city images and on the impact of image construction interventions upon individuals and collectivities, to uncover the way in which these images are contested, reworked and opposed by those who feel excluded by their representation.

This book examines practices of urban image construction in the particular context posed by the hosting of global-scale mega-events. These exceptional circumstances represent a privileged moment to observe urban transformations in an accelerated manner. Preparations to host large sporting events provide an ideal laboratory for the study of large-scale urban redevelopment and urban image construction projects in a condensed timeframe. Host cities typically have seven years to prepare themselves to receive and entertain the world, and this accelerated context exacerbates existing trends and tensions and magnifies them so as to make them more readily observable. While mega-events can be viewed as accidents in the 'normal' development of a city, they nonetheless represent rare moments and unique opportunities to study urban change, especially as cities transition from regional centre to global metropolis.

Literature review

This book aims to fill an important gap in the existing literature, especially regarding the process of urban image construction and the unique conditions posed by the hosting of mega-events. Although I consider urban image construction practices to be of utmost importance to the understanding of contemporary urban phenomena, the issue has gained little attention in the contemporary academic context, with the exception of city marketing specialists, who seek practical applications (Karavatzis and Ashworth 2015; Karavatzis 2007), or of visual studies specialists, who approach it as a cultural phenomenon (Hannigan 1998; Julier 2005). Rarely has the issue received the critical analysis it deserves, especially from a political-economy point of view (Vale and Bass Warner 2001; Colomb 2012). While multiple publications, especially in the fields of planning and urban studies, examine issues of city marketing, branding and the spectacularization of the urban environment through 'starchitecture', few serious studies centre on the phenomenon of urban image construction *per se*.

Recent years have seen growing academic interest in the urban aspects of mega-events, especially with respect to their role as catalysts for mega-projects, magnets for investors and tourists and instruments of city marketing (Gold and Gold 2011; Hiller 2000, 2006, 2012; Lefebvre and Roult 2008; Essex and Chalkey 2004; Roult and Lefebvre 2013). Urban research on mega-events is generally concerned with the socio-spatial implications of event-led redevelopment, the impacts of mega-events on local politics and public policy, the economic legacy of mega-events and their role in city marketing (Gold and Gold 2008; Burbank *et al.* 2001; Chalkey and Essex 1999; de Lange 1998). Research has demonstrated how mega-events exacerbate local disparities, drive up inflation, place tremendous pressure on housing markets and lead to some of the largest state-sponsored eviction programmes in the world (Hayes and Horne 2011; Davis 2007, 2011; Lenskyj and Wagg 2011; Lenskyj 2000, 2002, 2008; COHRE 2007, 2008a, 2008b). While an increasing number of researchers are starting to ask critical questions about how mega-events impact local inhabitants, many studies remain at a macroscopic level, and focus on large-scale spatial reconfiguration and economic development, rarely examining the impacts of these events and their related mega-projects upon population groups at the micro-level (Davis 2007; Raco and Tunney 2010; Greene 2003). Only rarely are the important image construction campaigns that accompany these initiatives examined (Choi 2004; Greene 2003; Lenskyj 2002; see also Rojek 2013).

Moreover, there is a dearth of publications on the impacts of mega-events in cities of the semi-periphery; the bulk of the recent literature on mega-event-led urban redevelopment is carried out in the context of Western cities (Owen 2005; Matheson and Baade 2004; Nauright 2004). The historical bias for First World cities in the selection of hosts for these events has resulted in the relative paucity of empirical data on these so-called peripheral cities. Few empirical studies examine the impacts of these events upon urban neighbourhoods and their inhabitants in cities of the developing world (Shin 2008, 2012; Cottle 2011; Davis 2011; Pillary 2009; Black and van der Westhuizen 2004; Dimeo and Kay 2004).

Although recent years have seen a surge in the number of emerging countries hosting sporting mega-events, with the 2010 New Delhi Commonwealth Games, the 2010 South Africa World Cup, the 2008 Beijing Olympics, and Rio's 2014 and 2016 events, relatively little is known about the specific urban impacts of hosting mega-events in the Global South. A growing number of reports suggest that negative impacts in terms of housing rights violations, job security and access to resources happen on a much larger scale (COHRE 2008b; Blunden 2007; Alexandridis 2007). However, academic understanding of the social and spatial effect of these intense urban interventions remains limited, with only a few published studies on South Korea, South Africa and China (Shin 2012; Davis 2011; Alegi 2008; Brady 2009; Broudehoux 2007; Black and van der Westhuizen 2004). Serious Brazilian studies of mega- events and urban transformations are emerging (Mascarenhas *et al.* 2011; Oliveira 2011; Lima Jr. 2010; Vainer 2010; Lima Jr. *et al.* 2007) but few have so far been published in English (Sánchez and Broudehoux 2013; Sylvestre and Oliveira 2012; Curi *et al.* 2011; Gaffney 2010; Freeman 2012, 2014). This book thus helps fill an important gap in contemporary research by providing a better understanding of the particular dynamics of mega-event-led redevelopment in nations plagued by vast social inequalities.

Methodological approach

The approach used in this book mixes a cultural studies critique with a political-economic analytical framework, which I find essential to the study of a multifarious object such as the image of the city. As both a social, economic and political entity, with territorial, legal and cultural characteristics, the city requires innovative, multidisciplinary analytical tools to explain urban phenomena in their complexity. This integrative approach allows capture of the reality of image-related power struggles at the economic and political level, without losing sight of the social and cultural implications of ongoing urban transformations.

This book draws upon research conducted over the last 20 years, which analysed a variety of urban issues related to the hosting of mega-events, including the social, spatial and symbolic dimensions of architectural mega-projects, notions of identity and representation in tourism development, and housing rights issues related to urban redevelopment.[4] The present book builds upon this expertise to further current understanding of the construction of the event-city and expand current theorization of its image component. Reflecting back on this work, the book extracts insights about issues pertaining to the phenomenon of urban image construction, a topic that always underscored my analysis without necessarily being at the forefront.

The methodology used in my research rests upon a multidisciplinary conceptual approach, which integrates the study of social and spatial phenomena by combining ethnography – a traditionally anthropological method – with an analytical framework derived from critical human geography in an approach that could be termed *spatial ethnography*. With its ability to capture the complexities of people's daily lives, ethnography allows individual experiences to inform the research process. It bypasses the shortcomings of studies which privilege global causes over local ones or assume the primacy of broad structural forces over socio-political agency. Spatial ethnography also reveals fine layers of social change not reflected in more general considerations and helps situate specific practices within a spatial context.

To minimize possible biases and inaccuracies and to paint the most informed, comprehensive, accurate and balanced picture of the event-related image construction process, the research relies on a variety of sources and approaches. The present book is thus based on repeat, on-site observation conducted over the course of several years, which included photographic surveys, field notes and spatial analysis, before, during and after the events. Participant observation was also carried out on the occasion of various local events, including festivals, forums, public consultation meetings, street demonstrations, informal gatherings and political protests held during the study period. Formal and informal interviews were conducted with actors involved in local urban transformations, at the city administration level and in private consortiums, as well as local-resident activists, workers and business owners, artists and members of diverse groups and associations. Information was supplemented by the consultation of a wide range of resources, including extensive press reviews, in the printed and web media, documentary sources, scholarly literature, media reports, official bid documents, event propaganda, planning documents, official websites, activist blogs, NGO reports and other relevant secondary sources.

Beijing and Rio de Janeiro as Faustian cities

This book draws upon insights garnered from over two decades of empirical research on the process of urban image construction in the context of mega-event preparations, particularly in Beijing, host of the 2008 Summer Olympics, and Rio de Janeiro, host of the 2014 FIFA World Cup and 2016 Summer Olympics. My interest in events-related urban image construction stems from my early work studying the transformation of Beijing from a socialist capital into a world metropolis and an Olympic city (Broudehoux 2004). Over a 16-year period that spanned from the early 1990s to the Olympic Games, I witnessed the construction of a potemkin city, a highly controlled, make-believe dreamworld of unproblematic success, wealth and prosperity. I documented the diverse imaging strategies and manipulations that were associated with the construction of this façade, and the projection of a disciplined, crisis-free and cohesive civic order.

After 2008, my interest shifted to Rio de Janeiro, a city with an entirely different geopolitical makeup. The reasons for this shift were easy. In 2009, Rio de Janeiro was chosen as host of the 2016 Olympics just a few years after Brazil had been selected to hold the 2014 Fédération Internationale de Football Association (FIFA) World Cup, with Rio hosting the finals. Rio de Janeiro's unique status as one of the rare cities in recent history to receive the world's two top sporting mega-events, within a two-year span, made it an attractive object of study. The impacts of this unprecedented 'double whammy' in terms of infrastructure projects and the transformation of the city's urban landscape were bound to be tremendous, and to have important social, political and economic ramifications.

In spite of their great difference, both cities share similarities. First, their condition as ambitious 'second cities' in powerful, emerging nations make the stakes for hosting mega-events all the higher in a national, inter-urban competition dynamic, as well as on the broader international plane. In both Beijing and Rio, spectacular mega-events were clearly driven by an image imperative, pursued as a way to improve their country's position on the global geopolitical stage, to further their integration in the league of 'advanced' nations and to strengthen their stature as rising economic powers. But if Beijing's Olympic transformations were geared towards changing the world image of China as a whole, by turning a derelict socialist capital city into a futuristic capitalist metropolis, in Rio considerations were more deeply rooted in internal political strife. Rio de Janeiro's mega-events were much less about showing the world Brazil's capabilities as a new economic player, than they were an occasion to privatize state land and to consolidate power into the hands of a few local actors through legal and territorial reconfigurations. Power consolidation was also a central issue in Beijing, where the Olympics were largely instrumentalized as a tool of legitimation for the ruling party, but this was carried out at the national level and centred around the rekindling of a strong national consciousness. Other similarities can be found in the image construction strategies deployed, especially those seeking to conceal problematic aspects of their society, rather than acting upon resolving them.

Although the book largely draws from these two examples, it is not exactly comparative in its approach, and issues are not necessarily discussed in a symmetrical manner. The book rather calls upon examples from one or the other city to illustrate concepts or strategies, at times underlining differences between them, at others exposing similarities. It thus avoids systematic comparison, which would not be productive, cause redundancy and needlessly complicate the narrative.

Structure of the book

The book is structured around six main chapters. Chapter 1 paints a general portrait of the practice of urban image construction and discusses its growing role in contemporary urban policy. It examines the transformative effects of mega-events on the urban landscape of their host cities and discusses how these events contribute to the coalescence of neoliberal policies in the service of capital. The chapter presents two dominant paradigms commonly used in the realization of the event-city and the construction of its image: the city as spectacle, and the city of exception, and explains the ideological and political underpinnings of each approach, respectively illustrated by the case of Beijing and Rio de Janeiro.

The following three chapters examine each of the three levels of intervention in the construction of urban representations. Chapter 2 focuses on the conceived image of the city as a cognitive product, made of mental, abstract and discursive representations. This first level of intervention lies in the symbolic realm and is based on the construction of an intangible, conceptual urban image through rhetorical means and virtual representations. It seeks to communicate ideas about places through advertising strategies, the creation of a brand image and their diffusion in the media. Chapter 3 centres on the city's physical landscape, both natural and man-made, which is subjected to a transformation process in order to conform, as much as possible, to the picture-perfect vision imagined by city marketers. It examines the projection of a seductive place image, celebrating the city's best assets, as well as the construction of places of exclusion, with the deliberate concealment of aspects of the urban landscape that could cause prejudice to the city's image. Chapter 4 focuses on social image construction and is concerned with the conscious and planned management of human activity and the control, regulation and normalization of the city's social environment. It discusses social beautification initiatives, social engineering programmes and civilization campaigns, as well as initiatives that target the ordering of bodies in space through classification, documentation and surveillance.

In Chapter 5, the diverse modes of resistance that have emerged to contest event-led transformations in reaction to exclusionary image construction strategies are examined. The chapter describes a wide range of strategies devised to challenge ill-advised decision-makers, to subvert hegemonic discourse and to hijack the event spectacle. The chapter details three common modes of resistance to event-related image construction. They range from organized forms of mass resistance and city-wide protests, to locally based demonstrations, either collective or individual, all the way to more creative, micro-political dynamics of contestations and web-based resistance strategies.

Chapter 6 returns to some of the book's main findings to discuss the wider consequences of urban image construction practices. It first draws upon the work of Neil Smith to explain some of the realities that have characterized the urban image construction practices described in the book, especially regarding the 'revanchist' aspects of the neoliberal event-city. The book concludes with a reflection on the impact of exclusionary processes of urban image construction on urban democracy, raising questions about the constitution of citizenship, the right to the city and the simple right to be seen and exist in the city's urban spaces.

Notes

1 'Image': www.merriam-webster.com/dictionary/image; http://www.vocabulary.com/dictionary/image; www.macmillandictionary.com/dictionary/british/image_1, accessed 5 November 2015.

2 The new disciplinary field of visual culture studies was largely developed by cultural studies specialists like Nicholas Mirzoeff, Stuart Hall, Jessica Evans, William Mitchell and Chris Jenks, who believed that the visual aspect deserved its own separate discipline (see Mirzoeff 2002).
3 The 'method of loci', also called the *memory palace* or *mind palace* technique, is a method of memory enhancement known to the Ancient Greeks and Romans which uses visualization to organize and recall information. It is by associating information to a mental image of a place (or loci) that one can store and recall long-term memories. See, for example Lyndon and Moore (1994).
4 A portion of text, argument and examples found in this book has previously appeared in conference papers, published contributions to edited volumes and periodical articles.

References

Alegi, P. (2008) 'A Nation to be Reckoned With: The Politics of World Cup Stadium Construction in Cape Town and Durban, South Africa', *African Studies*. Vol. 67, pp. 397–422.

Alexandridis, T. (2007) *The Housing Impact of the 2004 Olympic Games in Athens*. Geneva: Centre on Housing Rights and Evictions (COHRE).

Ashworth, G. and Graham, B. (2005) *Senses of Place: Senses of Time*. Aldershot: Ashgate.

Ashworth, G. and Voogd, H. (1990) *Selling the City: Marketing Approaches in Public Sector Urban Planning*. London: Belhaven Press.

Benedict, B. (1983) *The Anthropology of World's Fairs: San Francisco's Panama Pacific International Exposition of 1915*. Berkeley, CA: Lowie Museum of Anthropology.

Berman, M. (1983) *All That is Solid Melts into Air: The Experience of Modernity*. London: Verso.

Black, D.R. and van der Westhuizen, J. (2004) 'The Allure of Global Games for 'Semi-peripheral' Polities and Spaces: A Research Agenda', *Third World Quarterly*. Vol. 25, pp. 1195–1214.

Blunden, H. (2007) *The Impacts of the Sydney Olympic Games on Housing Rights*. Geneva: Centre on Housing Rights and Evictions (COHRE).

Brady, A.M. (2009) 'The Beijing Olympics as a Campaign of Mass Distraction', *The China Quarterly*. Vol. 197, pp. 1–24.

Broudehoux, A.-M. (2004) *The Making and Selling of Post-Mao Beijing*. London: Routledge.

Broudehoux, A.-M. (2007) 'Spectacular Beijing: The Conspicuous Construction of an Olympic Metropolis', *Journal of Urban Affairs*. Vol. 29, pp. 383–399.

Broudehoux, A.-M. (2015) 'Mega-Events, Urban Image Construction and the Politics of Exclusion', R. Gruneau and J. Horne (eds), *Mega-Events and Globalization: Capital and Spectacle in a Changing World Order*. London: Routledge, pp. 113–130.

Burbank, M., Andranovich, G. and Heying, C. H. (2001) *Olympic Dreams: The Impact of Mega-Events on Local Politics*. Boulder, CO: Lynne Rienner.

Carter, T.F. (2006) 'Introduction: The Sport of Cities Spectacle and the Economy of Appearances', *City & Society*. Vol. 18, pp. 151–158.

Chalkey, B.S. and Essex, S.J. (1999) 'Urban Development Through Hosting International Events: A History of the Olympic Games', *Planning Perspectives*. Vol. 14, No. 4, pp. 369–394.

Choi, Y.S. (2004) 'Football and the South Korean Imagination: South Korea and the 2002 World Cup Tournaments', W. Manzenreiter and J. Horne (eds), *Football Goes East: Business, Culture and the People's Game in East Asia*. London: Routledge, pp. 133–147.

COHRE (Centre on Housing Rights and Eviction). (2007) *Fair Play for Housing Rights: Mega-Events.* Geneva: COHRE.

COHRE (Centre on Housing Rights and Eviction). (2008a) 'Housing Rights and the 2010 Football World Cup', *Business as Usual? Housing Rights and 'Slum Eradication' in Durban, South Africa.* Geneva: COHRE.

COHRE (Centre on Housing Rights and Eviction). (2008b) *One World, Whose Dream? Housing Rights Violations and the Beijing Olympic Games.* Geneva: COHRE.

Colomb, C. (2012) *Staging the New Berlin: Place Marketing and the Politics of Urban Reinvention Post-1989.* London: Routledge.

Cottie, E. (2011) *South Africa's World Cup: A Legacy for Whom?* Scottsville: University of KwaZulu-Natal Press.

Curi, M., Knijnik, J. and Mascarenhas, G. (2011) 'The Pan American Games in Rio de Janeiro 2007: Consequences of a Sport Mega-event on a BRIC Country', *International Review for the Sociology of Sport.* Vol. 46, pp.1–16.

Davis, L.K. (2007) *Housing, Evictions and the Seoul 1988 Summer Olympic Games.* Geneva: Centre on Housing Rights and Evictions.

Davis, L.K. (2011) 'International Events and Mass Evictions: A Longer View', *International Journal of Urban and Regional Research.* Vol. 35, No. 3, pp. 582–599.

de Lange, P. (1998) *Games Cities Play: The Staging of the Greatest Socio-Economic Event in the World.* Pretoria: Sigma Press.

Debord, G. (1967) *La société du spectacle.* Paris: Folio.

Deutsche, R. (1996) *Evictions: Art and Spatial Politics.* Cambridge, MA: MIT Press.

Dimeo, P. and Kay, J. (2004) 'Major Sports Events, Image Projection and the Problems of "Semi-periphery": A Case Study of the 1996 South Asia Cricket World Cup', *Third World Quarterly.* Vol. 25, pp. 1263–1276.

Emmison, M., Mayall, M. and Smith, P. (2000) *Researching the Visual.* London: SAGE.

Essex, S. and Chalkley, B. (2004) 'Mega-Sporting Events in Urban and Regional Policy: A History of the Winter Olympics', *Planning Perspectives.* Vol. 19, No. 2, pp. 201–204.

Faccioli, P. (2007) 'La sociologie dans la société de l'image', *Sociétés.* Vol. 95, pp. 9–18.

Freeman, J. (2012) 'Neoliberal Accumulation Strategies and the Visible Hand of Police Pacification in Rio de Janeiro', *Revista de Estudos Universitários.* Vol. 38, No. 1, pp. 95–126.

Freeman, J. (2014) 'Raising the Flag over Rio de Janeiro's Favelas: Citizenship and Social Control in the Olympic City', *Journal of Latin American Geography.* Vol. 13, No. 1, pp. 7–38.

Gaffney, C. (2010) 'Mega-events and Socio-spatial Dynamics in Rio de Janeiro, 1919–2016', *Journal of Latin American Geography.* Vol. 9, No. 1, pp. 7–29.

Goffman, E. (1976) *Gender Advertisements.* New York: Harper & Row.

Gold, J.R. and Gold, M.M. (2008) 'Olympic Cities: Regeneration, City Rebranding and Changing Agendas', *Geographical Compass.* Vol. 2, No. 1, pp. 300–318.

Gold, J.R. and Gold, M.M. (2011) *Olympic Cities: City Agendas, Planning, and the World's Games, 1896 to the Present.* London: Routledge.

Gombrich, E. (1996) 'The Visual Image: Its Place in Communication', R. Woodfield (ed.), *The Essential Gombrich: Selected Writings in Art and Culture.* London: Phaidon, pp. 41–64.

Gotham, K.F. (2005) 'Theorizing Urban Spectacles Festivals: Tourism and the Transformation of Urban Space', *City.* Vol. 9, pp. 225–247.

Greene, S.J. (2003) 'Staged Cities: Mega-Events, Slum Clearance and Global Capital', *Yale Human Rights and Development Law Journal.* Vol. 6, pp. 161–187.

Hannigan, J. (1998) *Fantasy City: Pleasure and Profit in the Postmodern Metropolis.* London: Routledge.

Hannigan, J. (2003) 'Symposium on Branding, the Entertainment Economy and Urban Place Building: Introduction', *International Journal of Urban and Regional Research*. Vol. 27, No. 2, pp. 352–360.

Harvey, D. (1989) 'From Managerialism to Entrepreneurialism: The Transformation in Urban Governance in Late Capitalism', *Geografiska Annaler, Human Geography*. Vol. 71, pp. 3–17.

Harvey, D. (2001) *Spaces of Capital: Towards a Critical Geography*. New York: Routledge.

Hawkes, D. (1996) *Ideology (The New Critical Idiom)*. London: Routledge.

Hayes, G. and Horne, J. (2011) 'Sustainable Development: Shock and Awe? London 2012 and Civil Society', *Sociology*. Vol. 45, No. 5, pp. 749–764.

Healey, P. (2002) 'On Creating the "City" as a Collective Resource', *Urban Studies*. Vol. 39, pp. 177–179.

Hiller, H.H. (2000) 'Mega-Events, Urban Boosterism and Growth Strategies: An Analysis of the Objectives and Legitimations of the Cape Town 2004 Olympic Bid', *International Journal of Urban and Regional Research*. Vol. 24, No. 2, pp. 449–458.

Hiller, H.H. (2006) 'Post-Event Outcomes and the Post-Modern Turn: The Olympics and Urban Transformations', *Journal of European Sport Management Quarterly*. Vol. 6, No. 4, pp. 317–332.

Hiller, H.H. (2012) *Host Cities and the Olympics: An Interactionist Approach*. London: Routledge.

Holcomb, B. (2001) 'Place Marketing: Using Media to Promote Cities', L.J. Vale and S.B. Bass Warner Jr. (eds), *Imaging the City: Continuing Struggles and New Directions*. New Brunswick, NJ: Center for Urban Policy Research.

Hudson, S., Wang, Y. and Moreno Gil, S. (2011) 'The Influence of a Film on Destination Image and the Desire to Travel: A Cross-Cultural Comparison', *International Journal of Tourism Research*. Vol. 13, pp. 177–190.

Jay, M. (1993) *Downcast Eyes: The Denigration of Vision in Twentieth-Century French Thought*. Berkeley, CA: University of California Press.

Jenks, C. (1995) *Visual Culture*. London: Routledge.

Julier, G. (2005) 'Urban Designscapes and the Production of Aesthetic Consent', *Urban Studies*. Vol. 42, pp. 869–887.

Karavatzis, M. (2007) 'City Marketing: The Past, the Present and Some Unresolved Issues', *Geography Compass*. Vol. 1, pp. 695–712.

Karavatzis, M. and Ashworth, G. (2005) 'City Branding: An Effective Assertion of Identity or a Transitory Marketing Trick?', *Tijdschrift voor Economische en Social Geografie*. Vol. 96, No. 5, pp. 506–514.

Kearns, G. and Philo, C. (1993) *Selling Places: The City as Cultural Capital, Past and Present*. Oxford: Pergamon.

Lasch, C. (1991) *Culture of Narcissism: American Life in an Age of Diminishing Expectations*. New York: W.W. Norton.

Lefebvre, H. (1991) *The Production of Space*. Malden, MA: Blackwell.

Lefebvre, S. and Roult, R. (2008, October) 'L'après-JO: Reconversion et réutilisation des équipements olympiques', *Revue Espaces, tourisme et loisirs*. Vol. 263.

Lenskyj, H.J. (2000) *Inside the Olympic Industry: Power, Politics, and Activism*. Albany, NY: State University of New York Press.

Lenskyj, H.J. (2002) *The Best Olympics Ever? Social Impacts of Sydney 2000*. Albany, NY: State University of New York Press.

Lenskyj, H.J. (2008) *Olympic Industry Resistance: Challenging Olympic Power and Propaganda*. Stanford, CA: Stanford University Press.

Lenskyj, H.J. and Wagg, S. (2011) *A Handbook of Olympic Studies*. London: Palgrave Macmillan.

Levin, D.M. (1993) *Modernity and Hegemony of Vision*. Berkeley, CA: University of California Press.

Lima Jr, P.N. (2010) Uma estratégia chamada 'planejamento estratégico'. *7 Letras*.

Lima Jr, P.N., Oliveira, F., Bienenstein, G. and Sánchez, F. (2007) 'Grandes Projetos Urbanos: panorama da experiência brasileira', *Annals of the XVe ENANPUR National Conference*. Belém: ANPUR.

Lyndon, D. and Moore, C. (1994) *Chambers for a Memory Palace*. Cambridge, MA: MIT Press.

Mascarenhas, G., Bienenstein, G. and Sánchez, F. (2011) *O Jogo Continua. Megaeventos e Cidades*. Rio de Janeiro: Press of the State University of Rio de Janeiro (EDUERJ).

Massey, D. (2005) *For Space*. London: SAGE.

Matheson, V. and Baade, R. (2004) 'Mega-Sporting Events in Developing Nations: Playing the Way to Prosperity?', *The South African Journal of Economics*. Vol. 72, No. 5, pp. 1085–1096.

McCann, E.J. (2009) 'City Marketing', R. Kitchin and N. Thrift (eds), *International Encyclopedia of Human Geography*. London: Elsevier, pp. 119–124.

Mirzoeff, N. (2002) 'What is Visual Culture', N. Mirzoeff (ed.), *The Visual Culture Reader*. New York: Routledge, pp. 3–13.

Mitchell, W. (1986) *Iconology: Image, Text, Ideology*. Chicago, IL: University of Chicago Press.

Nauright, J. (2004) 'Global Games: Culture, Political Economy and Sport in the Globalised World in the 21st Century', *Third World Quarterly*. Vol. 25, No. 7, pp. 1325–1336.

Oliveira, N. (2011) 'Força-de-lei: rupturas e realinhamentos institucionais na busca do "sonho olímpico" carioca', *14th National ANPUR Conference*. Rio de Janeiro.

Owen, J. (2005) 'Estimating the Costs and Benefits of Hosting Olympic Games: What Can Beijing Expect from its 2008 Games?', *The Industrial Geographer*. Vol. 3, No. 1, pp. 1–18.

Palmer, R. and Richards, G. (2010) 'Why Cities Need to be Eventful', *Eventful Cities: Cultural Management and Urban Revitalization*. London: Butterworth-Heinemann, pp. 1–37.

Pillary, U., Tomlinson, R. and Bass, O. (eds) (2009) *Development and Dreams: The Urban Legacy of the 2010 Football World Cup*. Cape Town: Human Science Research Council (HSRC).

Powell, H. and Marrero-Guillamón, I. (2012) *The Art of Dissent: Adventures in London's Olympic State*. London: Marshgate Press.

Prakash, G. and Kruse, K.M. (2008) *The Spaces of the Modern City: Imaginaries, Politics, and Everyday Life*. Princeton, NJ: Princeton University Press.

Raco, M. and Tunney, E. (2010) 'Visibilities and Invisibilities in Urban Development: Small Business Communities and the London Olympics 2012', *Urban Studies*. Vol. 47, pp. 2069–2091.

Rojek, C. (2013) *Event Power: How Global Events Manage and Manipulate*. London: SAGE.

Rose, G. (2001) *Visual Methodologies: An Introduction to the Interpretation of Visual Materials*. London: SAGE.

Roult, R. and Lefebvre, S. (2013) 'Stadiums, Public Spaces and Mega-events: Cultural and Sports Facilities as Catalysts for Urban Regeneration and Development', Michael E. Leary and J. McCarthy (eds), *The Routledge Companion to Urban Regeneration*. London: Routledge, pp. 548–557.

Sánchez, F. and Broudehoux, A.-M. (2013) 'Mega-Events and Urban Regeneration in Rio de Janeiro: Planning in a State of Emergency', *International Journal of Urban Sustainable Development*, Vol. 5, No. 2, pp. 132–163.

Shin, H.B. (2012) 'Unequal Cities of Spectacle and Mega-Events in China', *City: Analysis of Urban Trends, Culture, Theory, Policy, Action.* Vol. 16, pp. 728–744.

Smith, A. (2005) 'Reimaging the City: The Value of Sport Initiatives', *Annals of Tourism Research.* Vol. 32, pp. 217–236.

Smith, A. (2006) 'Assessing the Contribution of Flagship Projects to City Image Change: A Quasi-Experimental Technique', *International Journal of Tourism Research.* Vol. 8, pp. 391–404.

Stavrides, S. (2014) 'Athens 2004 Olympics: An Urban State of Exception which Became the Rule', Keynote presentation, *Second International Conference on Mega-Events and the City.* Rio de Janeiro.

Sylvestre, G. and de Oliveira, N. (2012) 'The Revanchist Logic of Mega-Events: Community Displacement in Rio de Janeiro's West End', *Visual Studies.* Vol. 27, No. 2, pp. 204–210.

Upton, D. (1991) 'Architectural History or Landscape History?', *Journal of Architectural Education.* Vol. 44, pp. 195–199.

Urry, J. (2002) *The Tourist Gaze,* 2nd edition. London: SAGE.

Vainer, C.B. (2010) 'Megaeventos e a Cidade de Exceção', *Mega-Events and the City International Conference.* Niterói.

Vale, L.J. and Bass Warner, S. (2001) *Imaging the City: Continuing Struggles and New Directions.* New Brunswick, NJ: Rutgers University Center for Urban Policy Research.

Ward, S.V. (1998) *Selling Places: The Marketing and Promotion of Towns and Cities, 1850–2000.* London: Routledge.

Wright, T. (1997) *Out of Place Homeless Mobilizations, Subcities, and Contested Landscapes.* Albany, NY: State University of New York Press.

1 Mega-events and urban image construction

A tale of two cities

It is no exaggeration to state that sporting mega-events have as much to do with sports as they have to do with image. These events are exceptional moments for the production and consumption of images, and their organization is all about image management and planning. They represent great image-construction endeavours for nations, cities, politicians, brands, corporations and athletes. In recent decades, the staging of mega-events such as world exhibitions, international conferences or major sports competitions like the FIFA World Cup or the Olympic Games has become both an instrument of urban image construction and a justification to initiate large-scale urban transformation.

This chapter is concerned with the role played by mega-events in the transformation of their host cities and the development of urban image-construction practices. It examines how mega-events serve as opportunities to impress a new reality upon the existing city, contributing to the crystallization of public policies that serve some to the detriment of others. The first part of the chapter discusses the main forces that motivate the hosting of such global-scale events and which make event-led image-construction practices both highly political and artfully deceptive. The second part introduces two dominant paradigms commonly used in the realization of the event-city and the construction of its image: the city as spectacle and the city of exception, each illustrated in detail by the distinct experience of Beijing and Rio de Janeiro. These cities' social, political and economic climate and their particular urban conditions are examined to assess what part mega-events may have played in determining the urban image-construction strategies developed.

The motives and benefits of hosting mega-events

The candidacy of a city to host a mega-event is usually initiated by a coalition of public and private sector actors at the national, state and local levels, whose motives differ according to the benefits they seek in this venture. National leaders usually support the hosting of mega-events for the role they play as part of public diplomacy strategies and a way to broaden their global sphere of influence (Rojek 2013). Grix and Lee (2013) describe the strategic use of sporting mega-events to alter one's poor international image as a form of *soft power*, defined by Joseph

Nye (2004) as the ability to attract and co-opt instead of using force, money or coercion (*hard power*). National leaders also view such events as a relatively affordable way to improve their country's image, credibility, stature, economic competitiveness and ability to take on a leadership position in the global arena. For them, mega-events represent a rare occasion to exhibit statecraft, showcase a unified citizenry, demonstrate economic abilities and display technological advances (Rojek 2013).

At the city level, the need for economic survival and anxieties about one's position in the dominant world order are among the main factors that motivate local leaders to seek out mega-events. With their vast media coverage and strong branding power, world-class sporting events are seen as an unparalleled source of recognition and prestige. Harnessed by cities looking for a competitive advantage in the global economy, the hosting of mega-events represents a rare and unique opportunity to advertise their assets and to enhance their global visibility. Mega-events are perceived as a stamp of approval from the international community that will attest to a city's economic performance, organizational efficiency and cultural sophistication. They are also viewed as instruments of economic regeneration, stimulating domestic consumer markets while capturing mobile sources of capital. Furthermore, the tremendous symbolic weight placed upon these events endows local authorities with great leverage in the spectacular reorganization of urban space and the aesthetic control of the city's image. Hosting mega-events thus allows local authorities to secure funding from different levels of government to help finance key urban projects that may have long laid dormant (Hiller 2006; Smith 2005; Chalkey and Essex 1999).

Local economic elites in the tourism, hospitality and real-estate sectors are often among the main promoters of a city's candidacy as future host of a sporting mega-event. Apart from their obvious economic interests, local entrepreneurs and business owners covet mega-events as means to increase their power within local politics, to influence the decision-making process and reprioritize the urban agenda. They use the pretext to push for policies that are advantageous for them while discharging any blame on the needs of mega-events and the demands of International Sporting Federations. Mega-events are thus entrenched in a complex politics of representation, shaped by the interests and desires of multiple actors, both internal and external to the city, whose irreconcilable demands and divergent viewpoints about policy orientations and development priorities can exacerbate existing tensions within their host city.

Performance anxiety in the hosting of mega-events

Things get more complicated once the city becomes selected as host and must accommodate the demands of external players such as International Sporting Federations, global event sponsors and other foreign interests, who have a stake in the successful hosting of the event. Their objectives are often aligned with those of local elites, and their institutional orientation towards commercial profits means they favour place images that connote order, security and organizational sophistication. Not only are reputations at stake, but a lot of investments and potential benefits also depend upon the projection of an impeccable place image. Telecommunication companies, broadcasting right holders and the press also play a role in the image-conscious remodelling of the host city as a fit background for their reporting. The media thrives on spectacle and demands grandiose urban settings that are both telegenic and visually consumable. Event-led image construction thus relies on the production of an image of the city that embodies the expectations of visitors, serves the interest of stakeholders such as event franchise owners, foreign visitors, television broadcasters and event sponsors and resonates with the aspirations of local economic and political elite.

Local hosts are thus exposed to a lot of pressure to do everything in their power to brush up their image and control every aspect of the event. Sustained exposure to the critical, scrutinizing gaze of the global media explains the defensive nature of many event-related image-construction efforts, which focus on correcting perceived flaws, redressing a reputation and addressing the particular concerns of an external audience. Aware that no city is immune from negative reporting that exposes inefficiencies and embarrassing episodes of mismanagement, few event promoters want to run the risk of making Olympic history as a symbol of poor planning, and to inherit the reputation of a barely averted disaster as their greatest Olympic legacy, such as in the cases of Montreal and Athens.

The pressure to perform is even greater for cities of the East and Global South, confronted with a biased Western media bent on confirming negative stereotypes about local inclinations for crime, violence, disorganization and delays (Dimeo and Kay 2004). While event organizers wish to project a positive image of good management and effective organizational capacity, journalists on the ground are often more likely to highlight the host city's 'competency deficit' (Dimeo and Kay 2004). Not only do cities of emerging nations face important hurdles in their efforts to project a positive urban image, but the stakes in hosting mega-events are especially high (Rivenburg 2004). When countries facing massive poverty and housing shortages spend their limited resources on hosting mega-events, it is not only in the hope of promoting economic development, but more importantly to escape marginalization, to overcome a precarious position in the symbolic ranking of nations, and to acquire global respect (Black and van der Westhuizen 2004).

For countries on the margin, hosting mega-events is seen as a test of modernity, a performance indicator, and an occasion to establish their credibility as worthy economic players. Rose and Spiegel (2011) suggest that these cities bid to host mega-events as a way to send economic signals that could help launch them into the global economy by boosting national exports and international trade. More than merely an instrument for measuring the health of a city, a region or a nation, participation in mega-events has become a mark of responsible citizenship, a statement of a country's identity and collective aspirations. On 2 October 2009, when Brazil won its bid to host the 2016 Olympics, president Lula expressed with a rare clarity the historical significance of this event for his nation:

Brazil has left its second-class status behind and has joined the first class. Today we received respect. This is a victory for 190 million souls, a victory for Latin America, a victory for the Olympics.... Brazil today won her international citizenship, we broke the last barrier of prejudice.

(Redação Estadão 2009)

Smoke screens and mirrors: potemkinism and other deceptions

It is in part in response to the multiple demands and enormous pressure associated with their realization that mega-events have come to be associated with a culture of covert deceit, replete with unrealistic predictions and unproven assertions. Proponents feel compelled to deploy a vast range of persuasion techniques to embellish reality, win over public opinion and rally investors. Julier (2005) talks of the creative repackaging of local reality, while Greene (2003) describes host cities as 'staged cities', promoted as models of success and prosperity to obscure grim urban realities. For David Harvey (1989), the façade of cultural redevelopment that results from the mass production of festivals and celebrations acts as a 'carnival mask' to conceal continuing disinvestment and divert attention from growing inequality. Rojek (2013) denounces the hypocritical façade of mega-events, easily co-opted by the entities that manage, operate and design them. He describes greedy, manipulative politicians and their hidden economic interests as backstage puppet masters who appropriate these events to pocket their massive short-term profits.

Cities resort to such stratagems when pressured to correct negative perceptions, to restore a damaged reputation or to perform in unfamiliar circumstances. Aspects of urban reality that suggest disorder or decline are often actively concealed or left out of representations because they may tarnish the city's carefully constructed image. Endemic problems that cannot be easily resolved are addressed by masking the issue, or diverting attention and putting emphasis elsewhere. Examples of deceitful tactics of event-led image construction abound. In Beijing in 2008, city leaders countered negative reporting in the international media regarding air pollution, traffic congestion and tainted food products by taking drastic actions for hygiene and pollution alleviation, but also by reducing urban mobility, shutting down factories and occasionally falsifying official pollution indices (Broudehoux 2011). In many cities, vast efforts are deployed to both hide and destroy the landscapes of the poor, simply and violently banishing them from sight (Kennelly and Watts 2011).

As Andranovitch *et al.* (2001) suggest, making a debut on the world stage requires looking the part. In my research, especially in the context of pre-Olympic China, I have used the term *potemkinism* to describe the projection of an idealized vision of the city that both beautifies and falsifies reality. This image construction strategy relies on deception and manipulation to project a highly controlled and overly positive image, and could be described, in popular parlance, as a kind of 'fake it till you make it' approach to modernization, where the city is 'pimped' for maximum effect.

The notion of *potemkinism* comes from Tsarist Russia, when Catherine the Great undertook a grand tour of the Crimea to witness the progress of her colonization efforts. To deceive the empress about the mixed success of his initiatives, Prince Grigory Potemkin allegedly used theatrical stage sets to erect imitation villages in the landscape, thus suggesting a more advanced rate of settlement. The Bolshevik revolution would later refine similar practices and develop new, carefully constructed representations of reality where 'the defects and contradictions of the present are overlooked and the world is described not as it is but as it is becoming' (Fitzpatrick 1999: 16).

As an image-construction practice, potemkinism sheds light on some of the mechanisms that underscore contemporary interventions, especially in the context of aspiring world cities. In the context of Athens 2004, Beriatos and Gospodini (2004) suggest that one should distinguish between attempting to change a city's image while changing its actual reality, and attempting to change its image without making any genuine, lasting improvements. In this sense, image construction is often no more than a mirage, an illusory promise whose benefits never quite materialize. While from a distance the impression may appear genuine and substantial, upon closer examination it turns out to be ersatz and evanescent.

As a manipulation of appearances to distort and embellish reality, potemkinism can also be seen as a self-preservation mechanism developed in response to the presence of an external, critical viewer, assessing one's worth and substance. It does not merely suggest a desire to mystify by disguising reality, but rather connotes an intention to please, to impress and to fulfil expectations, even through deception and disguise. More importantly, it conveys a certain unease, even embarrassment, at exposing what could be taken as proof of one's failure, inadequacy or, worse, inferiority.

In totalitarian regimes, potemkinism is not limited to visual manipulations, but also includes a wide range of discursive practices and strategies that rely upon the use of seductive rhetoric, superlative language, mystifying data and diverse forms of exaggeration to improve perceptions of reality. Going beyond simple window dressing and the construction of false façades, it involves the reconstruction of an entire reality, a whole potemkin world in which newspapers, movies, political speeches and official statistics conspire to dispel allegations of economic and cultural backwardness (Fitzpatrick 1999). This embellished vision is not strictly aimed at an external audience, but also seeks to convince local citizens of the righteousness of their leaders and the merits of the revolution.

Of course, image control is not exclusive to any political-economic system and can be found in different cultural contexts. In Brazil, a close equivalent to the idea of potemkinism lies in the expression 'para ingles ver' (literally 'for the English to see'), which could be translated as 'just for show' or 'for the sake of appearances'. The expression is said to date back to the second half of the nineteenth century, when England compelled Brazil to sign a series of treaties to stop slave trafficking. With no real intention of ending the lucrative trade, Brazil passed a number of abolitionist legislations to satisfy English demands, which were never put into effect. The expression is now used to denounce cosmetic modernization projects or to refer to Brazil's embracing of liberal ideas and institutions associated with developed countries for largely 'ornamental' purposes (Figure 1.1). This expression adds a new dimension to the idea of potemkinism, as it goes beyond the simple display of

Figure 1.1 UPP é pra gringo ver. Graffiti in one of Rio's favelas denouncing the police
    pacification programme (PPP) as being for the outside world's benefit (for the
    gringo to see) (photo by the author, 2013).

a false reality to impress outside viewers and evokes a covert resistance strategy,
akin to what James Scott (1985) calls *false compliance*. For Scott, by pretending to
comply with the demands of their superiors while carrying out their own intentions,
subordinate groups produce a 'veiled discourse of dignity and self-assertion',
thereby subverting power inequalities and skirting domination (Scott 1985: 137).

The Chinese also have an interesting expression to qualify potemkinist urban
practices. They talk of *mian* (face) projects, which allow their promoters to build
or save face, and thus to preserve their dignity, suggesting that a disappointing
performance may result in a loss of respect.[1] Underlying these different expressions
is the idea of an uneven power relationship between the subject and an external
assessor, which reveals deep insecurities about one's status in the world. Such
practices are also deeply entrenched into a complex politics of representation,
where images play a central role in the construction and maintenance of one's
status and position in a hierarchical system.

Event-led urban image construction: two dominant paradigms

The contemporary literature on mega-events identifies two main paradigms in the
realization of the event-city and the transformation of its image: the *city as
spectacle* and the *city of exception*. The city as spectacle draws upon Guy Debord
and other theorists to suggest that dramatic and ostentatious urban transformations
linked to the hosting of spectacular, global-scale events are instrumentalized by
ruling coalitions to consolidate their power (Shin 2012; Broudehoux 2010;
Gruneau and Horne 2015). This vision posits that by helping build popular

consensus around the grand collective endeavours that sporting events represent, the spectacle facilitates state manipulations and distracts popular attention from important political issues. The second paradigm, the *city of exception*, presents hosting mega-events as an opportunity seized by local political and economic elites to take advantage of the artificial crisis occasioned by the event's tight deadline. This crisis allows them to alter their city's juridico-legal makeup and implement 'exceptional measures' that accelerate the city's neoliberalization in ways that may appear temporary but have long-term implications (Stavrides 2010; Oliveira 2013; Vainer 2010; Powell and Marrero-Guillamón 2012).

Although most event cities combine aspects of both approaches in different proportions, each of the two cities studied in this book epitomize one paradigm in particular: Olympic Beijing represents the ultimate in the spectacularization of mega-events, while Rio de Janeiro perfectly embodies the city of exception. If both paradigms differ in their motives and application, they remain similar in their underlying logic, and both instrumentalize mega-events to serve particular interests and consolidate power. While the first approach is more concerned with national politics, image and prestige, and the other aims to respond to the demands of global capital, they both remain quite similar in terms of imaging strategies and concrete outcomes for the general population, as the following chapters will show.

The spectacle as instrument of power and control

Throughout history, the spectacle has served as an instrument of hegemonic power, a crucial weapon in the struggle to gain and maintain rule of people and territories, playing a significant part in the constitution of empires and nation states (Waitt 1999). Power-seekers, both religious and political, have relied on spectacular events to conquer the world and legitimize their rule, appropriating entertainment, art and festival to distract, appease and control the masses. From the proverbial *circenses* of imperial Rome, to the military parades and monuments of Empire and the Nuremberg rallies of Nazi Germany, the staging of spectacles for mass mobilization has served the interests of the ruling elite and helped secure their grip on power.

One of the chief roles of the spectacle is to maximize the visibility of the state in the landscape. As an intangible entity lacking materiality, the state depends upon physical embodiments and permanent markers to make its existence manifest (Low 2003). The built environment has come to play a central role in substantiating the state's presence in the city, as the constitutive element of urban space and the most visible expression of cultural and civic values. Through the manipulation of images and symbols, monumental spaces act as communicative mechanisms for state ideologies. More than a simple backdrop for elaborate rituals, protocols and other state choreographies, architecture and urban design are full participants in the machinery of power.

Leaders of autocratic regimes and democratically elected governments alike have used the urban landscape as an instrument of propaganda and statecraft, a medium through which they could seduce their followers and intimidate their opponents. In imperial China, new dynastic rulers rebuilt their capital city to erase traces of their predecessors, using symbolically charged spaces and highly codified architecture to signify the beginning of a new heavenly mandate. Autocratic regimes, from Mussolini to Ceauşescu and Kim Jong-il, relied on monumentalism, theatricality and excess to emotionally engage their supporters and to legitimize their dominant position in society (Fitzpatrick 1999). Late capitalist rulers across the political spectrum, from François Mitterand, to Tony Blair and Hu Jintao, similarly exploited the power of architecture, not only to immortalize their leadership, but also to secure a position in the world economy (Carter 2008; Sudjic 2005).

The spectacle has also been harnessed in support of economic power, helping capitalists secure their dominance and hegemony. Walter Benjamin (1968: 165–167) describes how mid-nineteenth-century universal exhibitions attracted pilgrims to the commodity fetish, and turned the commodity into a spectacle that transformed citizens into spectators and consumers. The phantasmagoria of window displays, advertising and commodity abundance became a ploy by which capitalism could ensure its own survival, by manufacturing consent and promoting consumption. Conspicuous consumption itself played an important depoliticizing role, distracting popular attention from public debate and assigning the masses a passive role in public affairs (Benjamin 1968). More recently, the spectacularization of the urban landscape has been championed by cities seeking global recognition. The spectacle is now seen as essential to the survival of twenty-first-century cities, as urban imagineers and city marketers capitalize upon spectacular architecture and alluring urban iconography as key generators of symbolic capital, helping market and advertise their city (Judd 2003; Ashworth and Voogd 1990). The spectacle is so central to the new urban economy that one of the most effective ways for cities to enhance their world image is by staging global-scale events that promote an image of the city as a vital and dynamic place.

But the spectacle's greatest asset remains its power of mystification: its capacity to mute criticism, to facilitate compliance, to pacify and depoliticize. Since the 1960s, critical theorists have reappraised the value of the spectacle in their critique of the alienation of Western capitalist society. In a post-modern world dominated by media-images and marked by the triumph of pseudo realities, Daniel Boorstin (1961), followed by Jean Baudrillard (1968), underlines the role of symbolic codes and visual phenomena in manipulating the masses, describing visibility, invisibility and images as the dominant modalities of contemporary power. For Baudrillard (1981), in a world of pure signs, disconnected from its referents, it is through seduction – a celebration of surface – that the image engages viewers, daunting any quest for meaning and preventing deeper levels of inquiry.

But it was Guy Debord (1967) who best exposed the spectacle as a manipulation of meaning-making processes to serve the production of economic and political power. Characterizing late capitalist society as the *Society of Spectacle*, Debord deplored his contemporaries' obsession with the superficial world of the commodified image, which he accused of displacing reality. For him, the power of the spectacle went beyond the simple domination of images and media saturation; it was an entire worldview that had materialized into an objective reality (Debord 1967).

Debord (1967) presents the spectacle as a tool of pacification and depoliticization, a 'permanent opium war' which uses the ideology of consumerism to ferment political indifference, stupefy social subjects and distract them from the more vital aspects of everyday life. Debord's notion of spectacle is integrally connected to ideas of alienation, passivity, submission and pacification, where the lifeless consumption of spectacles distances people from their creative and imaginative potential and estranges them from actively engaging in the production of their own life.

Debord theorized the multiple ways in which the spectacle serves power. For him, it is in the specialization of power that the spectacle takes its full force. In his 1988 *Commentaries*, Debord delineates three categories of spectacle, based on the specific form of power they embody. The *concentrated spectacle* is the spectacle of raw political power, the spectacle produced by centrally planned power, which favours an ideology condensed around a tyrannical personality or a totalitarian regime, such as those found in 1930s dictatorships. The *diffuse spectacle*, a particularly American brand of the spectacle, is the spectacle of economic power, associated with advanced capitalism and commodity abundance, akin to the commodity phantasmagoria described by Walter Benjamin (1968). If the concentrated spectacle operates mostly through violence, it is through seduction that the diffuse spectacle generally performs. According to Debord, since the late 1960s, global capitalism has brought about a rational combination of these two forms of spectacle into a new one, serving simultaneously economic and political power: the *integrated spectacle*, which represents the form of spectacular consumer society that has imposed itself globally. The late capitalist spectacle thus embodies a new, uniquely specialized form of power. Once a way for state and Church power to keep the masses under control, the spectacle now represents corporate capital's way of deluding and intoxicating people with the illusion of commodity culture.

More recently, some political theorists have built upon Debord's concept of the *integrated spectacle* to develop a new theory of the state. Philosopher Giorgio Agamben (2000) contends that the society of spectacle is the final stage of the evolution of the state form, and represents the ultimate condition of integration of state and economy. For Agamben, this society captures the commodity's last metamorphosis, in which exchange value has completely eclipsed use value. He locates the rise of this spectacular state in the development of late capitalism, where state and economy are interwoven to the point that the logic of capitalist development now determines the state. This latest form of the state is made manifest as capitalism takes over the state to become absolutely sovereign.

In the context of the mega-event-city, scholars have viewed the spectacle as a tool of distraction and control used by authoritarian leaders and power coalitions to pacify local residents and blind them from the multiple long-term costs of the event-city's socio-spatial reorganization (Broudehoux 2007, 2010; Caffrey 2013; Shin 2012; Gotham 2005). But the spectacle is also described as an instrument deployed to rally investors to finance the realization of the event-city. Drawing upon anthropologist Anna Tsing's (2000) notion of an 'economy of appearances', which presents the self-conscious making of a spectacle as necessary to attract investment funds, Carter (2006) views the dramatic demonstration of 'spectacular accumulation' as a prerequisite for cities wishing to assert their viability. According to Tsing (2000), those seeking financial capital must dramatize their growth potential and produce a spectacle of economic performance and profitability in order to attract the investment they need to operate and expand. For her, this economy of appearances, which relies on the conjunction of both economic and dramatic performance, has become a regular feature of the search for financial capital. Successful image-construction campaigns are thus premised on equal doses of urban development and public relations initiatives. In a kind of potemkin logic, cities have to 'appear' to be dynamic, progressive, modern and 'global' before actually economically becoming so.

Olympic Beijing, or the city as spectacle

Beijing's 2008 Olympic Games came in the midst of China's historical transition from a planned to a market economy under the autocratic leadership of the Chinese Communist Party. Since the early 1990s, China's state policy had been characterized by deregulation and by a rush to join the world market. China's particular configuration of market society led to the simultaneous waning of state capacity and its over-involvement in the workings of the market. For political analyst Wang Hui (2003), politics and economics became so intertwined that those who controlled China's domestic capital came to control political power, to the point that political and economic elites were completely conflated. Through the exchange of power for money, public property was placed in the hands of interest groups who used their monopoly power to seize market resources and earn substantial profits.

The Olympic transformation of China's 800-year-old capital city and centre of state power took place in the context of a post-socialist mode of urban governance, characterized by growing inter-urban competition, where cities sought to reposition themselves on the national and international scene in order to attract foreign investment and mobile capital (Wu 2000; Xu and Yeh 2005). Thanks to China's economic reforms, which devolved more political-economic power to localities, local governments enjoyed greater financial flexibility and increased autonomy and control over land disposal.

However, this new urban condition remained constrained by the legacy of state socialism (Wang 2003). Because local officials were appointed rather than elected and were promoted according to political loyalty, economic performance and achievements, they tended to favour high-visibility physical projects rather than less tangible social initiatives to make their accomplishments more noticeable and to help sustain their career advancement (Ma and Wu 2005). As a result, new urban strategies focused on large projects as a means of promoting economic development and projecting a new, dynamic urban image.

In the heydays of socialism, China had developed a sophisticated image-construction strategy, largely modelled on Soviet practices, and perfected the art of embellishing reality, using diverse potemkinist approaches to alter appearances. In Beijing, at the rare occasion of a visit by foreign heads of state, aspects of the city that could question the success of the socialist revolution were either dressed up or carefully concealed, using rapidly erected walls, billboards or shrubbery, while dissidents and indigents were safely placed out of sight (Broudehoux 2004). In his memoir, Henry Kissinger (1979: 1056) describes his 1972 visit to China as 'a carefully rehearsed play in which nothing was accidental and yet everything appeared spontaneous'.

The 2008 Olympic Games provided a great impetus to accelerate the modernization of China's capital city, initiated in the previous decades, especially on the occasion of the 1990s Asian Games. Soon after Beijing's selection as Olympic host in 2001, the city undertook a series of large-scale projects that sought to transform its image from a sleepy socialist capital into a world-class metropolis. This facelift not only aimed to enhance the city's economic performance by attracting international tourists and foreign investors; it also sought to restore China's international image and to legitimize the power of its ruling elite (Broudehoux 2004).

Keen to show its openness and modernity, and desirous to reform its image as a conservative gerontocracy, the Chinese leadership quickly embraced global trends in the marketing of cities to update and re-brand their capital city. They called upon avant-garde designers and capitalized on the power of architecture to endow Beijing with a distinctive image that would outdo rival destinations. Members of the international design elite found the perfect patrons in the image-conscious Chinese leadership, for whom face, prestige and symbolic capital were easily converted into political power (Broudehoux 2010).

While other cities have monumentalized the Olympics, the extent of Beijing's transformation was unprecedented and remains unrivalled to this day. After winning the bid, Beijing commissioned more than a dozen iconic projects whose ostentatious character was expressed in their size, cutting-edge design and extravagant cost. Beijing's delirious Olympic transformation contributed to the extraordinary building boom that is transforming China's landscape at a velocity perhaps unequalled in human history (Broudehoux 2007). Within a few years, 31 competition venues, 50 training venues and related facilities, a 42-building athlete village and a 16-building media village, as well as new transportation infrastructure with the construction of 62 new roads, 4 bridges, the expansion of the subway and a new light rail network were built (Beijing 2008). This impressive transformation was supplemented by the construction of the world's largest airport terminal, several spectacular cultural projects and important neighbourhood renewal initiatives, as well as countless environmental beautification and landscaping projects (Broudehoux 2007).

As the material expression of the rising power of a coalition of political leaders and their capitalist allies, this recent exercise in image construction was the embodiment of Debord's integrated spectacle. Beijing's new image testified to ongoing changes in the dominant power structure, composed of a one-party state increasingly conflated with a rising capitalist class, and sought to maximize both private profits and social control. The Olympic Games did not only radically transform the physical image of this ancient city, they also helped reconfigure its political-economic structure as well. Over 1.5 million people lost their homes and were relocated to make way for Olympic projects. In many ways, Beijing's seductive urbanism acted as a smokescreen to conceal the consolidation of autocratic power while legitimating the powerful interests of property developers.

Beijing's Olympic projects were mostly built through public–private partnerships, which made private sector actors, often with close ties to the Party, the main beneficiaries of public investments. Beijing's rapid and largely unregulated transformation allowed private investors to serve their own economic interests in the reconfiguration of the urban landscape. After the Games, many facilities were privatized as the entrepreneurs responsible for overseeing their construction became their managers, operators and effective owners for a set contract period. By clustering capital in certain sectors of the city, Olympic restructuring helped concentrate economic assets in the hands of a few economic and political elites. It also increased the prominence of these new economic players in the city's symbolic economy, and allowed them to play a growing role in the decision-making process.

Beijing's approach to urban image construction on the occasion of the Olympic Games has proven the potency of the city as a spectacle paradigm (Broudehoux 2010; Shin 2012). The vast success of the 2008 Olympics, widely acclaimed as one of the most spectacular in history, has consecrated the rise of China as a prominent player on the world stage, demonstrating both its organizational capacity and unlimited economic resources. The glorious national image that the event projected allowed the state to regain its grip on power in the face of growing social discontent and political instability linked to the stark inequalities and exploitation that had marked China's rapid transition to a market economy. In the aftermath of the event, the state's newfound self-confidence and reclaimed authority sustained the accelerated transformation of the nation: speculative urbanization was amplified, while ever-rising inequalities went largely uncontested (Shin 2012, 2014).

The city of exception paradigm

The second paradigm in the realization of the event-city and the transformation of its image, the *city of exception*, was developed specifically to explain the urban effects of mega-events. This characterization draws upon Agamben's (2005) theorization of the 'state of exception', which describes the exercise of an authority's right to suspend laws and rights in order to face the unexpected 'necessity' posed by an imminent external or internal threat. Agamben claims that rather than being a provisional measure developed to cope with an emergency situation, the state of exception has become a common technique of government, increasingly used in a range of non-war situations, such as financial crises or general strikes. The state of exception is characterized by the state's unilateral power to bypass the pre-existing juridical order, to take preemptive measures or to rule by decrees, a process that Agamben describes as the 'suspension of law by law' (Agamben 2005).

In recent years, scholars from emerging nations that have hosted mega-events, especially from Greece, Brazil and South Africa, have applied Agamben's theory to the mega-event-city (Stavrides 2010; Oliveira 2013; Vainer 2010; Powell and Marrero-Guillamón 2012). They maintain that neoliberal leaders have managed to generate popular consensus for major urban interventions, especially in the context of mega-events, by generating an artificial crisis prompted by a discourse of fear, violence, economic decline or imminent catastrophe (Vainer 2009; Arantes 2009). Akin to the 'shock doctrine' described by Naomi Klein (2007), where disasters are used to push local economies to adapt to the needs of a neoliberal agenda, mega-events' fixed deadline and tight schedule are used to legitimate the imposition of a state of emergency upon cities, and to impress a new, exceptional mode of governance.

It is this very capacity to generate a generalized sense of urgency – what Stavrides (2010) calls an 'Olympic state of emergency' – that has legitimized the adoption of an exceptional politico-institutional framework, often in total disregard for existing legal and spatial realities. The exceptional situation created by the imminent realization of mega-events has allowed growth coalitions to exploit both the mobilizing and consensual power of the spectacle to dodge lengthy political discussions and public consultations, and take unilateral decisions to enact policy changes (Oliveira 2013).

For Vainer (2010), this state of emergency deeply impacts local planning conditions, turning host cities into 'cities of exception', where exceptions literally become the rule. Powell and Marrero-Guillamón (2012) talk of an 'Olympic state of exception', where event-promoting coalitions have been granted great leeway in reshaping the city for the needs of the event, its sponsors and their local partners. The 'event-city of exception' is thus characterized by a radical transformation of the city's legal and spatial landscape, both of which are marked by a high level of exceptionalism (Powell and Marrero-Guillamón 2012). Nunes (2014) claims that the state of exception has become the common *modus operandi* of both FIFA and the IOC, whose basic business model include the predatory privatization of profits and socialization of costs. He describes how these two private, unelected bodies, which are not accountable to any constituencies, travel the world selling 'state of exception packages' to preferably undemocratic, investment-hungry nations, in what he views as the most continuously victorious example of shock doctrine capitalism (Nunes 2014).

The Olympic city of exception thus exacerbates some of the determining features of the neoliberal city as it came to be known in the late twentieth century. Among those features is 'ad-hoc planning', which Ascher (2001) defines as contemporary urban interventions where select projects are regulated by contract rather than by law and where negotiation and compromise replace majority rule and standardized norms. Ascher (2001) also calls 'cities of exception' those cities where corporate agents play an increasing role in the transformation of urban space.

In the event-city of exception, mega-events represent essential tools to help bypass the democratic political process in the implementation of mega-projects. They legitimize the adoption of an exceptional politico-institutional framework that authorizes the relaxation of certain rules and obligations in the implementation of urban interventions that will benefit the event. The event-city is thus characterized by the disruption of accepted legal and social norms; the suspension of established procedures, restrictions and controls; the reformulation of planning regulations; the circumvention of existing laws; the lifting of safety standards; and the introduction of highly restrictive regulatory instruments to ensure compliance with the stipulations of local and global organizers and to better serve investor interests (Hayes and Horne 2011; Lima Jr 2010).

Furthermore, this state of exception facilitates the imposition of extra-legal forms of governance, allowing unelected agents, including beneficiaries of international capital sponsorship like the IOC and FIFA, to play a key role in local decision-making (Oliveira 2011). The promises made by aspiring host cities in their desperate attempt to be selected become binding after the city has been selected, even if they are often highly unrealistic and were made years before the actual hosting of the event. As a result, urban redevelopment and the use of public space is largely dictated by FIFA and the IOC, and public–private coalitions enjoy extraordinary powers to carry out massive urban transformations without any form of accountability. The scope of event-related projects to be undertaken and the magnitude of demands made by international organizations have given these coalitions licence to take exceptional measures in order to reshape the city for the needs of the event, its sponsors and local partners.

Corrarino has described in detail the extraordinary legal regime adopted to facilitate event preparation, which enables event organizers to suspend the pre-existing legal order and to impose new rules and sanctions that circumvent the normal decision-making process. This legal exceptionalism has allowed the introduction of highly restrictive regulatory instruments that govern speech, the use of public space, employment, housing and numerous other facets of life while diverting normal rights protections (Corrarino 2014). It also facilitates the fast-tracking of special laws to ensure compliance with the stipulations of local and global organizers and to better serve investor interests (Hayes and Horne 2011; Lima Jr 2010).

In this 'regime of legal exceptionalism' (Corrarino 2014), laws are not applied equally for all citizens. Actors involved in event preparation are given special treatment and allowed to bypass the competitive bidding process, suspend established procedures, reformulate planning regulations and lift safety standards. Not only do such legal exceptions benefit some more than others, but many new laws are passed in exceptional circumstances to protect the rights and interests of private corporations, and are in direct violation of local citizens' rights. This exceptional legal regime leads to a great power imbalance between local and foreign interests, and result in uneven rights protection in favour of international organizations and their sponsors. Other forms of legal exemptions granted to private entities are used to justify free speech bans or to evict or displace people without due process. It has become common practice for Olympic host cities to introduce restrictive legislation specifically directed at population groups considered undesirable to the city's image (COHRE 2007).

The exceptional circumstances that characterize mega-event planning are also affecting governmentality, with the establishment of an authoritarian form of urban governance, characterized by the direct interference of executive powers in the act of legislation. Olympic redevelopment is often marked by a total lack of transparency, where decisions are made behind closed doors, and citizen groups are denied information about the project implementation process. Mega-events are also the source of great ruptures in the local political process. Describing the unprecedented political and judicial autonomy enjoyed by organizations like FIFA and the IOC, Nelma Gusmão de Oliveira (2013) talks of the emergence of a 'parallel form of government and a parallel form of justice'. Mega-events thus facilitate the creation of a state within the state, where political and ethical responsibilities are blurred and sovereign law is suspended.

Not only do mega-events produce a legal vacuum, they have also given rise to new territorial expressions in the form of self-governing enclaves, which can be seen as the spatial manifestation of the city of exception. These pockets of extraterritoriality echo Weizman's (2005) 'archipelagos of exception', defined as discontinuous territorial fragments where sovereign power is deposed or challenged. They are considered extraterritorial because of their position outside local and national jurisdiction. For Weizman (2005), the term 'extraterritoriality' refers to those instances where a state extends its jurisdiction or effective control beyond its borders. The concept may apply to military movements on foreign soil as well as to embassies or diplomats in the form of diplomatic immunity.

In the Olympic city of exception, territorial enclaves are constituted as special autonomous zones, controlled and regulated by corporate or intergovernmental entities, where normal legal processes do not apply. For example, Olympic Parks as well as the area surrounding stadia and other venues are often isolated, both physically and legally, from their immediate context. Designated as special legal zones where political and ethical responsibilities are lifted, they function like corporate embassies and benefit from a certain form of sovereignty akin to diplomatic immunity. These zones of exception are not governed by the laws of the land, but by those of corporate or intergovernmental entities, which allows them to operate by their own rules. Although publicly funded and benefiting from generous fiscal conditions, these newly created territories are often privately owned and managed. In the South African World Cup context, Kolamo and Vuolteenaho (2013) describe the contractual rights that FIFA had over the strict delineation of official event-controlled areas as part of an 'enclavization' process, which fractioned cities and resulted in a hierarchization of public space that deeply altered accessibility.

Even if these territories of exception are characterized by the suspension of the normal legal process, it does not mean they are unregulated spaces. Quite the contrary, they have become some of the city's most regulated areas. For example, many territories of exception rely on stringent antiterrorist-like regulations to provide security for capital and to protect the rights and privileges of major stakeholders. The fact that mega-event revenues rely on exclusive broadcasting and sponsorship contracts explains some of the extreme measures deployed to protect the sponsors' acquired 'monopoly rights', especially against ambush marketing. So vast is the sovereignty of these territories of exception that they are immune to the rules of the free market. Indeed, many of them could be qualified of 'zones of protected monopoly', and represent places where market rules of fair competition no longer apply.

Among different types of territories of exclusion that have emerged in the city of exception are 'brand exclusion zones', areas surrounding event venues which are designated as special legal zones and where commercial product placement for approved branded sponsors is protected (Hall 2012). Exceptional legislation adopted in sight of the coming mega-events thus allow the conversion of part of the city's public spaces into privatized, exclusive and monopolistic commercial territories. These exclusive zones typically correspond to an area delimited by a 1 km radius from event venues. Inside, commercial and advertising rights are restricted to event sponsors, while the sale of products and the placement of publicity from companies other than official sponsorship rights holders are proscribed. These brand exclusion zones therefore make illegal a host of activities and practices normally conducted in the city's public space, such as vending unofficial products, wearing non-sanctioned commercial brands, consuming non-sponsor drinks and food, which are seen as breaches in the exclusivity contracts signed by cities. The existence of these zones prevents the operation of countless independent sales points that would have generated significant revenue for local residents.

Examples of such exclusion zones include FIFA Fan Fest zones, which are public viewing areas where fans are invited to watch football games on giant screens, to attend staged performances and to consume sponsored products. These densely mediated enclaves, saturated with event-related images and narratives, are dedicated to branded product placement and to the festive celebration of the event. According to FIFA propaganda, they represent 'unique opportunities to build brand relationships'. Those fenced-off portions of the city's public spaces are highly controlled contractual spaces (Augé 1995), protected by legal contracts and carefully monitored against the violation of intellectual property rights by both private security agents and local police. This kind of reality has led Boykoff (2014) to describe mega-events not as a strictly neoliberal affair, marked by growing deregulation and privatization, but as a stringent regime of rules and regulations emanating from mega-event franchise owners like the IOC or FIFA. He charges these remarkably powerful institutions as being against the free market, forcing host cities to bend local laws to conform to commercial imperatives, for example by enforcing stringent brand protections (Boykoff 2014).

In his description of the state of exception as a technique of government, Agamben (2005) warns that rather than being a provisional measure, this vision has a tendency to impose itself permanently and to become a regular feature of state rule. Although adopted in an urgent manner, the changes provoked by the state of exception can have lasting impacts. In the context of mega-events, one major risk of this paradigm is that in spite of being presented as temporary, many exceptional measures implemented in the months leading to the event and during the weeks of the event themselves become permanent after the event and come to be seen as the 'new normal' (Fussey *et al.* 2011).

Rio de Janeiro as Olympic city of exception

Rio de Janeiro is a city long concerned with the production and dissemination of a positive urban image. Endowed with a unique topography, a spectacular shoreline and a rich urban culture, the city has historically enjoyed a great reputation as Brazil's prime tourism destination. But over the last few decades, Rio's image has suffered a series of blows, beginning with the loss, in 1960, of its 200-year-old status as capital of Brazil. The transfer of government functions to Brasilia profoundly affected the local economy, compounded by the ascent of São Paulo as the economic and financial centre of Brazil. In the 1990s, the city's reputation further suffered from drug-related violence and criminality, widespread poverty and rampant social inequality, and the incapacity for the local state to manage this crisis.

The coming of Rio's moment in the global spotlight, with the hosting of two of the world's most important sporting mega-events, was facilitated by several factors, including the adoption, in the 1990s, of strategic planning, a neoliberal mode of governance. In Brazil this managerial approach was perceived as the only viable option to face the new conditions imposed by globalization (Vainer 2009). The debt crisis of the 1980s and the end of the military dictatorship facilitated a major shift towards neoliberalism in Brazil's political economy. Faced with falling property tax revenues and growing deficits, municipal governments moved away from policies that meet the basic needs of the population in favour of policies to attract investment. This marked the disappearance of the old model of rational, technocratic and centralized planning, where urban strategies focused on collective consumption and land use, in favour of an 'entrepreneurial' mode of urban management (Arantes 2009; Harvey 1989). In this vision, a market logic was applied to the organization of urban space and the city became at once a product sold on the market and a profit-generating enterprise.

In 1995, Rio de Janeiro adopted Latin America's first strategic plan, modelled after the approach pioneered in Barcelona, whose acclaimed Olympic revitalization was widely emulated in Latin America. Barcelona's success in mobilizing private sector resources to revitalize its urban infrastructure, and its use of mega-events to rejuvenate a depressed urban image, attract external capital and position itself in the global economy, greatly influenced Rio de Janeiro's new urban vision (Ferreira 2010). The strategic plan vowed to restore tourism as the city's 'natural' vocation and to insert Rio in the mega-events circuit as a viable way to enhance the city's global image and stimulate inward investment (Acioly 2001). Planning strategies focused on improving the city's image, repackaging its assets and marketing its competitive advantages to foreign investors, wealthy residents, international tourists and members of the creative class. The period saw a new rapprochement between the city's public and private sectors, which revived an old alliance between real-estate capital and the city's executive power (Oliveira 2013; Lima Jr 2010).

This neoliberal planning vision was marked by an authoritarian conception of the exercise of power, based on the construction and consolidation of consensus, on selective popular participation, and on the growing involvement of the private sector in urban management. It corresponds to a vision of neoliberalism that Žižek (1999) qualifies as 'post-political', where open debate around urban issues is discouraged, and dissent is replaced by compromise and pacification (Oliveira 2013). This competitive urban vision requires a reconfiguration of the political order, with the inclusion of members of the private sector and other non-elected participants in the act of governing. According to Vainer (2009), Brazil's own brand of strategic planning radicalized the Catalan model by reinterpreting the integration of public and private sectors advocated by Castells and Borja (1996) and eliminating the rigid separation between public and private sectors, a move that Brazilian critics have equated to the submission of the common good to private interests (Vainer 2009). Another aspect of the neoliberal planning vision adopted by Rio de Janeiro is institutional flexibility, which allowed authorities to reformulate planning regulations by adapting zoning and land use plans to specific projects in an ad-hoc fashion and granting tax breaks and legal exemptions to serve investor interests (Lima Jr 2010).

Rio de Janeiro's incursion into the realm of mega-events began with the hosting of the 1992 World Summit on the environment. Over the next decades, the city would more firmly embrace mega-events as a core promotional strategy to attract global capital, hosting, among others, the 2007 Pan American Games, the 2010 World Urban Forum, the 2011 Military World Games, the 2013 World Youth Day, the 2014 FIFA World Cup, the 2015 celebration of the city's 450th anniversary and the 2016 Olympic Games. The hosting of mega-events was pursued as a means of positioning itself among great world cities and as a unique opportunity to attract global interest, to stimulate inward investment and to improve the city's 'primitive accumulation of symbolic capital' (Torres Ribeiro 2006). These events were part of the 'trophies' the city had been collecting, to use the state governor Cabral's terminology, attempting to buttress its stature, to consolidate the local brand and elevate its position in the global hierarchy by accumulating accolades and recognitions (Gaffney 2016). For example, the selection of Cristo Redentor as one of the seven contemporary Wonders of the World in 2011 and the designation of Rio de Janeiro's landscape as a UNESCO World Heritage in 2012 were considered as aggregators of value for the city (Gaffney 2016).

Rio's embrace of sporting mega-events as a development strategy was facilitated by a rare political alignment at the municipal, provincial and federal levels, with a strong political alliance between President Lula's Worker's Party, Rio de Janeiro's state governor, Sergio Cabral, and Rio's mayor, Eduardo Paes. This unified political front was behind Rio's successful Olympic bid after two failed attempts (2004, 2012), and the successful hosting of the 2007 Pan American Games. Local economic agents took advantage of this favourable social, economic and political conjuncture to push the adoption of many opportunistic projects, while the municipal government used these projects for self-promotional purposes.

Projects planned for the 2014 World Cup and 2016 Olympics confirmed Rio's strategic plan orientation, with market-friendly policies that promoted the concentration of power and capital and the privatization of public space and services. More than 20 billion dollars of public funds would be spent on Olympic-related investments, which strengthened the role of a handful of private companies in transforming the city's urban landscape, especially in transportation management. These companies control most major event-related projects, including the construction of the new Bus Rapid Transit (BRT) corridors, Rio's subway expansion, the Maracanã Stadium makeover and Porto Maravilha, the city's vast port revitalization project.

These few key enterprises have expanded their influence in urban affairs and now play a growing role in the exercise of state power, to the point that Rachel Rolnik (2014), special UN reporter on housing issues, described the Brazilian state as having been *absolutely privatized*. A series of reports made public in 2014 demonstrate how the firms who benefited from the mega-event construction boom, which include Andrade Gutierrez, Camargo Corréa, Odebrecht and OAS, figure among the greatest political donors to the leading Worker's Party campaigns (Oliveira and Vainer 2014).[2] The *O Globo* newspaper claims that for every R$1 donated to the 2010 campaign funds, these companies gained R$8 in public projects. An independent research group that in 2014 released a document called 'Who are Brazil's real owners?' pushes allegations further by suggesting the existence of a cartel between the aforementioned enterprises, which have dominated mega-event construction and were involved in more than 20 event-related public projects (Instituto Mais Democracia 2014).[3]

Conclusions

This chapter has underlined the role of mega-events in processes of urban image construction and introduced some of the actors, motives and benefits that drive their realization. The chapter also introduced two dominant paradigms that characterize the event-led transformation of host cities, illustrated by detailed examples of each paradigm, respectively embodied by Beijing and Rio de Janeiro.

In the city as spectacle example, mega-events were shown to serve as an occasion to remake the city's image in a way that will secure the leadership's grip on power. The construction of ostentatious mega-projects, world-class architecture and top-of-the-line infrastructure were used to facilitate the accumulation of symbolic capital in the eye of an outward audience. In Beijing, event-led urban development was less about functionality, economic rationality and growth than about power, image and prestige. The world's most famous designers were thus invited to brand their landscape and endow their city with impressive visual icons that would provide highly coveted symbolic capital. Rio de Janeiro's mega-event transformation was much less concerned with spectacle, and relied very little on 'economy of appearance' strategies, drawing more upon a city of exception approach, using the juridico-legal reframing of the urban landscape to facilitate the city's territorial reconfiguration and its control. Its greatest impacts were in the accelerated privatization of the urban landscape and its elitist reconfiguration, with long-term legal, social and spatial consequences.

In spite of their great differences, both approaches display similarities. In both cases, mega-events represent important agents of change that accelerate transformations in the distribution and geometry of power, while providing the tools and arguments to help disguise these transformations as urgent and necessary endeavours meant to improve collective wellbeing. Both approaches were marked by a democratic deficit and were led by authoritarian regimes bent on taking whatever necessary measures not merely in order to stage a successful event but to facilitate the reconfiguration of urban territory to serve the needs of state-assisted capital accumulation. In both cases, local governments have relied on private entrepreneurs to help finance these projects. Those investors often had privileged relationships with government leaders and viewed such investments as opportunities for rent seeking and speculation, and benefited from enhanced property values and a growing influence upon policy-making. As a result, event-related projects prioritized the economic benefits of private investors and the political visibility of their public sponsors over the amelioration of local urban conditions.

This first chapter introduced some of the complex issues that cities face as they prepare to host world-class sporting mega-events. The following chapters will examine in more detail the process of image construction that accompanies these events and the strategies developed to maximize their potential benefits. Each of the next three chapters focuses on a particular dimension of event-led urban image construction: the cognitive dimension, the material dimension and the social dimension.

Notes

1 This usage is generally limited to the colloquial language. Official discourse is generally more cautious about the use of the term 'face' (*mian* or *mianzi*), for which it usually substitutes the words for 'honour' and 'dignity' (see Brownell 1995: 296–302).
2 For example, Andrade Gutierrez was involved in the construction of the Olympic Park and the athletes' village, the port's light rail system, and both the Transolimpica and Transcarioca BRT systems. It was also involved in the construction of several World Cup stadia around Brazil. AOS, for its part, was contracted for Rio's new subway line, the port revitalization project, the Transolimpica and Transcarioca BRT lines and the new light rail system. Odebrecht worked on Rio's international airport upgrade, the transformation of the Maracana Stadium, the construction of new subways lines, cable car systems, light rail and BRT lines, as well as in the Porto Maravilha project, the Olympic Park and village. It is also involved in the construction of three other World Cup stadia in Brazil.
3 This group is made up of the Instituto Mais Democracia and the Cooperativa Educaçao, Informaçao e Tecnologia para au Autogestao.

References

Acioly, C. (2001) 'Reviewing Urban Revitalisation Strategies in Rio de Janeiro: From Urban Project to Urban Management Approaches', *Geoforum*. Vol. 32, No. 4, pp. 501–530.

Agamben, G. (2000) 'Marginal Notes on Commentaries on the Society of the Spectacle', *Means Without End: Notes on Politics*. Minneapolis: University of Minnesota Press, pp. 73–90.

Agamben, G. (2005) *State of Exception*. Chicago: University of Chicago Press.

Andranovich, G.J., Burbank, M.J. and Heying, C.H. (2001) 'Olympic Cities: Lessons Learned from Mega-Event Politics', *Journal of Urban Affairs*. Vol. 23, pp. 113–131.

Arantes, O. (2009) 'Uma estratégia fatal A cultura nas novas gestões urbanas', O. Arantes, C. Vainer and E. Maricato (eds). *A cidade do pensamento único: Desmanchando consensos*. Petrópolis: Vozes, pp. 11–74.

Ascher, F. (2001) *Les Nouveaux Principes de l'urbanisme: La fin des villes n'est pas à l'ordre du jour*. La Tour d'Aigues: Éditions de l'Aube.

Ashworth, G. and Voogd, H. (1990) *Selling the City: Marketing Approaches in Public Sector Urban Planning*. London: Belhaven Press.

Augé, M. (1995) *Non-places: Introduction to an Anthropology of Supermodernity*. London: Verso.

Baudrillard, J. (1968) *Le système des objets*. Paris: Gallimard.

Baudrillard, J. (1981) *Simulacres et simulation*. Paris: Galilée.

Benjamin, W. (1968) 'The Work of Art in the Age of Mechanical Reproduction', *Illuminations: Essays and Reflections*. New York: Schocken, pp. 217–252.

Beriatos, E. and Gospodini, A. (2004) '"Glocalising" Urban Landscapes: Athens and the 2004 Olympics', *Cities*. Vol. 21, No. 3 , pp. 187–202.

Black, D.R. and van der Westhuizen, J. (2004) 'The Allure of Global Games for "Semi-peripheral" Polities and Spaces: A Research Agenda', *Third World Quarterly*. Vol. 25, pp. 1195–1214.

Boorstin, D.J. (1961) *The Image: A Guide to Pseudo-Events in America*. New York: Atheneum.

Boykoff, J. (2014) *Celebration Capitalism and the Olympic Games*. London: Routledge.

Broudehoux, A.-M. (2004) *The Making and Selling of Post-Mao Beijing*. London: Routledge.

Broudehoux, A.-M. (2007) 'Spectacular Beijing: The Conspicuous Construction of an Olympic Metropolis', *Journal of Urban Affairs*. Vol. 29, pp. 383–399.

Broudehoux, A.-M. (2010) 'Images of Power: Architectures of the Integrated Spectacle at the Beijing Olympics', *Journal of Architectural Education*. Vol. 63, pp. 52–62.

Broudehoux, A.-M. (2011) 'The Social and Spatial Impacts of Olympic Image Construction: The Case of Beijing 2008', H. Lenskyj and S. Wagg (eds), *A Handbook of Olympic Studies*. London: Palgrave Macmillan, pp. 195–209.

Brownell, S. (1995) *Training the Body for China: Sports in the Moral Order of the People's Republic*. Chicago, IL: University of Chicago Press.

Caffrey, K. (2013) *Beijing Olympics: Promoting China, Soft and Hardpower in Global Politics*. London: Routledge.

Carter, T.F. (2006) 'Introduction: The Sport of Cities Spectacle and the Economy of Appearances', *City & Society*. Vol. 18, pp. 151–158.

Carter, T.F. (2008) 'Of Spectacular Phantasmal Desire: Tourism and the Cuban State's Complicity in the Commodification of its Citizens', *Leisure Studies*. Vol. 27, pp. 241–257.

Castells, M. and Borja, J. (1996) 'As cidades como atores politicos.', *Novos Estudos CEBRAP*, Vol. 45, pp. 152–166.

Chalkey, B.S. and Essex, S.J. (1999) 'Urban Development Through Hosting International Events: A History of the Olympic Games', *Planning Perspectives*. Vol. 14, No. 4, pp. 369–394.

COHRE (Centre on Housing Rights and Eviction). (2007) *Fair Play for Housing Rights: Mega-Events*. Geneva: COHRE.

Corrarino, M. (2014) 'Law Exclusion Zones: Mega-Events as Sites of Procedural and Substantive Human Rights Violations', *Yale Human Rights & Development Law Journal.* Vol. 17, pp. 180–204.

Debord, G. (1967) *La société du spectacle.* Paris: Folio.

Dimeo, P. and Kay, J. (2004) 'Major Sports Events, Image Projection and the Problems of "Semi-periphery": A Case Study of the 1996 South Asia Cricket World Cup', *Third World Quarterly.* Vol. 25, pp. 1263–1276.

Ferreira, A. (2010) 'O Projeto "Porto Maravilha" No Rio De Janeiro: Inspiração ee Barcelona e Produção a Serviço do Capital?' *Revista Bibliográfica de Geografía Y Ciencias Sociales.* Vol. 15, p. 895.

Fitzpatrick, S. (1999) *Everyday Stalinism: Ordinary Life in Extraordinary Times. Soviet Russia in the 1930s.* New York: Oxford University Press.

Fussey, P., Coaffee, J., Armstrong, G. and Hobbs, D. (2011) *Securing and Sustaining the Olympic City: Reconfiguring London for 2012 and Beyond.* London: Ashgate.

Gaffney, C. (2016) 'Geo-porn: Selling the City Through Mediated Spectacle', *Urban Transformation Processes: The Role of Flagship Architecture as Urban Generator (American Association of Geographers Conference).* San Francisco.

Gotham, K.F. (2005) 'Theorizing Urban Spectacles Festivals: Tourism and the Transformation of Urban Space', *City.* Vol. 9, pp. 225–247.

Greene, S.J. (2003) 'Staged Cities: Mega-Events, Slum Clearance and Global Capital', *Yale Human Rights and Development Law Journal.* Vol. 6, pp. 161–187.

Grix, J. and Lee, D. (2013) 'Soft Power, Sports Mega-Events and Emerging States: The Lure of the Politics of Attraction', *Global Society.* Vol. 7, pp. 521–563.

Gruneau, R. and Horne, J. (2015) 'Mega-Events and Globalization: A Critical Introduction', *Mega-Events and Globalization: Capital and Spectacle in a Changing World Order.* London: Routledge, pp. 1–48.

Hall, Emma. (2012, 4 July) 'London Outdoes China in Brand Crackdown at Summer Olympics: Restrictions to Protect Sponsors even Stricter than Beijing Games', *Ad Age.* Available at: http://adage.com/article/global-news/brand-police-full-force-london-olympics/235136 (accessed 24 October 2016).

Harvey, D. (1989) 'From Managerialism to Entrepreneurialism: The Transformation in Urban Governance in Late Capitalism', *Geografiska Annaler, Human Geography.* Vol. 71, pp. 3–17.

Hayes, G. and Horne, J. (2011) 'Sustainable Development: Shock and Awe? London 2012 and Civil Society', *Sociology.* Vol. 45, No. 5, pp. 749–764.

Hiller, H.H. (2006) 'Post-Event Outcomes and the Post-Modern Turn: The Olympics and Urban Transformations', *Journal of European Sport Management Quarterly.* Vol. 6, No. 4, pp. 317–332.

Hui, W. (2003) *China's New Order: Society, Politics, and Economy in Transition.* Cambridge, MA: Harvard University Press.

Instituto Mais Democracia and Cooperativa Educaçao, Informaçao e Tecnologia para au Autogestao. (2014) *'Quem sao os proprietarios do Brasil?'* www.proprietariosdobrasil.org.br/index.php/en (accessed 24 October 2016).

Judd, D. (2003) *The Infrastructure of Play: Building the Tourist City.* New York: M.E. Sharpe.

Julier, G. (2005) 'Urban Designscapes and the Production of Aesthetic Consent', *Urban Studies.* Vol. 42, pp. 869–887.

Kennelly, J. and Watts, P. (2011) 'Sanitizing Public Space in Olympic Host Cities: The Spatial Experiences of Marginalized Youth in 2010 Vancouver and 2012 London', *Sociology.* Vol. 45, No. 5, pp. 765–781.

Kissinger, H. (1979) *White House Years*. Boston, MA: Little Brown & Co.

Klein, N. (2007) *The Shock Doctrine: The Rise of Disaster Capitalism*. Toronto: Alfred A. Knopf.

Kolamo, S. and Vuolteenaho, J. (2013) 'The Interplay of Mediascapes and Cityscapes in a Sports Mega-event: The Power Dynamics of Place Branding in the 2010 FIFA World Cup in South Africa', *International Communication Gazette*. Vol. 75, pp. 502–520.

Lima Jr, P.N. (2010) Uma estratégia chamada 'planejamento estratégico'. *7 Letras*.

Low, S.M. (2003) 'Embodied Space(s): Anthropological Theories of Body, Space, and Culture', *Space and Culture*. Vol. 6, pp. 9–18.

Ma, L.J. and Wu, F. (2005) *Restructuring the Chinese City: Changing Society, Economy and Space*. New York: Routledge.

Nunes, R. (2014, 30 May) 'There Will Have Been No World Cup', *Aljazeera*. Available at: www.aljazeera.com/indepth/opinion/2014/05/brazil-world-cup-protests-201452910299437439.html (accessed 12 July 2016).

Nye, J.S. (2004, June) 'Soft Power: The Means to Success in World Politics', *Foreign Affairs*. Available at: www.foreignaffairs.com/reviews/capsule-review/2004-05-01/soft-power-means-success-world-politics (accessed 11 July 2016).

Oliveira, N. (2011) 'Força-de-lei: rupturas e realinhamentos institucionais na busca do "sonho olímpico" carioca', *14th National ANPUR Conference*. Rio de Janeiro.

Oliveira, N. (2013) *O Poder Dos Jogos e Os Jogos De Poder: Os Interesses Em Campo na Produção De Uma Cidade Para O Espetáculo Esportivo*. Doctoral Dissertation in Urban and Regional Planning, Federal University of Rio de Janeiro.

Oliveira, N.G.D. and Vainer, C.B. (2014) 'Megaeventos no Brasil e no Rio de Janeiro: uma articulação transescalar na produção da cidade de exceção', F. Fernada Sánchez, G. Bienenstein, F. Oliveira and P. Novais (eds), *A copa do mundo e as cidades: políticas, projetos e resistências*. Rio de Janeiro: Universidade Federal Fluminense, pp. 81–117.

Powell, H. and Marrero-Guillamón, I. (2012) *The Art of Dissent: Adventures in London's Olympic State*. London: Marshgate Press.

Redação Estadão. (2009) 'Lula exalta vitória do povo brasileiro com a escolha do Rio 2016', *Estadão*. Available at: www.estadao.com.br/noticias/esportes,lula-exalta-vitoria-do-povo-brasileiro-com-a- escolha-do-rio-2016, 444826,0.htm (accessed 24 October 2016).

Rivenburgh, N.K. (2004) *The Olympic Games, Media, and the Challenges of Global Image Making*. Geneva: Centre d'Estudis Olímpics (UAB).

Rojek, C. (2013) *Event Power: How Global Events Manage and Manipulate*. London: SAGE.

Rolnik, R. (2014) 'Keynote Presentation', *Second International Conference on Mega-Events and the City*. Rio de Janeiro.

Rose, A.K. and Spiegel, M.M. (2011) 'The Olympic Effect', *Economic Journal, Royal Economic Society*. Vol. 121, pp. 652–677.

Scott, J.C. (1985) *Weapons of the Weak: Everyday Forms of Peasant Resistance*. New Haven, CT: Yale University Press.

Shin, H.B. (2012) 'Unequal Cities of Spectacle and Mega-Events in China', *City: Analysis of Urban Trends, Culture, Theory, Policy, Action*. Vol. 16, pp. 728–744.

Shin, H.B. (2014, 4 May) 'Contesting Speculative Urbanisation and Strategising Discontents', *The City at Time of Crisis*. Available at: http://crisis-scape.net/conference/item/186-contesting-speculative-urbanisation-and-strategising-discontents (accessed 13 July 2016).

Smith, A. (2005) 'Reimaging the City: The Value of Sport Initiatives', *Annals of Tourism Research*. Vol. 32, pp. 217–236.

Stavrides, S. (2010) 'The Athens 2004 Olympics: Modernization as a State of Emergency', *Mega-Events and the City International Conference*. Niterói.

Sudjic, D. (2005) *The Edifice Complex: How the Rich and Powerful Shape the World.* New York: Penguin Press.

Torres Ribeiro, A.C. (2006) 'A acumulação primitiva do Capital Simbólico', H.P. Jeudi and P.J. Berenstein (eds), *Corpos e Cenários Urbanos: Territórios Urbanos e Políticas Culturais.* Salvador: Federal University of Bahia Press (EDUFBA).

Tsing, A. (2000) 'Inside the Economy of Appearances', *Public Culture.* Vol. 12, No. 1, pp. 115–144.

Vainer, C.B. (2009) 'Pátria, empresa e mercadoria: notas sobre a estratégia discursiva do Planejamento Estratégico Urbano', O. Arantes, C. Vainer and E. Maricato (eds), *A cidade do pensamento único: Desmanchando consensos*, Petrópolis: Vozes, pp. 75–103.

Vainer, C.B. (2010) 'Megaeventos e a Cidade de Exceção', *Mega-Events and the City International Conference.* Niterói.

Waitt, G. (1999) 'Playing Games with Sidney: Marketing Sydney for the 2000 Olympics', *Urban Studies.* Vol. 36, No. 7, pp. 1055–1077.

Wang, H. (2003) *China's New Order: Society, Politics, and Economy in Transition.* Cambridge, MA: Harvard University Press.

Weizman, Eyal (2005, 10–11 November). 'On Extraterritoriality'. *Archipelago of Exception. Sovereignties of Extraterritoriality Conference.*

Wu, F. (2000) 'Place Promotion in Shanghai, PRC', *Cities.* Vol. 17, pp. 349–361.

Xu, J. and Yeh, A.G. (2005) 'City Repositioning and Competitiveness Building in Regional Development: New Development Strategies in Guangzhou, China', *International Journal of Urban and Regional Research.* Vol. 29, pp. 283–308.

Žižek, S. (1999) *The Ticklish Subject: The Absent Centre of Political Ontology.* London: Verso.

2 The autonomous and concerted production of mental place images

Whether embracing a city as spectacle approach or leaning towards the city of exception, civic leaders use different strategies to transform the image of their city. This book identifies three levels of intervention in the construction of urban representations: the conceived image of the city; the built image of the city; and the lived image of the city. This chapter focuses on the conceived image of the city as a cognitive product, made of mental, abstract and discursive representations. This first level of intervention in the representation of places lies in the symbolic realm and is based on the construction of an intangible, conceptual urban image through rhetorical means and virtual representations.

Cognitive place images are first and foremost the product of an organic process that develops over time, through association with historical events or characters, as a result of direct personal experimentation, or filtered through the experience – real or imagined – of others, as reported in newspapers, travel accounts, photographs, songs, films and television shows and other cultural vectors such as paintings and novels. Mental representations of places result from an amalgam of impressions, images, memories and evocations that evolve over time and become identified with a specific city or place. They can stem from a deep level of emotional engagement, linked to close knowledge and experience, or can be superficial, filled with clichés and faint notions, especially when the place is little known. This cognitive representation corresponds, at least in part, to the 'image of the city' that Kevin Lynch (1960) was exploring in his seminal study. This organically and independently produced image-construction process is said to be 'autonomous' in the sense that it is not controlled by goal-driven promoters (Gartner 1994).

But mental place images are also the result of 'concerted' actions by city leaders and local economic, political or religious elites who stand to benefit from a positive urban image and want to influence perceptions by imposing their own vision and interpretation. As Holcomb (1999) rightly notes, while Kevin Lynch sought to understand people's mental place images, image promoters seek to change and control them. Urban image construction has thus become a planned and highly controlled process, devised at the initiative of public entities or commissioned by private agents and local interest groups, often related to the tourism sector. In the context of mega-event preparations, this form of concerted urban image construction has become a standard practice and a crucial element in warranting the success of the event.

This chapter is divided into five parts. The first one centres upon the controlled production of cognitive urban images, and explores some of the strategies used by city promoters to build and project a particular place image, however fabricated, selective and utopian. The second part examines more closely instances when the production of a mental place image falls outside the control of image producers, especially in the case of film and media productions. The third part of the chapter discusses the production of mental place images in the context of sporting mega-events, and examines the role played by the media in controlling these representations. The following part discusses how the development of a new mediascape and the use of new information technologies have impacted the formation, diffusion and control of event-related place images, drawing on examples from Olympic Beijing. The case pre-Olympic Rio de Janeiro is finally discussed in the last section to exemplify the complex production of mental place images and the political implications of this process.

Selectivity and control in the production of a marketable place image

Concerted actions to instil a mental place image are generally of a discursive nature. The earliest image of a city is the one dreamed by its creators, whether planners, architects, urban designers or power-holders, who first envision the city before concretizing its realization. This initial image is communicated rhetorically, often in highly symbolic and evocative terms, to convey a particular impression to patrons or supporters.[1] This early vision is then further developed and rationalized, with the production of detailed representations, in the form of plans, perspective drawings and scaled models, as well as bylaws and regulations that will determine what can be built, where and how.

In such highly abstract, deterministic and comprehensive conceptualization, the city is conceived from above, as a series of spatial, geometric and economic relationships rather than from ground level as a lived, inhabited place, endowed with experience and emotions. This vision corresponds to Henri Lefebvre's notion of 'conceived space', defined as the planned, administered and consciously constructed terrain of engineers, city planners and architects, expressed in numbers and intellectually worked out verbal signs. This vision also recalls James Scott's (1999) characterization in *Seeing Like a State*, of how modern states view the world as rational, quantifiable and standardized in order to make society 'legible' and thereby controllable. Based on standardized techniques and statistics rather than on common knowledge, local circumstances and lived experience, this vision still dominates the way many urban interventions are envisioned today by contemporary planners and city administrators.

In the contemporary climate of intensified inter-urban competition, discursive urban image construction is less concerned with conceptualizations of the city as an abstract 'space', regulated, measured and quantified. It rather seeks to project an image of the city as a relatable 'place', imbued with particularity and qualitative density. Place image producers are usually driven by specific motives, whether profit making and bureaucratic control, and work with hired specialists in advertising, place marketing and destination branding, to imprint a strong and powerful image that will trump other mental representations and dominate collective imaginings. It is through repetition, redundancy and media saturation that these representations achieve their full potential.

The construction of mental place images relies upon persuasion techniques directly borrowed from the field of advertising. Destination branding is one of the main tools of city marketing and rests upon the constitution of a vivid and coherent place image at once attractive, inspiring and stimulating. Kavaratzis and Ashworth (2005) define the brand as a multidimensional construct, consisting of functional, emotional, relational and strategic elements that collectively generate a unique set of associations in the public mind. The message communicated by the brand is usually a mixture of objective reality that reflects the unique qualities of place and its best assets, and of fantasy, with attributes that marketers believe will make the city more attractive to its target audience. Branding thus includes a part of fiction and the most successful marketing campaigns rest upon great story-telling and myth making.[2]

The construction of a mental representation of place rests upon the combination of verbal and visual elements, with a rich, evocative narrative and a superlative rhetoric that sustains the aesthetic appeal of places. Such articulations between discourse and representation are replete with enthusiastic, hyperbolic attributes, creating a stimulating rhetoric with maximum visual impact. This discourse rests upon vivid descriptions that emphasize colour, exoticism, excitement, and uniqueness, with the use of a deterministic, synthetic language that is at once euphoric, apolitical and highly populist. It relies upon a predictable vocabulary that uniformly describes the city as forward-looking, dynamic, festive, vibrant, hospitable and charming. The 'idea' of the city thus constituted is later given expression in the form of a slogan, a logo and a visual palette which help repackage the intended message in a more communicable way.

The visual images that accompany these verbal descriptions are carefully chosen for their safe and positive connotations. For de Moragas (1992), a critical aspect in the planning of urban imaging strategies is the identification of the city's 'visual identity'. This involves the selection of visually striking urban landmarks such as monuments and grandiose landscapes, features invoking human genius like art or architectural cannons, and the identification of key popular culture attributes that embody the city's unique values and personality. While the explicit goal of a city marketing campaign is to give the city brand an edge, marketers and their clients are often risk averse and usually err on the safe side. Elements chosen in these representations are usually tried-and-true assets that have exemplar, universal appeal, and steer away from controversial, risky or politically sensitive topics.[3]

City marketing tends to view the city as an objectifiable, marketable entity; a product that can be packaged and sold on the market. Turning the city into a unified brand and a consumable product with its trademark characteristics requires an explicit positioning, with a consistent message that will guide all marketing efforts. Like all types of advertising, the constitution of a unified place image entails a certain manipulation of reality. The sleek, postcard-perfect urban images that fill glossy tourism magazines are carefully composed representations, using professional models and staged photographs that show a city's iconic features from the most favourable angles and in the best possible light. Intended for specific target audiences, generally young professionals, middle-class families and wealthy visitors, they are reassuring in their predictable and sanitized familiarity, yet offer a measured touch of exoticism and originality to arouse curiosity.

The desire to program and predetermine the way places are consumed and to draw a flattering portrait of the city thus entails a simplification of the complex social, political and economic reality that the city represents, reduced into a consensual, easily digestible and stereotyped form. City brand construction rests upon calculated efforts to highlight only the most attractive aspects of the city's culture, as if it were its totality. Briavel Holcomb (1999) views the marketed images of cities as selective fragments of urban reality, presented through rose-tinted glasses that obscure the city's many flaws, thereby negating a diversity of urban dynamics to produce an image that is much more generic than its material reality (Holcomb 1999). As a result, he writes, the people depicted in marketing images are overwhelmingly not poor, not minorities and not unhappy. Also absent from these representations are ubiquitous retail chain outlets, outdated suburbs, derelict industrial districts and poor neighbourhoods. Old urban quarters are only shown when properly renovated and sanitized to suggest a glorious past, with a rich historical heritage and attractive preservation districts.

Uncontrolled place image formation: the role of film

One of the great paradoxes of urban image construction is that those who want to plan and dictate the image of their city often have to rely upon modes of diffusion, which are autonomous and increasingly difficult to control. As previously mentioned, the construction of a positive mental place image remains largely the work of autonomous agents who cannot be controlled by image producers. Independent media coverage and popular vectors of representation like literature, theatre, film, song, visual arts and television can be powerful image-construction agents, which often have a greater impact than purpose-made advertising. Because they lack the perceptual bias of promotional material and appear closer to the truth than blatantly controlled publicity campaigns, they are important to brand recognition and cast a wider net than conventional advertisement (Vagionis and Loumioti 2011). With the potential to be seen by millions, they give exposure to audiences that could never be reached by traditional propaganda and targeted tourism promotion. Films, in particular, have a longer shelf-life and persist for decades in providing publicity, often with less investment than place marketing campaigns (Kim and Richardson 2003).

Motion pictures filmed on location are increasingly seen as effective marketing tools, which can play up the image of a city and turn it into a fashionable destination. As powerful myth-makers, films have the power to inscribe emotions and desire onto place, and help create seductive fantasy worlds that a visit promises to actualize. The on-screen imaging of cities in movies and television does not only make these locales more desirable as tourist destinations, but as places of residence as well, as testified by the ever-growing number of people wanting to move to New York or Los Angeles (Flanagan *et al.* 2010).[4]

In the sphere of city marketing, a film that portrays a destination in a favourable light has come to be seen as the ultimate in place-based product placement. One could talk of a 'Woody Allen effect', in reference to the boost in popularity enjoyed by cities like Paris, Barcelona, and London featured in this directors' recent films. Cities are becoming proactive in leveraging their film potential, targeting filmmakers in the pre-production stage, offering grants, tax credits and free scouting trips to encourage producers to film in their city (Hudson *et al.* 2011; Hudson and Ritchie 2006). In 2013, Rio de Janeiro's mayor declared he would give Woody Allen 'whatever he wants' to get him to film in his city (Shoard 2013).

Some local governments have tried to control the content of such autonomous image-building processes, going as far as dictating the way their city should be portrayed and attempting to censor negative depictions. In early 2015, Mexico City's mayor offered an extra six million dollars to the 14 million already paid to the James Bond movie franchise if the city was to be shown as a booming modern metropolis rather than a decaying, ancient colonial capital (Estevez 2015). He also specified that the villain should not be Mexican, while demanding that the Bond girl should be (Estevez 2015). However, researchers have found that investing money in film remains risky for cities because there is no guarantee of a positive outcome (Hudson and Ritchie 2006). Critics claim that drawing film production companies with taxpayer subsidies and concessions can be a drain on city finances and indirectly contribute to urban inequality and gentrification (Osterweil 2014).

Mega-events, mental place image construction and the media

A major player in the construction and diffusion of mental place images that remains largely uncontrolled is the media. The media has long played a major role in global and national perceptions of cities, disseminating ideas about place identity, and at times dictating the meaning of images projected. Global and local media alike have served as the main vehicles to market, design and consolidate desired place narratives, while also helping raise both standards and expectations in terms of place image. It is in this context that the staging of sporting mega-events has become part of many cities' image-construction strategies, as a unique opportunity to gain media exposure and to be in the global spotlight.

Global athletic events are first and foremost mass-media events, consumed as 'peak spectacle of the global mediascape' (Dayan and Katz 1992). Broadcast live to billions of people in most of the world's countries, the World Cup and the Olympics have long competed for the title of 'most watched event on earth' (Whitson and Macintosh 1996) and for the status of 'defining event of their era' (Kellner 2003). Sporting mega-events also occupy an ever-growing proportion of media airtime. The short alternating cycle of the FIFA World Cup and Winter and Summer Olympics have made these events quasi-permanent features in the media, with continuous news coverage of the bidding process, athletes' qualifications, host city preparations and actual competition (Horne 2014). During the event, media coverage reaches near saturation, and dominates the headlines.

Mega-events partake in urban image construction both via their pre-event marketing campaigns and by means of the event itself, which offers their host city a privileged, worldwide visibility and a guaranteed moment in the limelight. Just as event sponsors proudly exhibit their own branding symbols during the event, host cities have learned to use sporting mega-events as a marketing opportunity to flaunt their iconic features and profit from their global diffusion to attract inward investors and tourists.

Mega-event image strategies typically include the production of a large array of collateral material that presents the host setting in a favourable light. The candidacy files of potential host cities are great exercises in urban image construction. Filled with an aestheticized visual discourse, they project a highly seductive image of the city in the public relations and media packages widely distributed by host committees in pre-event campaigns and during the event. This promotional material is often the work of consultancy companies specialized in so-called 'overlay design' for sporting mega-events.[5] According to dictionary definitions, to overlay signifies to embellish superficially and to cover a given surface with a decorative veneer in order to change its appearance. Working with multidisciplinary teams of marketing specialists, filmmakers, architects, ex-athletes, sport advisers and graphic designers, they assist with sport facility planning and design, bid file compilation and project management, as well as media production. In this propaganda material, computer-generated images of future event sites construct the idealized image of a festive, convivial, easy-going city, leaving out the heavily secured, crowded and segregated atmosphere that characterizes such mass events. Traffic congestion, security checkpoints, perimeter fences, crowd-control corridors, long lines, empty seats, ticket scalpers, rowdy fans and overflowing garbage cans, which are also part of the event experience, are rarely shown.

One common strategy for host cities to maximize the media exposure of their greatest assets while controlling how their city is portrayed includes providing a selection of judiciously placed beauty shot locations around the city during the event. Images from these cameras feed directly to a centralized broadcast centre and are made available for use by rights-paying international broadcasters. Even more powerful as a place promotion strategy is the careful scheduling of activities and competitions in key urban settings. Many sporting events, especially those held outdoors, become ideal pretexts to showcase iconic urban features. Beach volleyball competitions, such as those held in Whitehall at London's 2012 Olympics or in Copacabana at the occasion of the 2016 Summer Games in Rio de Janeiro, were designed as tools of urban promotion, exploiting the cityscape as a picturesque backdrop. Also particularly spectacular are kinetic events like the torch relay and the marathon, which travel through the urban fabric, acting as hour-long tourism advertisements. Seen by some as the ultimate telegenic sporting event, the marathon best exemplifies the merging of sporting event and city marketing.

The case of the 2012 Olympic marathon exemplifies the use of a sporting event as a privileged moment of controlled image construction. The London marathon route was originally planned to go through Tower Hamlets and other East End working-class boroughs, ending at the Olympic Stadium at Stratford. However, in October 2010 the route was changed amid much controversy in favour of a new course, entirely staged in central London around the city's greatest landmarks. The shorter circuit started and finished at the Mall and looped several times past Buckingham Palace, Birdcage Walk, St. Paul's Cathedral and the Houses of Parliament, giving great television exposure to London's most famous sights, especially the ubiquitous Big Ben. Local representatives accused the Olympic Organizing Committee of changing the route because they were ashamed to show the less scenic, poorer East End (BBC News 2010).

Mega-event opening and closing ceremonies also represent exceptional vectors of image construction and unique opportunities to exhibit the host culture and setting. Figuring among the world's greatest marketing events, along with the Superbowl halftime, Olympic ceremonies are tightly controlled media events, planned as visually dramatic celebrations of the host nation through carefully selected music, dance, graphics, costumes and celebrities. In Beijing, the 2008 Opening Ceremony was a perfectly synchronized choreography and a stunningly designed venture into China's multiple contributions to world civilization, which featured sweeping views of the city's major landmarks gleaming under spectacular fireworks.

More than a mere vehicle for urban images, the media has come to play a major part in production of urban images and has a substantial impact upon the way cities are imagined and portrayed. The media acts both as a medium and an agent of urban image construction, especially in the context of sporting mega-events. The televisual dimension of these events has exacerbated their essentially visual and aesthetic dimensions and made them opportunities to promote a place image that can instil a desire to visit a city and to consume local goods and services (Traganou and Kang 2009).

In his analysis of the social construction of the Olympic spectacle, sociologist Pierre Bourdieu (1998) describes the Olympics as first and foremost a televised show, or, in marketing terms, a 'means of communication'. Bourdieu views the televised event as a commercial, marketable product and a prop for advertising that must be tailored to meet audience demands in terms of content and diffusion time. For him, the producers of images and commentary for television, radio and newspapers condition the representation of the Olympics by influencing how images are selected, framed and edited, and how the commentary is elaborated. The constraints of television broadcasting also influence the choice of sports included in Olympic competition, the site and time slot awarded to each sport, and even the ways in which matches and ceremonies take place. Bourdieu (1998) ends his commentary by underlining the double concealment that characterizes the Olympic broadcast: no one can see the spectacle in its entirety, and no one should sense this impossibility. Every television viewer must have the illusion of seeing 'the Olympics' as a whole.

It is thus through the filter of media representations that the great majority of the world's audience follows the event. Most people, including host-city residents and out-of-town visitors, watch the show on screens, at home, in bars or at live sites.

Even the lucky few to attend live events follow part of the action on giant screens through pre-selected and carefully framed images. Striving to compensate remote viewers for not being present in the stadium during the competition, television rights holders have refined the on-screen experience, using close-up shots, vertiginous perspectives, divided screens and detailed commentary to make sure that no live audience will ever experience the event with the all-seeing eye of the broadcast. State-of-the-art imaging techniques allow to them to package each event to their own specifications, with the best light, the best frame, the most representative angle to showcase their sponsors' main object of interest.

In recent decades, the cost of broadcasting rights for major sporting event and membership in their sponsorship programmes have grown exponentially, translating into greater corporate control over the way these events are organized and mediatized. As a result, the media, especially official rights holders, now largely control, digest, frame and filter how the event and its host city are represented. They are the ones who determine what is to be seen and what is kept out of sight, and the ones who dictate how images should be read and what they mean. Their version of reality is highly selective, and responds to their own biased interpretation and desired effect.

Once again, local and national hosting coalitions are faced with a conundrum when relying on uncontrolled image producers. Because they have a stake in the event's success, official broadcasters have a tendency to encourage positive coverage, to avoid criticism and to let controversies go unreported. But this is not necessarily the case with those image producers who do not hold exclusive rights (Horne 2007). No matter how carefully planned and designed, city images will be digested by independent, national and international media organizations to serve their own interests, concerns and national discourse.

If the central goal of an event-related image strategy is to overcome certain stereotypes, especially those relayed by the mainstream media, general event coverage often contributes to the confirmation and solidification of stereotypes rather than challenging or defeating them. For Traganou and Kang (2009), mega-event coverage responds to global audiences' demands for the consumption of the 'other' through registers of difference that follow stereotypical iconographies. Journalists covering mega-events – often sports journalists who have little inclination or interest in understanding local culture – use many short-cuts in their descriptions, drawing upon familiar allusions or exotic imagery thought to appeal to relevant to Western audiences (Rivenburgh 2004). They make quick judgements about the worth and potential of people and the places they inhabit and produce a variety of interpretations that are very difficult to control (Rivenburgh 2004). And because bad news sells better, the media has a tendency to focus on negative news and to reproduce enduring negative stereotypes.

No matter how much event hosts try to guide, deflect and control the narrative, negative reporting remains unpredictable. In the months preceding an event, preparation coverage routinely centres on local protests, human rights concerns, rising construction costs, security issues and delays in venue delivery and event preparation (Rivenburgh 2004; Horne and Whannel 2011). Closer to the event, journalists on the ground turn their focus to organizational and logistical problems.

When the event begins, sports competitions take up most media time and attention, and interest for the locale quickly fades, especially after the end of the event (Horne and Whannel 2011).

Image production, control and manipulation in the age of the new mediascape

In recent decades, the development of advanced communication technologies such as mobile networks, the internet and the blogosphere has prompted the apparition of what Appadurai (1996) calls a new 'mediascape', which now provides ever more material for modelling thought and behaviour, and for constructing place images and identities. For Kellner (2003), the internet-based economy has multiplied promotional opportunities and helped develop sophisticated multimedia technology to dazzle consumers and maximize both power and profits.

Kolamo and Vuolteenaho (2013) define the mega-event mediascape as the channels and concentrations of media publicity through which the event brand is communicated. They talk about the role of the media in the production of branded spatial identities and the construction of media-dense urban spaces as sites of construction and diffusion of the event spectacle. Kolamo and Vuolteenaho (2013) claim that the organization of sporting mega-events enhances the presence of media technologies and their use in the urban landscape: they promote the construction of media infrastructure, advance the connectivity of specific urban nodes to global communications networks and equip public spaces with state-of-the-art interactive devices and giant screens for media diffusion. The provision of new media technology infrastructure, including broadcast and media centres, data cables and digital networks to support and enhance connectivity, has become a central part of the contract-based obligations with which cities need to comply. However, event franchise owners draw no distinctions between First World and Third World hosts; poorer countries often feel burdened to provide all necessary services and infrastructure, at the expense of more pressing local services, even if there will be little use for such technology after the event.

No longer merely a stage for the mega-event spectacle, the host city is now also an array of a site of media production and a broadcasting studio, equipped with technologies that allow for the vast and continuous diffusion of the event spectacle on various platforms and at various scales. Mega-events have also become unique laboratories to develop groundbreaking communication systems and act as testing grounds for cutting-edge media technologies. Nick Couldry and Anna McCarthy (2004) maintain that mega-events have themselves engendered a new media space, which they describe as 'both the kind of spaces created by media, and the effect that existing spatial arrangements have on media forms as they materialize in everyday life'. Host cities and image producers have seized the opportunity to exploit new digital platforms to help shape, enhance and alter public perceptions of places, often creating a virtual simulacra of the built city. For Lawrence Vale (in Vale and Bass Warner 2001), this mediascape has facilitated the production of utopias and sustained attempts to design new imagined worlds and communities.

The advent of this new mediascape has deeply transformed the dynamics of image construction, simultaneously opening up new possibilities for controlling representations of places while also making the diffusion of images and information more difficult to constrain. The emergence of new media forms such as the internet and mobile telecommunications has complicated attempts to command the tightly orchestrated representations produced by mega-event hosts, making them susceptible to both disintegration and subversion (Marshall *et al.* 2010). Post-broadcast television audiences are no longer passive recipients or homogeneous spectators, but are now more actively engaged in the production and distribution of event images. As we will see in Chapter 5, the new media allows room to contest or rework mainstream media representations controlled by event producers, sponsors and broadcasters.

But advances in information technology, the development of new imaging techniques and the multiplication of diffusion platforms have also facilitated the production and manipulation of place images, and the development of digitalized potemkin practices. Media representations rely on sophisticated computer program and advanced imaging software to selectively construct visual narratives, reframe reality and reinterpret place images. During the event itself, broadcasters employ similar processes to enhance the perception of places, using digital technology to seamlessly refashion local geography, and hide discontinuities and eyesores thereby broadcasting a fictional city to armchair spectators around the world.

In Beijing, these technologies facilitated the projection of Photoshopped visions of the urban environment, enhancing some features, erasing others, even at time creatively 'augmenting' reality to maximize the potency of the media spectacle (Broudehoux 2010). The Beijing Olympics were replete with CGI representations, which included sweeping atmospheric views of the city in a delusional juxtaposition of its most iconic spaces, collaged, compressed and recomposed into a totally improbable geography (Anonymous 2008). The dazzling giant footprint-shaped fireworks that exploded along Beijing's central axis at the end of the Opening Ceremony were later revealed to be a computer-generated, three-dimensional animation. Footage was inserted with a slight wobble to simulate a helicopter fly-by, and transmitted by hundreds of compliant international broadcasters, including the BBC. Other digital manipulations allegedly used in Beijing included 'crowd cheerers', a computer-generated special effect used at major sporting events to fill up empty stadium seats and boost the festive aspect of the event.

The 2008 Beijing Olympics exemplified the great difficulty faced by host cities in the ideological control of the global media, in the face of new media technology (Marshall *et al.* 2010). In pre-Olympic Beijing, damage control about the city's image was achieved through the careful monitoring of information made available to the press and general public. In the months leading to the Olympics, the city withheld crucial information about pollution levels, using a euphemistic 'newspeak' to soften perceptions (publishing 'haze' levels rather than pollution indexes) and refusing to make public actual air pollution data, going as far as falsifying reports and exaggerating the number of so-called 'blue sky' days (Bonneau 2008). There was also much secrecy around the use of the city's rare freshwater resources for competition purposes, even though the city suffered near-drought conditions (Bonneau 2008).

The Beijing Games were marked by efforts to contain the new media landscape and to limit the circulation of non-sanctioned Olympics-related content in a way that subverted the state's nationalistic discourse and compromised exclusive broadcasting deals (Billings 2008). Attempts by new-media users to provide a more diversified coverage of the event, with fewer state-filtered images of the Games, were partly compromised by official efforts to control 'piracy'. Global sporting bodies, the IOC, the Beijing government and official broadcasters coordinated their efforts to control the mediascape and maintain exclusive broadcasting rights by monitoring Olympic content on the internet. But new-media users struck back with their own innovative ways to bypass corporate media control, circulating information about accessing pirated material, especially through online peer-to-peer streaming. The IOC was so alarmed by the frequency at which the Opening Ceremony was illegally downloaded that it asked for the Swedish government's assistance to block The Pirate Bay and Bittorrent users from sharing Olympic content (van der Sar 2008a). But the censorship strategy backfired, and Peter Sunde, co-founder of The Pirate Bay, defied the IOC to take legal action, with the Swedish court's approval. Sunde seized the opportunity to take a stand against the Chinese government, temporarily renaming his site The Beijing Bay and issuing this statement: 'Our weapons of mass distribution are pointed towards China' (van der Sar 2008b). Ultimately, China's efforts to restrict illegal coverage of the Games, in combination with the IOC's automatic monitoring system, managed to greatly reduce unauthorized broadcasting, especially on YouTube. According to Marshall *et al.* (2010), the combined efforts of the IOC and the Chinese government proved effective in actively eliminating many instances of piracy, and the overall level of censorship achieved remained remarkable.

In Brazil, too, the close relationship between the state and the media, and media concentration in the hands of a few conglomerates, especially the right-leaning *O Globo* media empire, facilitated the control of information and weakened the power of those wishing to contest image-construction efforts. *O Globo* played a central part in manipulating public opinion against Olympic evictees, siding with state efforts to expel them and misconstruing their struggle as the actions of greedy individuals wishing to cheat the system in order to divide residents, weaken their solidarity and delegitimize their resistance efforts. This proximity also helped keep other damning issues, such as the failed depollution of Guanabara Bay, out of the public eye until international uproar forced authorities to admit its laxity, blaming the use of a different way of calculating contamination levels.

The politics of Rio de Janeiro's Olympic mental image construction

Pre-Olympic Rio de Janeiro provides a great example of the complex politics of event-related mental image construction. As Brazil's primary tourist attraction and one of the most visited cities in the Southern Hemisphere, Rio de Janeiro has long capitalized upon its image to attract visitors and investment (Tavener 2012). It was the French poet Jeanne Catulle Mendes, author of *Rio: La ville merveilleuse* (1912), who cornered what would become the city's most enduring slogan: *Cidade Maravilhosa*, the Marvellous City. The phrase was immortalized in different songs, including André Filho's 1935 homonymous carnival march, declared the city's official anthem in the 1960s. Other agents – in film, literature, sports and culture – also contributed to the imposition of *Cidade Maravilhosa* as a brand, and played an important role in the diffusion of images and representations of the city that would consecrate its claim to be the 'most beautiful city in the world' (Ramos Machado 2004).

Since the 1970s, stereotypical elements of the city's image, such as its exuberant tropical nature, vast cultural effervescence and proverbial bohemian lifestyle, had dominated both controlled and uncontrolled representations of the city, conveying a sense of exotic buoyancy and laid-back cosmopolitanism. In defining its competitive advantage, the city capitalized upon the diversity of its unique natural assets, including its beaches, lagoons, waterfalls, mountains and tropical forest, as well as upon its rich cultural tradition, in terms of music, architecture, carnival and gastronomy. Successive tourism image-construction campaigns led by Riotur, the city's tourism bureau – namely *Rio Incomparavel* in 1997 and *Rio Maravilha* in 2002 – in conjunction with government-led civic pride campaigns like *Orgulho de Ser Carioca* (pride of being carioca) in the 1990s, overemphasized the sea, sex and sand stereotype long attached to the city's image. They clearly strove to maintain a consensual representation of the city as a light-hearted, easy-going tropical paradise of carefree excitement and leisure, in the face of rising violence, poverty, social inequality and environmental degradation.

As local conditions deteriorated at the turn of the millennium, it became increasingly difficult to conceal the fact that such representations of Rio de Janeiro only reflected the reality of a tiny portion of the city, concentrated along the southern littoral, where elite neighbourhoods and tourist attractions are located. The majority of *carioca* lived in an entire different world, many in informal, poorly serviced, substandard settlements known as *favelas*, subjected to growing violence at the hands of armed drug traffickers and paramilitary militia groups.

In the years preceding its two sporting mega-events, Rio de Janeiro's image-construction efforts focused on toning down the visibility of poverty in the city's landscape. These initiatives had to work against the foreign community's growing fascination with the favela, whose powerful, exotic appeal was supplanting more idyllic visions of the city (Zeiderman 2006). Over the last decade, the favela had acquired a sort of cult status and become an object of fetish in the global geographical imaginary, where it now occupies a unique position as both a trendy trademark and a fashionable commodity (Freire-Medeiros 2008). For Tom Philips (2003), the word 'favela' came to stand as a tropical prefix capable of turning the most diverse products into something exotic. Researchers located *Favela Chic* nightclubs in London, Paris, Glasgow, Montreal and Miami (Sterling 2010). Upscale design stores around the world sell the *favela chair*, designed by Brazilian-Italian designers

Umberto and Fernando Campana, which retails for US$5,185. The favela even represents a state of mind, as suggested by a 2005 exhibition of favela resident Maurio Hora's photographs titled *Favélité*, held in a Paris subway station.

This sudden attraction for the favela has been attributed, in part, to the global popularity of Brazilian 'reality' movies such as *City of God* (2002),[6] and to the use of such neighbourhoods as a backdrop in mainstream Hollywood films,[7] a trend branded *slumsploitation* (Gilligan 2006; Jaguaribe 2004). The favela's glamorization in the global mass media, especially as an exotic stage set for music videos by African-American pop stars, also had a great impact on mental image formation, especially abroad. First popularized by Michael Jackson in 'They don't care about us' (1996), directed by Spike Lee, the favela was later featured in videos by Beyoncé Knowles, Alicia Keys and Snoopdog, among others. The favela also became a fashionable site for international art projects, such as Dutch artists Haas and Hahn's 2010 *favela painting* project, or French artist JR's 2008 *Women are Heroes* installation.

Local authorities have long condemned such over-visibilization of the favela, for fear it could tarnish Brazil's international image. In the 1990s, the filming of Michael Jackson's video was widely opposed by the state, which argued that its display of local poverty would damage the local tourism industry and ruin Rio's chances to host the 2004 Olympics (Schemo 1996). They also despised the distopic image of Rio de Janeiro portrayed in recent films, as a place of lawlessness, abandoned by God, where bandits came to spend their ill-acquired loot.

Consequently, Olympic and World Cup preparations were both marked by a desire to limit the visibility of the favela, in spite of its growing recognition as a trademark of the city's image. They strove to divert attention from the poverty, violence and social inequality that were tearing the city apart. Rio de Janeiro's winning Olympic candidacy file, deposited in 2007, was a great exercise in image control, carefully avoiding urban realities that could negatively affect global perceptions and suggest underdevelopment. Of the 174 images that appear in the candidacy file, an overwhelming proportion (45 per cent) show the city's littoral South Zone (Zona Sul), home to Rio's wealthiest residents and host to only two events. The entire file includes only one image of a favela, in spite of the ubiquitous presence of these neighbourhoods in Rio's landscape. In most propaganda clips and illustrations, favelas are airbrushed, cropped out, fast-forwarded, digitally erased or washed out by powerful sunrays, mist or haze. Venues located in Rio's poor Zona Norte are shown in close-up views, as isolated objects, to avoid revealing the working-class communities that surround them. Representations of Rio's famous Maracanã stadium are always shot from the same angle, so that the nearby Mangueira favela does not appear in the background.

Drawing upon enduring clichés and predictable assets, the bid document focused on the natural beauty of the city's scenery, mixing images of its curvaceous landscape with shots of the perfect bodies of its citizens practising a variety of sports to project an attractive and reassuring image of the city. Such aestheticized representation played a triple role, acting as a sensual titillation for potential visitors while naturalizing Rio's vocation as Olympic host and diverting attention from more sensitive urban issues. Based on a definition of pornography as 'the sensational depiction of acts so as to arouse a quick, intense emotional reaction', Chris Gaffney (2016) introduces the notion of geoporn to describe the specific ways in which geographic imaginaries are mobilized to create desire and manufacture consensus about the event-city. Pointing to erotically loaded images of Rio de Janeiro's urban landscapes in the marketing of mega-events, which portray the city's sensual playgrounds of beaches, samba, football and carnival, he describes the use of representational techniques of possession and domination which extend the privileged masculine gaze and respond to consumer fetishes. For him, the superficial and consensual narrative portrayed in these geopornographic images fuels the mega-event spectacle while simultaneously disguising the unbalanced power relations that make the image possible and masking the violence, domination, perversity and exploitation that are embedded in the landscape (Gaffney 2016).

After Rio de Janeiro was awarded the status of host city for both the 2014 FIFA World Cup and the 2016 Olympic Games in 2009, local elites' desire to negate the existence of favelas in visual representations of the city intensified. In 2011, major newspapers in Rio de Janeiro ran a full-page advertisement from Petrobras, showing an idealized birds-eye view of the city in which all favelas had been replaced by lush vegetation. In April 2013, a little over a year before the 2014 World Cup, Rio de Janeiro's favelas also disappeared from Google Maps. Since 2009, Google had been pressured by City Hall and Riotur, who lodged a formal complaint against the company's mapping service for giving favelas more visibility and prominence than formal neighbourhoods. Google finally agreed to replace the word favela by the euphemism *morro* or hill (Figure 2.1), a decision that was widely contested by citizens groups like the Comitê Popular da Copa for contributing to the symbolic erasure of these territories from the virtual landscape.

In 2011, Rio de Janeiro received an unexpected boost to its image with the release of the animated film *Rio*, which did more for the city's image than countless propaganda campaigns by the city's tourism office had done in years. The film's upbeat, positive depiction of the city helped Rio regain some of its old glory as a green, ecological paradise, and allowed it to reclaim its title as one of the most beautiful cities on earth, thereby eclipsing years of negative representations. The release of a sequel, *Rio 2*, in 2014, allowed the city to ride the wave of its glorious, if short-lived, petroleum-fuelled economic boom, which, from 2010 to 2015, made Rio Latin America's new Promised Land. Sadly, by 2015 reporting about Rio turned to the dire state of Brazil's political and economic systems and in the months preceding the Olympics the main tag lines were all about the mosquito-propagated Zika virus, the polluted Guanabara Bay, the tragic bicycle path collapse and president Dilma's impeachment scandal.

Rio de Janeiro's Olympic Opening Ceremonies, held on 5 August 2016, were yet another exercise in mental image construction. Media around the world praised Brazil's openness in addressing so transparently some of the most problematic aspects of its history, from colonialization and slavery to the constitution of one of the most unequal societies in the world, exemplified by the ubiquity of favelas in the urban landscape. If the favela was omnipresent during the ceremonies, the difficult issues that underscore its existence, from its marginal condition to the

Before (2011)

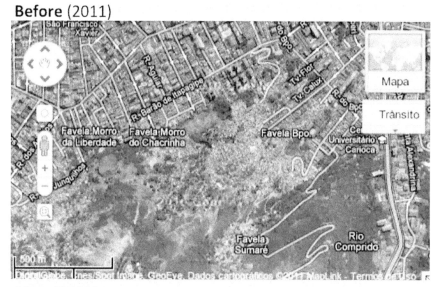

After (2013)

Figure 2.1 Google Maps censors Rio de Janeiro's favelas. These two screen-captures from Google Maps show the same area of Rio de Janeiro's North Zone. The one dating from 2011 identifies several favelas, while in the other, taken in 2013, the name of those favelas has disappeared.

economic exploitation and discrimination endured by its residents, to state abandonment and exclusion from public services, were whitewashed, depoliticized and deproblematized behind an aestheticized representation as a happy, festive, easy-going and light-hearted urban construct. Like other pressing urban issues, the favela was pushed into the background as an uncomfortable reality that should not get in the way of this great global-scale celebration.

One should not underestimate the effects of such cognitive image-construction strategies, not just on place images, but on places themselves, as they materialize on the ground in the actual reconfiguration of existing locales and transform the city's physical landscape. For example, in the case of Rio de Janeiro, by giving primacy to certain spaces historically privileged by the elite and urban features valued as residential status symbols by the real-estate market (such as beaches, lagoons and forests), these representations helped disqualify other sectors of the city, marked by urban obsolescence, poverty and other social problems. They also justified continuous investment in the privileged neighbourhoods of the littoral and South Zone, which remain the principal poles of expansion of the city, with the greatest concentration of cultural, leisure and event-related infrastructure.

Conclusions

This chapter focused on the conceived image of the city as an intangible, cognitive product, made of mental, abstract and discursive representations. Two visions of the city were juxtaposed: an abstract vision, conceived from above, that simplifies reality in order to make it legible and manageable; and a more complex, organic vision that rises from below, is based on lived reality and is more difficult to control. The chapter exposed the deep contrast between these conceptualizations of the city's image, and demonstrated that conflicts necessarily arise when the two visions collide. It also proved that no matter how much power-holders try to guide, deflect, control, even dictate the narrative, using diverse persuasion techniques and imaging technologies to impose a fabricated and easily digestible image of the city, these actions will be met with resistance, alternate representations and contradictory interpretations.

The chapter thus underlies the difficulty of controlling mental place images, which are multiple, complex, ephemeral and unfixed. It is a process that is constantly remade and negotiated, and is contingent upon a host of factors that are not necessarily within the reach of image producers. It is also very difficult to measure the actual effect of promotional campaigns and costly image-construction initiatives, which often prove ineffective, even counterproductive, as positive urban images can rapidly be obscured by new uncontrollable and unforeseen events. Olympic Vancouver's successful image as a convivial city where residents joyfully displayed their pride during the 2010 Winter Games quickly dissolved a few months later when its downtown was ransacked by rioters following the local hockey team's loss at the Stanley Cup tournament.

But in spite of dubious results in terms of global perception and unproven impacts upon the local economy, local governments will continue to invest in urban image construction, even if only to demonstrate their dynamism. In their fear of losing out in the global inter-urban competition, they are under tremendous pressure to remain proactive in helping position their cities on the global stage, and will do all in their power to avoid being left behind. The difficulty of evaluating the real positive impacts of these investments is actually beneficial for local authorities, as it prevents local taxpayers from judging their relevance and measuring their costs, thereby allowing ruling coalitions to pursue their initiatives unimpeded.

Notes

1 For example, in Brasilia, designers Lucio Costa and architect Oscar Niemeyer talked of a city of the future, built in the shape of a flying bird, or an airplane, the head of which would be the site of government activities (see Holston 1989).
2 These fictional representations can have a concrete impact upon reality and influence local identity formation, as the local population internalizes the constructed vision and adopts it as their own. For example, many aspects of Quebec City's identity, as both a Nordic capital and a piece of France on the North American continent, were constructed by the railway hotel industry to promote winter tourism at the turn of the twentieth century. It has been internalized as part of the invented traditions that now define the city's collective practices and representations (see Broudehoux 2004b). Similarly, reductive, essentializing and stereotypical place representations, as found in the Sinicized reconstruction of San Francisco's Chinatown after the great fire of 1906, can be assimilated and later reproduced as part of one's own cultural representation (see Broudehoux 2001).
3 Some daring approaches have paid off, like the widely successful 'I am sterdam' campaign, which exploited Amsterdam's hip diversity and openness in the construction of the city brand, depicting racially diverse same-sex parents holding a sign with the city's new slogan. But this kind of approach remains exceptional.
4 Of course, only films where the location plays a substantial part and is favourably differentiated and positively positioned from its competition will have a positive effect on image construction. Cities are often unrecognizable in film, and are often travestied as other locales. Montreal, for example, is widely used as a cheaper film location for movies taking place in Paris, New York or London.
5 One of the most successful of these firms is Designsports, based in Doha, which has advised most recent Olympic hosts, including London, Sochi and Qatar.
6 Other Brazilian feature and documentary films include *Favela Rising* (2005), *Five Times Favelas* (2011), *Elite Squad* (2007), *City of Men* (2007), *City of Favelas* (2010) and *Elite Squad II* (2011).
7 These Hollywood productions include *Fast and Furious 5* (2011), *The Hulk* (2008), *Rio* (2011) and *Rio 2* (2014).

References

Anonymous. (2008) 'Streetsweeper', *Urban Design International.* Vol. 13, p. 208.
Appadurai, A. (1996) *Modernity At Large: Cultural Dimensions of Globalization.* Minneapolis, MN: University of Minnesota Press
BBC News. (2010, 5 October) 'London 2012 Olympic Marathon Route a "Travesty"'. Available at: www.bbc.com/news/uk-england-london-11471541 (accessed 12 July 2016).
Billings, A. (2008) *Olympic Media: Inside the Biggest Show on Television.* London: Routledge.
Bonneau, C. (2008) 'Pékin 2008: La face cachée des JO', *Science & Vie.* Special edition, pp. 34–63.
Bourdieu, P. (1998) *On Television.* New York: The New Press.
Broudehoux, A.-M. (2001) 'Learning from Chinatown: The Search for a Modern Chinese Architecture, 1911–1998', N. AlSayyad (ed.), *Hybrid Urbanism: On the Identity Discourse and the Built Environment.* Westport, CT: Praeger, pp. 156–180.
Broudehoux, A.-M. (2010) 'Images of Power: Architectures of the Integrated Spectacle at the Beijing Olympics', *Journal of Architectural Education.* Vol. 63, pp. 52–62.
Couldry, N. and McCarthy, A. (2004) *MediaSpace: Place, Scale and Culture in a Media Age.* London: Routledge.

Dayan, D. and Katz, E. (1992) *Media Events: The Live Broadcasting of History.* Cambridge, MA: Harvard University Press.

De Moragas, S.M. (1992) *Communication, Cultural Identities and the Olympic Games: The Barcelona'92 Experience.* Bellaterra: Centre d'Estudis Olimpics, Universitat Autonoma de Barcelona.

Flanagan, S., Gilbert, D. and O'Connor, N. (2010) 'The Use of Film in Re-imaging a Tourism Destination: A Case Study of Yorkshire, UK', *Journal of Vacation Marketing.* Vol. 16, pp. 61–74.

Freire-Medeiros, B. (2008) 'And the Favela Went Global: The Invention of a Trademark and a Tourist Destination', M. Valença Marico, E. Nel and W. Leimgruber (eds), *The Global Challenge and Marginalisation.* New York: Nova Science, pp. 33–52.

Gaffney, C. (2010) 'Mega-events and Socio-spatial Dynamics in Rio de Janeiro, 1919–2016', *Journal of Latin American Geography.* Vol. 9, No. 1, pp. 7–29.

Gartner, W.C. (1994) 'Image Formation Process', *Journal of Travel & Tourism Marketing.* Vol. 2, pp. 191–215.

Gilligan, M. (2006) 'Slumsploitation: The Favela on Film and TV', *Metamute.* Available at: www.metamute.org/en/Slumsploitation-Favela-on-Film-and-TV (accessed 8 April 2015).

Holcomb, B. (1999) 'Marketing Cities for Tourism', D. Judd and S. Fainstein (eds), *The Tourist City.* New Haven, CT: Yale University Press, pp. 54–70.

Holston, J. (1989) *The Modernist City: An Anthropological Critique of Brasilia.* Chicago, IL: University of Chicago Press.

Horne, J. (2007) 'The Four "Knowns" of Sports Mega-Events', *Leisure Studies.* Vol. 26, pp. 81–96.

Horne, J. (2014) *Leisure, Culture and the Olympic Games.* London: Routledge.

Horne, J. and Whannel, G. (2011) *Understanding the Olympics.* London: Routledge.

Hudson, S. and Richie, J.R.B. (2006) 'Promoting Destinations via Film Tourism: An Empirical Identification of Supporting Marketing Initiatives', *Journal of Travel Research.* Vol. 44, pp. 387–396.

Hudson, S., Wang, Y. and Moreno Gil, S. (2011) 'The Influence of a Film on Destination Image and the Desire to Travel: A Cross-Cultural Comparison', *International Journal of Tourism Research.* Vol. 13, pp. 177–190.

Jaguaribe, B. (2004) 'Favelas and the Aesthetics of Realism: Representations in Film and Literature', *Journal of Latin American Cultural Studies.* Vol. 13, No. 3, pp. 327–342.

Karavatzis, M. and Ashworth, G. (2005) 'City Branding: An Effective Assertion of Identity or a Transitory Marketing Trick?', *Tijdschrift voor Economische en Social Geografie.* Vol. 96, No. 5, pp. 506–514.

Kellner, D. (2003) *Media Spectacle.* London: Routledge.

Kim, H. and Richardson, S.L. (2003) 'Motion Picture Impacts on Destination Images', *Annals of Tourism Research.* Vol. 30, No. 1, pp. 216–237.

Kolamo, S. and Vuolteenaho, J. (2013) 'The Interplay of Mediascapes and Cityscapes in a Sports Mega-event: The Power Dynamics of Place Branding in the 2010 FIFA World Cup in South Africa', *International Communication Gazette.* Vol. 75, pp. 502–520.

Marshall, D.P., Russo, N. and Walker, B. (2010) 'Mediating the Olympics', *Convergence.* Vol. 16, pp. 263–278.

Osterweil, W. (2014, 10 August) 'How "Movie Tourism" Hurts American Cities', *Aljazeera.* Available at: http://america.aljazeera.com/opinions/2014/8/movies-gentrifica tionfilmindustrycorruption.html (accessed 11 July 2016).

Philips, T. (2003) 'Brazil: How Favelas Went Chic', *Brazzil.* Available at: www.brazzillog. com/2003/html/articles/dec03/p105dec03.htm (accessed 8 April 2015).

Ramos Machado, T. (2004) *Para a "Cidade Maravilhosa", um "Plano Maravilha": uma análise crítica sobre produção da imagem turística e marketing urbano no Rio de Janeiro.* Rio de Janeiro: Universidade Federal do Rio de Janeiro.

Rivenburgh, N.K. (2004) *The Olympic Games, Media, and the Challenges of Global Image Making.* Geneva: Centre d'Estudis Olímpics (UAB).

Schemo, D.J. (1996, 2 November) 'Rio Frets as Michael Jackson Plans to Film Slum', *New York Times.* p.3.

Scott, J. (1999) *Seeing like a State.* New Haven, CT: Yale University Press.

Shoard, C. (2013, 19 August) 'Woody Allen is Offered "Whatever It Takes" to Film in Rio', *Guardian.* Available at: www.theguardian.com/film/2013/aug/19/woody-allen-rio-film (accessed 11 July 2016).

Sterling, B. (2010, 19 August) 'Favela Chic as a Brazilian Cultural Tourism Issue', *Wired.* p. 3.

Tavener, B. (2012, 5 May) 'Brazil Reports Record Tourism', *Rio Times.* p. 5.

Traganou, J. and Kang, J. (2009) 'The Olympics as Media Space: The Beijing 2008 Olympic Games from the Interdisciplinary Perspective of Media and Design Studies', *Esporte e sociedade.* Vol. 4.

Vagionis, N. and Loumioti, M. (2011) 'Movies as a Tool of Modern Tourist Marketing', *Tourismos: An International Multidisciplinary Journal of Tourism.* Vol. 6, No. 2, pp. 353–362.

Vale, L.J. and Bass Warner, S. (2001) *Imaging the City: Continuing Struggles and New Directions.* New Brunswick, NJ: Rutgers University Center for Urban Policy Research.

van der Sar, E. (2008a) 'Millions Download Olympics Opening Ceremony'. *TorrentFreak.* Available at: https://torrentfreak.com/millions-download-olympics-via-bittorrent-080812 (accessed 24 October 2016).

van der Sar, E. (2008b) 'IOC Wants Olympic Torrents Off The Pirate Bay'. *TorrentFreak.* Available at: https://torrentfreak.com/ioc-wants-olympic-torrents-off-the-pirate-bay (accessed 24 October 2016).

Whitson, D. and Macintosh, D. (1996) 'The Global Circus: International Sport, Tourism and the Marketing of Cities', *Journal of Sport and Social Issues.* Vol. 20, No. 3, pp. 278–295.

Zeiderman, A. (2006) *The Fetish and the Favela: Notes on Tourism and the Commodification of Place in Rio de Janeiro, Brazil.* Stanford, CA: Stanford University Press.

3 Mega-events and physical image construction

Between seduction and exclusion

Images are always a compromise between an objective reality and a projected ideal. In his work on dramaturgy, Goffman (1976) talks of 'impression management' to describe the desire to manipulate how others view us, or to influence their impression of us, with the use of mechanisms called 'sign vehicles'. Goffman's (1976) notions of front and back stages as elements of impression management suggest the existence of two simultaneous realities in the process of representation. The official, front-stage façade presented to the world seeks to convey a particular impression, however staged or enacted. The back-stage reality is where the more fragile, private, messy and authentic self is preserved and where the front-stage identity is concocted and reproduced. For Goffman (1976), the disconnect between front and back stages carries a certain potential for alienation.

In the production of urban images, two complementary processes, loosely related to Goffman's theory, are at play: a process of *seduction*, and a process of *exclusion*. Seduction entails a desire to please and a willingness to manipulate reality, to deceive and mystify in order to succeed in this enticement. Drawing upon Baudrillard, architectural critic Neil Leach (1999), seduction is a last recourse used when all substance or meaningful discourse is gone. In the process of urban image construction, seduction is used to create a *space of illusion*, where the best assets the city has to offer are put to the fore and celebrated as a utopian, picture-perfect vision of reality. Seduction thus relies upon illusionism, theatricality and spectacle, with the construction of a prominent front stage, upon which reality is embellished, manipulated, reformed and glorified.

This process of seduction is complemented by a process of exclusion or *repulsion* that covers up social divisions and deliberately omits, silences and denies realities that could be detrimental to the city's reputation, relegated to a hidden back stage. It is a vision from which aspects that may cause prejudice to the city's image are cropped out of the picture, both symbolically and literally. In a form of visual eugenics, the existence of the poor, the ugly and the unphotogenic is negated, while the plain, banal, mundane and not so quaint are simply swept under the rug.

If the first approach to urban image construction presented in the previous chapter sought to communicate ideas about places through advertising strategies, and their diffusion in the media, the second approach exposed in this chapter focuses on improving the product itself, that is, the actual city, in its materiality and three-dimensional reality. This chapter examines concurrent processes of seduction and exclusion in the transformation of the city's physical landscape, both natural and man-made, in order to conform, as much as possible, to the picture-perfect vision imagined by city marketers and other image producers. The first process relies on the projection of a seductive place image, celebrating the city's best assets, and the implementation of spectacular beautification initiatives that include architecture, urban design and public art. The second process relies on the deliberate camouflage, concealment or obliteration of aspects of the urban landscape that could cause prejudice to the city's image, through diverse forms of erasure – real or symbolic. The chapter's two main parts each centres on one of these processes.

Part 1: seduction as an instrument of image construction

For Lawrence Vale, image making has long been a central aspect of city making (Vale and Bass Warner, 2001). The built environment, especially in the form of historical heritage, architecture and urban design, has always constituted the raw material of urban image construction. Through the ages, architecture has served as an instrument of mass communication, a kind of word in stone that could manifest civic values and shared ideals. Religious and political leaders alike have used the urban landscape to convey ideas about a regime, an ideology or a vision, generally to legitimize and reproduce their power. For example, the Grand Manner urbanism of the seventeenth-century baroque city assisted the resurgence of Catholicism and relied upon the visual and theatrical techniques of perspective, monumentality and allegories to emotionally engage followers and converts. Architecture also contributed to the consolidation of colonial rule and the constitution of post-colonial identities through the design and construction of new capital cities and parliamentary districts (AlSayyad 1992; Vale 1992; Wright 1991). Monumental architecture was an explicit visual statement that testified to the refinement, grandeur and cultural authority of their rulers, but also substantiated their wealth and moral superiority. Diverse autocratic regimes, from Napoleon III to Stalin and Mao Zedong, similarly employed grand architectural gestures, monumental urbanism and potemkinist scene-rigging to establish and consolidate their hold on power.

The physical construction of the event-city

In their struggle for economic survival, contemporary cities have learned to exploit the symbolic power of architecture to update, transcend and rebrand their cityscape while simultaneously invoking a distinctive identity. Today, most image-construction programmes intervene on three aspects of the built environment. They focus on the city's existing assets, especially by showcasing local heritage and investing in conservation. They also act upon contemporary architecture, endowing their landscape with new, spectacular monuments that will transform their skyline. Finally, cities invest in urban design at the district level, with the creation of themed neighbourhoods with a cosmopolitan appeal. These three approaches are detailed in what follows.

Most interventions to improve a city's physical image first concentrate on its existing assets, in terms of its natural and heritage resources. Heritage assets are thus enhanced through historical preservation or adaptive reuse, and are creatively transformed into positive urban amenities and factors of attraction and turned into what Krupar and Al (2012) call 'spectacularized heritage brandscapes'. History is a valued element of place image. It is positively connoted, conveys a sense of stability and continuity, and suggests deeply rooted traditions. Existing parks, waterfronts and open spaces are also updated to enrich the urban landscape and help diversify the offer in terms of city's leisure facilities.

Most cities, especially those lacking rich historical landmarks or scenic landscape features, recognize the important role played by architecture in the new political economy of signs and invest in the creation of new assets in the hope of boosting their profile. As tradable symbols of value, spectacular buildings have become essential tools of city marketing (Evans 2003). Avant-garde architecture is now valued for its advertising power, its ability to brand the urban skyline and its capacity to enhance the prestige and desirability of place (Miles and Miles 2004; Crilley 1993). Local governments have thus learned to capitalize upon the power of architecture as a source of symbolic capital, helping their cities capture a semiotic advantage over rival destinations (Julier 2005). Motivated by what is now widely known as the Bilbao effect,[1] cities around the world have embarked on a competition for global pre-eminence by building the tallest, most daring and technologically advanced structures. They invite the world's top designers, often referred to as 'starchitects', to brand their landscape with signature buildings and endow their city with impressive visual symbols. These monuments are often called 'iconic' buildings, thereby confirming their function as visual elements of image construction.

The marketing literature talks profusely of the construction of flagship projects, defined as newsworthy buildings whose original design, unique qualities or revolutionary technique make them instant media sensations (Holcomb 2001; Karavatzis and Ashworth 2015). These architectural trophies generally house cultural amenities like concert halls, theatres, museums and public libraries, which supplement the local cultural offer and dynamize the city's creative credentials. Flagship buildings also include convention centres and other leisure, shopping and entertainment centres, like aquariums and urban stadia, which are now part of what Kaika (2005) calls the 'urban dowry', or those must-have amenities and standardized equipment that all self-respecting global cities must possess. Gaffney (2016) refers to such expensive, sparkling structures, whose 'wow' factor trumps their functionality and durability, as elements of 'urban bling', which glorify consumerism and wealth ostentation in order to stimulate capital accumulation. If Bilbao's Guggenheim Museum remains the most cited example of such conspicuous architectural branding, countless other examples are found around the world (Figure 3.1).

Figure 3.1 Museu do Amanhã (Museum of Tomorrow). Designed by world-famous Spanish architect Santiago Calatrava, this futuristic museum, inaugurated a few months before the 2016 Olympic Games, is the cultural anchor of Rio de Janeiro's port revitalization project, Porto Maravilha (photo by the author, 2016).

Paradoxically, in their fear of losing out in the global inter-urban competition, cities are compelled to follow the same trends and fashions and to emulate one another's success by reproducing safe and proven solutions and hiring architects from a short list of usual suspects (Hannigan 1998, 2003; Ritzer 1999; Gottdiener 2000). On the other hand, they must conform to ideal models, especially those best practices praised in the planning rankings that are circulated worldwide by the consulting industry, while on the other hand presenting a distinctive image and singular identity. Seeking distinction within a spectrum of conformity often proves counterproductive, resulting in a pre-formatted urban image, that superficially commodifies local cultural assets, repackaged for easy touristic consumption. More authentic or ordinary aspects of urban life are often ignored and set aside because of their lack of conformity with hegemonic models of tourist-friendly urbanity. Rather than reinforcing their unique place identity, cities become increasingly similar and run the risk of fostering a more homogenized, standardized urban experience, becoming what Crilley (1993) calls 'places of global sameness'. Lawrence Vale (Vale and Bass Warner 2001) suggests that the constant inflation of the standards that define spectacle and novelty makes the extraordinary ordinary.

The hosting of mega-events has played a central part in the rising popularity of superlative architecture and image-enhancing projects on the global scene, which are entirely at the service of the media spectacle. More than mere showcases for sporting events, event venues are envisioned as events in their own rights. Designed with their televisual impact in mind, they are often flashy, façadist projects, built for maximum effect. They are conceived as global-scale objects, to be seen from afar, from a broadcast helicopter or on large television screens rather than experienced spatially in their third dimension, at street level. Many capture the global imaginary with highly evocative, engaging designs, meant to awaken emotional attachment and to mobilize people's affective ties and identification with the event. Drawing upon familiar cultural associations, design codes and patterns of textuality (Crilley 1993), their playful, mimetic form and telegenic quality ensure universal appeal: Beijing's Bird's Nest and Water Cube (Figure 3.2), the giraffes and zebras of Mbombela stadium in South Africa, the calabash gourd at Soccer City, near Johannesburg, and the woven straw basket of the Amazonias Stadium in Manaus, Brazil, are only a few examples. Drawing upon tradition and familiarity, this sugar-coated, culturally resonant architectural symbolism is exploited as an alibi to earn public acceptance for controversial urban projects entirely de-politicized so as to elicit pride and assent among local taxpayers.

Figure 3.2 Beijing's Bird's Nest and Water Cube. The striking image of the Olympic stadium and National Aquatic Centre became visual shorthands for the 2008 Games and lasting trademarks for China's national capital (photo by Johan Nilsson, 2008, with permission).

Olympic stadia are often conceived to best serve one particular event: the hours-long Opening Ceremony, which arguably figures among the most watched television broadcasts on earth. The stadium must accommodate the live transmission of this event, planned more for the benefit of global television audiences than for those present in the stadium. Broadcasters have been known to work in close collaboration with stadium architects to determine the optimal spatial layout and internal organization that will best serve the show's production. Spaces are conceived with camera placement in mind, to ensure the best light, the most representative angles and ideal visibility, free from obstructions. The localization of these venues is similarly dictated by the televisual imperative, and seeks to maximize the imageability of the surrounding landscape (Broudehoux 2010). Olympic Parks and their vicinities increasingly include 'live sites', or freely accessible areas where ticketless Olympic fans can watch events on giant screens in public, and help reproduce the spectacle by making spectacles of themselves for a global television audience (Gaffney 2016).

The controversy that surrounded the construction of Cape Town's stadium at the 2010 South African World Cup illustrates the tremendous influence that international sporting organizations and their broadcasters exert over the design and realization of event venues. FIFA delegates objected to the host's proposal to use the existing Athlone Stadium, located in a popular neighbourhood in need of new services and sources of employment, on the grounds that the low-cost social housing that surrounded the site was not photogenic (Alegi 2008). A FIFA delegate reportedly told a *Mail & Guardian* (Joubert 2007) journalist: 'A billion television viewers don't want to see shacks and poverty on this scale.' The city thus changed its plans in favour of a more scenic spot in an upscale sector at Green Point, whose spectacular background featuring Table Mountain and the open sea would make for great television.

Apart from heritage preservation and architecture, urban design is also deployed as an image-construction strategy. Similarly ruled by a logic of seduction is the creation of signature districts and branded neighbourhoods, which transform existing urban sectors into single-purpose quarters, specialized in business, leisure or the arts. Using a visual form of urbanism, they are endowed with a uniform look, unique signage, sleek public spaces and remarkable architecture. These design-enhanced districts are used as props to buttress claims to global city status and help insert the city into international tourism circuits while giving new value to economically obsolete places.

In the neoliberal era, dominated by the consumption of images and spectacles and driven by a constant quest for profits, it is not surprising that urban image construction would borrow from the 'imagineering' practices developed by the Disney Corporation for its theme-park designs. Imagineering – a portmanteau of the words imagination and engineering – is a practice that combines creative imagination with technical expertise in the theming of goods, services and places. It follows a 'total design' approach, which encompasses all aspects of the man-made environment in order to create seemingly authentic landscapes. As tools of urban image construction, imagineered neighbourhoods often draw upon nostalgia and selective memory to manufacture standardized and reassuringly historical, festive environments. Gottdiener (2001) described them as mock urban spaces, where social exchange is mainly driven by consumption. They echo Hannigan's *pleasurescapes*, those artificial landscapes manufactured for the leisure class and specialized in festive entertainment (Hannigan 1998: 65). Influenced by the rise of New Urbanism, these imagineering practices were more prominent in the 1990s and 2000s, especially with the widespread 'quaintification' of gentrified historic neighbourhoods (Flusty 2001). But contemporary interventions continue to apply the same guiding principles by creating upscale, sanitized urban environments with a distinct visual identity and clearly defined boundaries, albeit with a more contemporary, post-industrial aesthetic.

The success of such manufactured spaces lies in their sophisticated image, their illusionary authenticity and the reassuring predictability of the consumption options they offer. These consensual imitations of real urban spaces often amount to little more than open-air shopping malls, which provide multiple attractions in the comfort of a clean, controlled environment, and a safe escape from the gritty reality of urban life. Today, a predictable, short list of themed neighbourhoods, including museum and entertainment districts, waterfront redevelopment, festival marketplaces, creative clusters, artist colonies, international business districts, ethnic neighbourhoods, gay village and nightlife districts, have become the standard fare of aspiring world-class cities.

Olympic urbanism in Beijing and Rio de Janeiro

In the context of mega-event preparation, the staging of the urban landscape has taken the form of what Gravari-Barbas (2013) calls *Olympic urbanism*, a planning approach she describes as based on purely visual considerations rather than on a long-term development vision. For her, Olympic urbanism is the actualization of the festive city, through the transformation of many urban sectors into spaces of hedonistic leisure and touristic consumption (Gravari-Barbas 2013). Two neighbourhood revitalization projects linked to the Olympic Games embody the creation of such support spaces for the festive city: Qianmen in Beijing and Porto Maravilha in Rio de Janeiro. Aimed at upmarket users, both projects were accompanied by the displacement of the former residents of these previously degraded districts.

Beijing's Qianmen district was a popular shopping and nightlife neighbourhood, located a stone's throw from Tiananmen Square and known as the birthplace of Peking Opera. It was repackaged as a world-class consumption and entertainment hub, with up-to-date tourist facilities and a nostalgic, neo-traditional architecture more reminiscent of a Chinatown than of the eclectic landscape that characterized the original district (Figure 3.3). Inaugurated on the eve of the 2008 Olympic Opening Ceremony, the project accelerated the transformation of this historically and socially sensitive area, resulting in the eviction and displacement of hundreds of families and the disappearance of a rich urban fabric (Bristow 2011; Meyer 2009).

Figure 3.3 Recently 'renovated' Qianmen street, Beijing, 2008 (photo by Johan Nilsson 2008, with permission).

In Rio de Janeiro, Porto Maravilha, a controversial port rehabilitation project launched in June 2009 as part of the city's pre-Olympic facelift, is similarly displacing hundreds of people. The project seeks to turn a devalued post-industrial sector into a mixed-use entertainment district through the construction of cultural facilities, the development of tourist attractions and the stimulation of real-estate activity (Broudehoux and Freeman 2013). The project encompasses an area long known as 'Little Africa', home of the busiest slave market in the Americas and birthplace of many Afro-Brazilian cultural traditions such as samba and capoeira, now recognized by UNESCO as part of Brazil's immaterial heritage.

Once a dynamic commercial and industrial neighbourhood, the area experienced a decline in its traditional activities during the second half of twentieth century and suffered a long period of 'territorial stigmatization' (Wacquant 2007), especially after vacant sites and properties were occupied by the poor and converted into informal housing. The diverse communities who have long inhabited the port are now threatened by Porto Maravilha, which seeks to exploit the architectural qualities of the local built environment and to draw upon its valuation potential to attract high-paying residents, businesses and members of the creative class. While the area's rich cultural past is used as a marketing tool to boost its tourism appeal, local cultural practices, especially the area's unique heritage, are disregarded, obliterated or transformed into objects of consumption.

The project embodies many aspects of Olympic urbanism, with sleek up-to-date designs, glittering new towers by Trump and Loreal, glamorous entertainment facilities catering to the cruise-ship set and well-designed new urban spaces. The project's key attraction is the spectacular Museum of Tomorrow, build on Guanabara Bay by world-renowned architect Santiago Calatrava (see Figure 3.1). Other anchors include an art museum, a brand-new light-rail service, the largest urban aquarium in the Americas and multiple venues for fashion shows, concerts and other festivities located inside renovated warehouses.

More than a mere image-construction initiative, the project was an opportunity to transform the city according to the city of exception paradigm defined in Chapter 2. Although it did not figure in the original Olympic bid, Porto Maravilha (Figure 3.4) largely benefited from its subsequent recuperation as one of the great Olympic legacies for the city and is capitalizing upon its association with the Olympic brand to sell the project to investors. The 2016 target date also fostered a sense of imminence and helped justify the haste with which many planning decisions were taken. As the largest public–private partnership in Brazilian history, Porto Maravilha has literally put three urban neighbourhoods under private management. All infrastructure provision was contracted out to a private consortium made up of three of Brazil's largest engineering and construction firms (Odebrecht, OAS and Carioca Engenharia), responsible for managing the project, clearing the land and upgrading urban infrastructure, as well as providing basic services such as street lighting, drainage and garbage collection for a 15-year period. All project costs, including building expenses and the remuneration of the private consortium, were covered by the state using funds from the Federal Workers Retirement Fund (FGTS) and the speculative sale of public property.

The redevelopment process was facilitated by extraordinary political interventions, financial innovations and legal decrees passed in exceptional circumstances. The municipal edict that authorized the public–private partnership was passed within weeks of Rio winning its Olympic bid (Oliveira 2013). Although the decision to grant the responsibility for the realization of public works and the provision of public services in an entire urban district to a single contractor was largely unprecedented in Brazil, the decree was adopted in an emergency fashion that failed to allow sufficient time for public scrutiny. Other municipal laws, including those providing tax benefits to the consortium and to other businesses settling in the area, were adopted with similar urgency (Oliveira 2011). In 2015–2016, the three companies that make up the consortium were investigated as part of the Operaçao Lava Jato (Operation Car Wash), as the source of the corruption scandal and political crisis that erupted several months before the Olympics, for having allegedly paid kickbacks to Eduardo Cunha, the former president of the Chamber of Deputies, who had brokered the use of FGTS funds for the operation. The press also revealed the minister's relation with Odebrecht, who funded Cunha's 2010 campaign and those of mayoral candidates for Rio's 2012 municipal elections, thereby confirming the incestuous relationship that exists between Rio de Janeiro's construction and real-estate sectors and the executive branch of city government (Affonso *et al.* 2016; Gaffney 2016).

Figure 3.4 The changing face of Rio de Janeiro's port district. The glass towers built to be the new modern façade of Rio de Janeiro as part of Porto Maravilha port revitalization project ironically reflect the favela they were meant to conceal (photo by the author, 2015).

Seduction and the dematerialization of the built environment

In devising its strategies of seduction, the event-city has exacerbated the visual nature of contemporary urbanism. In the late-capitalist city, visibility and imageability have become determining criteria guiding urban interventions, and image-conscious priorities increasingly trump other considerations. The widespread use of mega-events as city marketing opportunities has heightened architecture's new role as a media object in the service of the spectacle. The pride and ambition invested in hosting such events inflame the vain desire to eclipse other sensational projects, contributing to the hyperinflation of self-conscious exceptionalism in an increasingly fragmented urban landscape.

In the process, the built environment has been subsumed into a visual marker, a convenient situation-setting, an iconic emblem or logotype, carried in the popular imagination to help 'envision' a city and place it on the world's cognitive map (Ghirardo 1991). This emphasis on surface and readable imagery has had an impact on the practice of architecture and urban design, and generated two-dimensional environments, designed for their photogenic effect and advertising power rather than their experiential potential. For critics, this means that, in an increasingly disembodied world, marked by the virtual, ephemeral and consumable, the built environment is no longer entrenched in materiality but has itself been reduced to a matter of superficial appearance (Crawford 1991; Leach 2004). Prioritizing appearance over substance means that visual impact now takes primacy over functionality.

In the context of event-led urban image construction, the main objective of this material form of advertising is to seduce a clientele of local elites, foreign investors and international tourists. Technological prowess, glittering surfaces and monumentalism connote stability, boldness, might, progress and prosperity, which resonate with qualities sought by financial and business leaders and wealthy professionals. This architecture also conveys a level of cultural sophistication, discriminating taste and distinction that speaks of the superior quality of the local citizenry. Brand-name designs confer an aura of glamour to the city's image and an avant-garde sheen that manifests bold confidence and unabashed modernity.

The superficialization of architecture and urban design and the spectacularization of the urban landscape carry an important depoliticizing effect. Neil Leach (1999) explains how the fetish of the image has trapped architectural discourse within a logic of aestheticization, where the aesthetic displaces the political. He views the proliferation of spectacular architectural images in the urban landscape as inducing a form of anaesthesia, whose narcotic effect diminished social and political awareness (Leach 1999). Long before Leach, Walter Benjamin (1968) had warned that the privileging of the image was not innocent, given the close relationship between aesthetics and politics. He suggested that aesthetics could dress up an unsavoury political agenda and turn it into an intoxicating spectacle (Benjamin 1968). Julier (2005) similarly maintains that turning architecture into a spectacle and a support for the ideology of consumption represents a powerful instrument of deception that masks and perverts reality in order to pacify, fascinate and mystify.

Beijing 2008: visual urbanism, monumentalism and architectural spectacle

In preparing to host the 2008 Summer Olympic Games, Beijing fully embraced spectacular architecture as an image-building strategy. The conspicuous construction programme initiated by President Jiang Zemin in sight of the Olympics was truly unprecedented in scale. It underscored China's spectacular re-emergence as a world superpower, and its desire to claim its rightful position in the new global economy. Drawing upon cutting-edge designs bearing the signature of global architectural celebrities, the city hoped to reform its world image with a series of architectural icons that could mark the global collective imagination with something bold, heroic and modern.

Beijing's Olympic projects were entirely at the service of the spectacle (Figure 3.5). They enjoyed instant global recognition thanks to their exceptional aspect and renowned designers, and were the object of several publications, critiques and analyses long before their realization. Beijing's Olympic urbanism was part of the theatrics of power used by the regime to reassert its legitimacy as China's sole leader, and exhibited many of the characteristics traditionally found in architectures of power. For a building to be noticed and testify to the

Figure 3.5 Beijing's National Grand Theatre (National Centre for the Performing Arts). Designed amidst great controversy by French architect Paul Andreu as part of Beijing's pre-Olympic makeover, this striking building sits a block away from Tiananmen Square, the Forbidden City and the Great Hall of the People (equivalent to the parliament building, visible in the background) (photo by Johan Nilsson 2008, with permission).

grandeur of its sponsor, it has to carry a strong aesthetic presence and imprint a compelling and memorable image upon collective consciousness. The colossal size of Beijing's Olympic-related projects left no doubt about the ambition and audacity of their sponsors, while their monumentalism testified to the government's dynamism, will power and desire to be taken seriously on the world stage. Their sheer number was also astonishing and underscored the event's importance as a showcase of Chinese's state capability.

Thanks to their daring forms and self-conscious innovation, these spectacular projects marked a radical break with history and reaffirmed the Chinese state's commitment to modernity. This new architecture, which made no concessions to the past or to socialist ideology, challenged China's old image as a poor, Third World, self-centred and retrograde nation. By calling upon the leaders of the international architectural avant-garde, Chinese political elites made a bold statement about their worldly dispositions and aspirations, thereby distancing themselves from their more conservative predecessors. It also afforded them a certain amount of symbolic capital while bearing witness to their openness, discernment and sophistication.

Furthermore, the ostentatious iconography of Beijing's Olympic projects sanctioned the power of capital in the new Chinese society, and unapologetically declared that it was, as Deng Xiaoping once suggested, indeed glorious to be rich.

With their extravagant price tag, lavish appearance and sleek design, they symbolized China's active pursuit of wealth and taste for luxury, and suggested that frugality was no longer a professed value. Beijing's spectacular architecture did not only help consolidate the political power of the state but also legitimized the rising role of capital in the reconfiguration of the urban landscape. It helped project the constructed reality of a well-functioning society where social conditions are improving, thus acting as a smoke screen to conceal the rising contradictions brought about by China's rapid marketization.

Part 2: exclusion as an image construction strategy

The first part of this chapter detailed the physical construction of a seductive urban image by putting to the fore the city's most remarkable assets and enriching the city's landscape with new, spectacular attractions. This process is generally accompanied by a complementary approach, which seeks to conceal and set aside aspects of the urban landscape that may tarnish the city's carefully constructed image. Spatial manipulations in the projection of a spectacular image of the city rely as much on the creation of spaces of illusion and seduction, as they require the relegation and concealment of less attractive aspects, through multiple mechanisms of exclusion.

The spectacular construction of the event-city condones several forms of exclusion, especially regarding aspects of urban reality that may suggest incompetence, disorganization, backwardness or decline. This second part of the chapter documents several mechanisms put in place by host cities to tackle the problem posed by the visibility of poverty or post-industrial wasteland and decay, and their material manifestations of informality and marginality, in the urban landscape. It details four strategies devised by local authorities and event organizers to exclude, crop out, hide or beautify unsavoury aspects of urban reality, including the poor, the uncivilized, the unsightly, the dangerous and the unmodern. They include *forced evictions*, with the bulldozing of material landscapes of poverty and the displacement of their population; *concealment*, which hides the blight that cannot be displaced with the use of screens or walls; *aestheticization*, which beautifies poverty and decay to make them more visually acceptable, thereby anesthetizing their political power; and *intentional design*, where spaces are purposely conceived to exclude specific categories of users. Each approach is defined in more details in what follows. But first, a brief analysis of the historical development of such exclusionary mechanisms is presented to shed some light upon what makes the visibility of poverty so offensive to contemporary society.

Symbolic erasure in historical context

Historically, the practice of concealing certain aspects of urban reality, especially those connoting poverty and indigence, could be linked to a desire, on the part of elites, to enjoy their wealth without remorse or culpability. In the nineteenth century, Engels described in detail the design of English mining towns, where shops and prominent buildings were located along major routes in order to hide the view of working-class neighbourhoods and to spare local bourgeois and mine owners the sight of the misery in which those whose labour enriched them lived. Haussmann similarly endowed nineteenth-century Paris with a spectacular image of luxury and progress by hiding compact workers' housing behind prestigious façades. In *Paris Spleen* (1869), Baudelaire highlights the discomfort felt by the Parisian elite at the sight of urban poverty. His poem 'The eyes of the poor' opposes the compassion-filled guilt of a young man, embarrassed by the opulence of the café where he sits, with the disgust and irritation of his fiancée, who cannot stand the stare of a poor 'family of eyes', and begs the waiter to chase them out of sight. This poem illustrates the conflicted attitude of the French bourgeoisie towards poverty: a vexatious mix of shame and culpability, and an insufferable repulsion tinged with resentment and hostility.

With the rise of modern liberal thought in the West, and the promise of a fair and equal society, the visibility of poverty raised uncomfortable questions about the egalitarian pretences of capitalism. As a flagrant proof of the deceptive nature of free market orthodoxy, conspicuous poverty imperilled social stability by threatening to expose the fallacy of a system based on exploitation and inequity. Acknowledging its existence would destabilize the status quo and the state of denial elites had long sought comfort in. Furthermore, manifest poverty questioned the very promises of modernity, which had painted enlightenment as a path to universal betterment. Urban poverty was thus perceived as antithetical to urban modernity: it connoted a shameful lack of progress and a primitive state of backwardness.

Conspicuous poverty had ethical and religious implications as well, and stood as a shameful symptom of a morally faulty society. To give good conscience to those opposed to an equitable distribution of wealth, early twentieth-century social reformers devised strategies that helped displace the blame on the victim, often by associating poverty to disease and moral degeneracy. By exciting the fear of contamination and emphasizing the need to isolate the poor, reformers justified policies of socio-economic segregation mixed with attempts at symbolic extermination meant to render poverty invisible (Rabinow 1989).

In the course of the twentieth century, the popularity of overseas travel and the rise of international tourism made nations more self-conscious the impression they made on others. The weight of what John Urry (2002) would call the 'tourist gaze' exacerbated the insecurities of local ruling elites, who feared being perceived as underdeveloped or lagging, and justified the implementation of measures to hide – or at least displace – an overly visible poverty. Over time, cities and nations developed sophisticated strategies to limit what was to be shown to the world, hiding what was deemed either irrelevant or detrimental to their image, and blotting out elements that could cause reputational damage.

In the late twentieth and early twenty-first centuries, especially in the context of the post-industrial urban crisis, similar strategies were put in place to make invisible the growing precariousness that was born out of neoliberal policies (Kidd and Braker-Plummer 2009). A revanchist urban discourse increasingly blamed those left behind by globalization and economic restructuring for the ongoing urban crisis (Smith 1996). Public space was made increasingly inhospitable for the poor and the marginal, and intensive policing denied the homeless the simple 'right to be seen' (Mitchell 1995). By focusing on public security and targeting troublemakers, urban policy helped divert attention from the real insecurities experienced in the city in terms of access to labour, housing or food (Garnier 2008).

Today, poverty does not only suffer from invisibilization in the physical public space, but in the broader public sphere as well, especially in the mainstream media where the poor are absent both as a subject and as a voice. An increasingly conglomerated and profit-driven news industry has reduced coverage of social issues and decreased the diversity of viewpoints in the news (Bagdikian 2004; Kidd and Barker-Plummer 2009; McChesney 2004). Such media blackout means that problems faced by poor communities go unreported, and official statistics about the extent of urban poverty are underestimated. Over the last decade, the American NGO Fairness and Accuracy in Reporting (FAIR) has revealed that poverty represented less than 0.5 per cent of the content of televisual news in the US (Kidd and Braker-Plummer 2009). In France, the Institut national de la statistique et des études économiques (INSEE) was accused in 2008 of having manipulated certain figures in order to minimize the actual extent of poverty on the French national territory (Concialdi 2008). Around the world today, the poor and their contribution to society continue to suffer from symbolic erasure as their visibility is seen as a potential disturbance in the peaceful and consensual progression of capitalism. In the context of cities preparing to host a mega-event, poverty becomes a disgraceful sign of underperformance and a potential threat to investments.

Slum clearance as exclusive image construction

Cities have thus devised a host of symbolic erasure strategies in order to minimize the appearance of poverty in their landscape. Among the most common responses to the excessive visibility of an embarrassing urban poverty is slum clearance, with the forced evictions of vulnerable city residents, their displacement to less visible sites and the demolition of their squatter settlements. Urban redevelopment has long relied upon a rhetorical association between urban decay and crime to justify the violent dislocation of the poor. This association helps conceal the economic motivations of these population displacements, as the less fortunate and their physical manifestations are seen as a liability in real-estate valuation. Slum clearance also represents an opportunity for capital to expand into new territories, with the transfer of high-value urban land from the urban poor to middle- and upper-income groups. In this process of 'creative destruction' (Schumpeter 1942), relabelled 'accumulation by dispossession' by Harvey (2004), speculators benefit from the potential rise in value of the land freed by squatters, while municipalities benefit from new tax revenues.

Mega-events both facilitate and accelerate the reclaiming urban territories from the poor, and their planned and engineered gentrification. Territories once considered substandard, undesirable or undervalued, and long abandoned by the state, are now taken from the poor to allow for the expansion of capital. This dispossession is often carried out in a brutal, opaque and disrespectful way, without proper advance warning or in absentia. Unlawful eviction practices have become such a pervasive feature of sporting mega-events that Vale and Gray (2013) have turned them into an Olympic discipline: the displacement decathlon. Recent instances have been charted in Seoul's hanoks, Athens' Roma settlements, Barcelona's Poblenou, Beijing's hutongs, New Delhi's jhuggis camps, South African hostels and shanties, London's Clays Lane Estate and Brazil's favelas. Mega-event franchise owners such as the IOC and FIFA often require the clearing of vast swaths of land around event venues to create safety perimeters, free up the views for global broadcast and protect visitors from a potentially dangerous and visually offensive urbanity. Unsightly slums said to be blocking the path of progress are thus systematically removed from high-profile areas such as along the route of the Olympic torch.

These displacements are generally justified by the construction of event-related infrastructure and venues, but many are obviously related to image and speculation. In Beijing alone, nearly 1.5 million people were evicted and had their quarters demolished to make way for Olympic-related projects (COHRE 2008). Demolition typically affected densely populated, central-city neighbourhoods, referred to as 'hutong' or alleyways, which have been the object of scorn by official planners who have long seen their traditional, low rise structure, run-down appearance and difficult access as inefficient and unmodern (Figure 3.6).

Since access to basic housing is recognized as a human right (Article 25 (1) of the Universal Declaration of Human Rights), it is becoming politically difficult for local and national governments to justify forced evictions and massive demolitions. An alternative way to displace the poor without resorting to slum clearance is to combine several small-scale urban interventions to effectively reduce the size of a settlement. For example, in Rio de Janeiro, as the city prepared to host the 2016 Olympics, the construction of cable cars, access roads, elevators and sanitation systems contributed to the gradual erosion of many favelas, especially those located in key tourist sectors. Displaced residents were generally rehoused in the far periphery, away from job opportunities and basic services, or without fair compensation. The long commute, added housing fees and transportation costs often result in a net impoverishment of these population groups. Massive displacements to the urban fringe also exacerbated socio-spatial segregation.

Those targeted by slum clearance are typically given a few month's notice and are offered two compensation options: a replacement housing unit in a new community, generally on the far periphery, or a cash lump sum, which rarely reflect the fair market value of the property or its original dimension. Disgruntled residents have few options other than to turn to the court to demand justice or to wait for a better offer by standing off and refusing to leave. In the case in pre-Olympic Beijing, lawsuits were rarely heard in court, and protesters were routinely intimidated into dropping charges by being detained, harassed or put under police surveillance.

Figure 3.6 Pre-Olympic demolition of Beijing's hutongs (photo by Johan Nilsson 1998, with permission).

Local authorities resort to a host of coercive tactics to facilitate speedy slum eviction, to convince people to sign away their homes and to wear out the resolve of the most stubborn residents. If legal persuasion strategies fail, authorities resort to more illicit approaches, often using terror tactics and violence to remove people from coveted territories. Denounced in Rio de Janeiro as 'strategies of war and persecution' (ANCOP 2011: 8), intimidation tactics include infrastructure denial, public service cuts, misappropriation and destruction of property, home invasions without court orders and the marking of houses for demolition without explanation. Some strategies border on state terrorism; bulldozers show up without notice, partially demolish people's homes with their contents inside, and leave the neighbourhood in rubble to become a breeding ground for vermin. The process by which displacement is negotiated is generally individualized, thereby reducing the possibility of collective bargaining (Sylvestre and Oliveira 2012). Another heartless strategy, which could be termed *disperse and rule*, consists in scattering displaced individuals from the same community over different urban sectors, so as to permanently sever solidarity bonds and thus prevent further legal recourse.

In Beijing, the demolition companies employed by developers to clear the land before its redevelopment routinely hired eviction squads to force 'stubborn nails' (recalcitrant residents) to leave. Some of their tactics included disconnecting utilities or deliberately damaging parts of a house so as to render it uninhabitable, as was the case in Beijing's Qianmen district. Resisting residents were also physically threatened and beaten by demolition squads to prevent them from speaking to the media or complaining to authorities. In one recorded incident, thugs conducted a night raid on a house in Beijing, tied up its residents and demolished the structure, leaving the family's possessions buried in the ruins (Lim 2003).

In 2004, Amnesty International's annual report highlighted the prevalence of such abuses and described how the sense of dislocation and social upheaval and the psychological impact of living in constant fear of eviction took its toll on Beijing residents, especially older inhabitants. The loss of beloved homes and communities was compounded by the distress of being powerless in the face of such blatant injustice and disenfranchisement. The problem grew to such an extent that it pushed several people to commit suicide to protest their eviction, sometimes in very spectacular, public displays (Pocha 2004).

In Rio de Janeiro, the hosting of mega-events exacerbated the differential treatment given to favelas, worsened the state's de-responsibilization towards their residents and consolidated their status as territories of exception. In preparations for the two coming mega-events, *favelados* (those who live in favelas) were subjected to a series of extra-legal measures to facilitate their removal from territories coveted for events-related projects. While there are no official records of the number of event-related evictions throughout Rio de Janeiro, civil society group Popular Committee for the World Cup and the Olympics estimate them to be close to 100,000 (AMPVA 2016). This is tremendous, given the massive housing deficit suffered by the Brazilian poor.

In pre-Olympic Rio, examples of violent dispossession include the 2010 razing of the Mêtro-Mangueira favela, near Maracanã Stadium, in order to build an open-air parking lot. After being presented with a take-it-or-leave-it offer, residents who refused to leave were cut off from state services and left to suffer among the rubble of their departed neighbours' homes, in unbearable living conditions that exposed them to health hazards. Drug addicts moved into abandoned ruins, increasing local insecurity. In 2010, the United Nations criticized these evictions on human rights grounds, causing Rio's government to moderate its approach (Campbell-Dollaghan 2013). In January 2014, a new wave of evictions was carried out with a rare violence at the same location, as special shock-troops prevented resisting residents from blocking the destruction of the remaining homes. At the time of the World Cup in June 2014, the site was still in rubble and no parking lot had been built. Another, more notorious case of heartless destruction and eviction in Rio de Janeiro, that of Villa Autódromo, is detailed in Chapter 5.

Days before the start of the Olympics, Carlos Vainer (2016) accused the city and state governments of the crime of urbanicide and claimed that the Games' greatest legacy will be a city with a broken soul. He thus denounced the worst expulsions of the poor the city has ever known, beating the record set during the Lacerte dictatorship of the 1970s, when close to 60,000 people were expelled, and the notorious Haussmann-style evictions of the great hygienist Perreira Passos at the dawn of the twentieth century. Not only did evictions destroy large portions of the urban fabric, but 49 days before the opening of the Olympic Games, the state of Rio de Janeiro declared it a 'state of calamity', implying it was nearly bankrupt and that all available state resources would be redirected to finishing Olympic preparations. Innumerable public services were cuts and thousands of state employees, from civil servants to university professors, stopped receiving their salaries, a situation that lasted until this book went to press in December 2016. Also part of the legacy was a host of unfinished projects whose ruins have already become monuments to greed, arrogance and self-serving ambition.

Concealment in the construction of exclusive place images

A second means of invisibilizing poverty and decay in the preparation for hosting sporting mega-events is visual concealment, with the help of screen walls, hedges or other visual filters. Built near tourist attractions and along major roadways linking event sites to the city centre and the airport, they block the view of slums or industrial wastelands that cannot be demolished. One can think of the thick 'bamboo curtain' planted in New Delhi in the months leading up to the Commonwealth Games of 2010 or of the kilometres of grey brick walls erected in Beijing before the 2008 Olympics.

Pre-Olympic Rio is filled with such camouflage strategies that seek to make territories of poverty less visually offensive either invisible or more presentable. Shortly after Rio de Janeiro was awarded the 2016 Olympics in 2009, mayor Eduardo Paes erected a series of 'acoustic barriers' along the freeway connecting the airport to downtown (Figure 3.7). Few residents of Maré, a favela built along this road, were fooled by claims that these screens were meant to protect them

Figure 3.7 Acoustic barriers along Rio de Janeiro's Linha Vermelha freeway. A portion of the acoustic barrier erected in Rio de Janeiro in 2010, redecorated with Olympic designs in 2016 (photo by the author, 2016).

against harmful highway noise. The wall was decried not only as a blatant attempt at concealing their existence, but also as a mode of containment, blocking access to the roadway where many earned a living, selling snacks to motorists stuck in traffic jams. Soon after their erection, the barriers were heavily vandalized. They were repaired in the months leading to the Games, and decorated with Rio 2016 brand identity motifs.

If the wall remains a common means of concealment, it is also highly controversial because of its strong ideological charge and negative connotations, linked to notions of separation, isolation and exclusion. Authorities thus resort to alternative, less symbolically loaded means to conceal poor neighbourhoods from high-profile areas. Other forms of visual filters include large infrastructures that block the view of poor neighbourhoods and mask eyesores in the urban landscape. This is the case of the elevator to the favela of Cantagalo in Rio de Janeiro, built in 2010. This disproportionately large tower, located in the street's axis, entirely blocks the view of the favela from world-famous Ipanema beach. Other costly infrastructure projects erected as part of mega-event preparations, like the Niemeyer footbridge in Rocinha and the German-made ski cable cars in Complexo do Alemão and Morro da Providência, play a similar function while also justifying the displacement of many residents. Residents of those neighbourhoods complain that their needs in terms of sanitation, healthcare and education were left unmet. They suspect that the maintenance on these shiny new projects, built in the same sleek architectural language as other Olympic investments, will wane in the years following the event (Broudehoux and Legroux 2013).

Beautification as a means of invisibilization

A third approach commonly used to minimize the visibility of poverty and decline in the urban environment combines several tactics of beautification and urban camouflage to tone down perceptions of decay, with a visual discourse that is both neutralizing and pacifying. Here, dereliction is neither hidden nor destroyed, but embellished so as to become visually acceptable. This aestheticization often takes the form of façadist projects that beautify the most visible portion of a neighbourhood, or landscaping interventions near the point of contact with the formal city, that soften the interface between two separate worlds.

In Beijing, in the months leading to the Olympics, it was common to see superficial improvements on the most visible parts of derelict buildings, usually in the form of fresh coats of grey paint applied on walls facing major thoroughfares. Broken windows were replaced, graffiti scrubbed away and new trees and flowerbeds planted. The Rio de Janeiro government used similar tactics to tame the image of the favela and limit its negative impact. Many façadist interventions were carried out across the city to soften the rough, unfinished look of informal settlements and suggest their incorporation into the formal city. In the months preceding the World Cup and the Olympics, street signs, house numbers, garbage collection and other public services were implemented in some of Rio's favelas, which some cynical residents claim may not be maintained in the mega-events' aftermath.

A beautification initiative developed in Rio de Janeiro in preparation for its two sporting events consists of painting the most visible part of individual favela houses in a vivid palette, turning the community into a cheerful pile of brightly coloured blocks that could be the work of a clumsy child. Reminiscent of naive representations of the favela first popularized in tourist art, this caricature is now imposing itself as the visual identity of the referent 'favela' in the collective imagination. In spite of its reductive character, a similar approach was adopted in 2010 by the state and imposed upon existing communities in various new housing projects, such as the Program for Accelerated Growth (PAC) in Rocinha. The patronizing and infantilizing nature of such representations, which objectify the favela, reduced to a mere object of visual consumption, contributes to the symbolic disqualification of the poor and perpetuates their subaltern position in contemporary society. Such practices anaesthetize the political power of the favela by masking the conditions of exclusion and exploitation from which these settlements were born and by concealing traces of the discrimination and abandonment that its residents have long suffered and which are still inscribed on its walls. The lyrics of 'Favela Amarela', a popular samba song written in 1960 by Junior e Oldemar Magalhaes, demonstrate how such aestheticization strategies are nothing new in Rio de Janeiro. 'Favela amarela, ironia da vida. pintem a favela, façam aquarela, da miséria colorida' (Yellow favela, irony of life, they paint the favela as a watercolour of colourful misery) (author's translation).

Exclusion by intentional design

A last strategy of erasure and exclusion in the production of urban place images lies in the creation of spaces that are inhospitable to the poor or that cannot be appropriated by undesirable users. Garnier (2008) talks of a preventive architecture of fear, where public spaces are laid out and landscaped to eliminate dark corners, shady spots, setbacks and screens behind which indigents could find refuge. The festive redesign of urban spaces as playful and convivial leisure spaces for people 'of the right sort' also facilitates the planned gentrification of city districts (Harvey 2001). In this substitution process, the poor and the marginal are expelled from urban sectors, which are sanitized, sterilized and re-appropriated by a 'more deserving' elite.

On the occasion of security-obsessed mega-events, Olympic Parks and areas surrounding stadia or other venues are conceived according to a defensive planning approach to 'design out' potential threats and 'plan for the worst'. At once introverted, aggressive and slightly paranoid, these sites are characterized by a fortress-like architecture and a military-inspired spatial layout. Event venues are isolated by the creation of a cordon sanitaire, an unbuilt buffer zone that keeps them at a safe distance from surrounding urban districts and the dangerous social elements they are presumed to contain. They are also protected by a multilayered safety perimeter and tightly controlled borders, with a series of barriers, in the form of gates, fences, moats or waterways and few, easily monitored entry points with airport-like security checkpoints that filter access, limit admission and keep undesirables at bay.

In the case of Rio de Janeiro's Olympic Park, the parameters established by the Rio 2016 Bid Book and the technical requirements of the IOC called for a 'geographically bounded site'. The Olympic Park in Barra da Tijuca is located on a triangular peninsula stretching far into a lagoon. Bordered on two-thirds of its periphery by water, this site facilitates the creation of what Gaffney (2016) calls an Olympic Fantasy Island. Access to the park is limited to the base of the triangle attached to the mainland, where the main entrance is located. While the site's natural borders facilitate security and control, its isolation from the city proper also limits the need for creating and monitoring a brand exclusion zone (Figure 3.9).

During the event itself, many measures keep certain categories of people at bay and effectively turn Olympic sites into territories of exclusion. With the rising popularity of sporting mega-events and growing security concerns, international sports federations fear that host cities may become overcrowded and overburdened. Using a complex filtering system, which limits or selectively denies access and determines who can or cannot enter based on their wealth, status or social capital, event sites are virtually closed off to public access during the event. Entry is reserved for specific categories of people, who are either part of the organization or have the rare privilege to hold event tickets. Ticket owners enjoy preferential treatment and are granted admittance on the basis of their close contact to event participants or organizers, their status as members of the press or their capacity to pay. By limiting both the accessibility and affordability of access, certain classes

Figure 3.8 Satellite photos of Beijing and Rio de Janeiro Olympic sites. Both Olympic sites are bounded by water bodies, unbuilt buffer zones and large motorways, which act as barriers to limit access and isolate the Olympic Park from the surrounding city (source: Google Earth, 2016).

Figure 3.9 Security buffer zone at Rio de Janeiro's Olympic Park. Protective layers guard access to Rio's main Olympic park along the lagoon. A series of fences, moats and unbuilt area act as a "cordon sanitaire" to isolate the park and limit illegal entry (photo by the author, 2016).

of people are efficiently priced out, and have to remain quietly at home to watch the event on television, thereby preventing a cluttering of public space and transportation networks.

To complement these spatial provisions, a host of other technologies ensure the securitization and militarization of mega-event sites and have a city-wide impact on the public accessibility of urban spaces, not just event sites.[2] Coaffee (2014) details the extraordinary security measures deployed at the Sochi Olympics, which turned the entire resort into an impassable fortress, or what some likened to a concentration camp, limiting access to the city and the capacity of protestors to lawfully demonstrate. In London, a similarly complex surveillance system was set up, of which the infamous 'rings of steel', a high-performance electrified fence enclosing the Olympic site, was one of the most notorious features.

Discussion: the impacts of exclusionary imaging strategies

Olympic anthropologist John MacAloon (1984) described the mega-event spectacle as being 'as much about sight as it is about oversight' and noted that the Olympic spectacle simultaneously relies upon visibility and concealment. This chapter explored the different approaches used by cities to build and transform their image through concrete and material interventions. It examined policies, strategies and interventions that sought to seduce and captivate through grandiose deployment of resources and ostentatious architectural projects. It also surveyed means used by cities to exclude and conceal aspects of their urban landscape that could be perceived as nefarious to their image. The chapter demonstrated how mega-events act as a powerful force to reshape the urban environment. While they may not be the main cause of these multiple forms of urban exclusion, global-scale sporting competitions certainly facilitate their implementation.

The chapter also suggests that the use of mega-events as a mechanism for stimulating urban transformations can lead to a range of exclusionary practices that have a direct and disproportionate impact upon the most vulnerable and marginalized members of society. The expedited, high-risk and market-driven urban projects prompted by the hosting of mega-events have justified the adoption of urban strategies that produce both physical and psycho-geographical ruptures in the everyday urban landscape, and cause important disruptions to the stability of the broader social fabric. The creation of interdictory spaces and practices of spatial cleansing through the removal of the 'other' facilitates the privatized appropriation and control of urban spaces. Not only are these image-construction strategies highly selective and exclusionary, but, by projecting an idealized, fabricated and unproblematic vision of the city, they play an important pacifying and depoliticizing role, thereby discouraging possible resistance or contestation.

The danger is that these interdictory spaces, designed to systematically exclude those judged to be unsuitable, are easily naturalized so as to become acceptable urban realities (Flutsy 2001). These measures thus reinforce the exclusionary nature of the neoliberal city, where elites and middle-class citizens are given privileged access to city spaces that are increasingly privatized for their benefit and enjoyment, while the poor and the marginal are targeted by new modes of exclusion. They exacerbate a phenomenon that Soja (2000: 299) called the splintering of neoliberal urban space, with the creation of urban archipelagos of fortified enclosures.

In the context of growing public de-responsibilization towards the poor, the visibility of urban poverty becomes a highly political issue. Politics, Rancière (2006) writes, is the struggle of an unrecognized party for equal recognition in the established order. Aesthetics is bound up in this battle, Rancière argues, because the battle takes place over the image of society, what it is permissible to say or to show. Politics is thus aesthetics in that it 'makes visible what has been excluded from a perceptual field and in that it makes audible what used to be inaudible' (Rancière 1995: 226). In this sense, the invisibilization of the poor does not merely mean their visual concealment, but represents a form of disenfranchisement and silencing that denies them their citizenship right as legitimate members of society. Don Mitchell (2003) talks of the right to be seen, the simple right to be present and visible in public space, as a fundamental right that allows the most economically deprived to exist as citizens and to participate in society. To invisibilize the poor is to attempt to silence them, to neutralize their voice and to deny them any political weight. To hide poverty is also to perpetuate it, to refuse to face the structural causes of social inequality and to sustain the myth that the free market is a fair system that can provide for all members of society.

Notes

1 In reference to the urban renaissance enjoyed by the Spanish city of Bilbao after the construction of a spectacular new art museum designed by architect Frank O. Gehry in 1997.
2 These included standard military fares such as air missile defence systems, restricted airspace, tighter national border controls, the stationing of warships and high-speed patrol boats, perimeter checkpoints with detectors for explosive and radioactive material, controlled zones for searching people and their belongings, over 5,500 CCTV cameras linked to a centralized control centre, passenger profiling at Sochi international airport, surveillance drones, robotic vehicles for bomb detection, telephone and online communications tracking devices and detection equipment to monitor emotional responses. Protests, demonstrations and rallies were also banned from all Olympic spaces, with the setting up of a so-called 'forbidden zone' established by presidential decree (Coaffee 2014).

References

Affonso, J., Brandt, R., Coutinho, M. and Macedo, F. (2016) 'Lava Jato acha superplanilha da Odebrecht com valores para 279 políticos e 22 partidos', *Estadao.* Available at: http://politica.estadao.com.br/blogs/fausto-macedo/veja-a-lista-de-politicos-na-contabilidade-da-odebrecht (accessed 24 October 2016).

Alegi, P. (2008) 'A Nation to be Reckoned With: The Politics of World Cup Stadium Construction in Cape Town and Durban, South Africa', *African Studies.* Vol. 67, pp. 397–422.

AlSayyad, N. (1992) *Forms of Dominance: On the Architecture and Urbanism of the Colonial Enterprise.* London: Avebury.

AMPVA (Associaçao de moradores e Pescadores da Vila Autodromo) (2016) *Plano Popular da Vila Autodromo: Plano de desenvolvimento urbano, economico, social e cultural.* Rio de Janeiro.

ANCOP (Articulaçao National dos Comitês Populares da Copa). (2011) *Dossiê Megaeventos e Violações de Direitos Humanos no Brasil: Dossiê da articulação nacional dos comitês populares da copa.* Rio de Janeiro: ETTERN/Fundação Heinrich Böll.

Bagdikian, B.H. (2004) *The New Media Monopoly.* Boston, MA: Beacon Press.

Benjamin, W. (1968) 'The Work of Art in the Age of Mechanical Reproduction', *Illuminations: Essays and Reflections.* New York: Schocken, pp. 217–252.

Bristow, M. (2011, 15 February) 'Beijing's Qianmen District: Rebuilt for Better or Worse', *BBC News.* Available at: www.bbc.co.uk/news/world-asia-pacific-12344304

Broudehoux, A.-M. (2010) 'Images of Power: Architectures of the Integrated Spectacle at the Beijing Olympics', *Journal of Architectural Education.* Vol. 63, pp. 52–62.

Broudehoux, A.-M. and Freeman, J. (2013) 'Appropriation et dépossession dans la ville néo-libérale: Le cas du Porto Maravilha, Rio de Janeiro', L.K. de Morisset (ed.), *S' Approprier la ville. Le devenir-ensemble, du patrimoine urbain aux paysages culturels.* Quebec: Presses de l'Université du Québec.

Broudehoux, A.-M. and Legroux, J. (2013) 'L'option téléphérique dans les favelas de Rio de Janeiro: Conflits d'intérêts entre méga-événements, tourisme et besoins locaux', *Téoros.* Vol. 32, No. 2, pp. 16–25.

Campbell-Dollaghan, K. (2013, 11 October) 'Make Way for the Olympics: The Paramilitary Clearance of Rio's Slums', *Guardian*. Available at: www.gizmodo.in/news/Make-Way-For-the-Olympics-The-Paramilitary- Clearance-of-Rios-Slums/articleshow/23991312. cms (accessed 24 October 2016).

Coaffee, J. (2014) 'The uneven geographies of the Olympic carceral: from exceptionalism to normalisation', *The Geographical Journal*. Vol 181, No. 3, pp. 199–211.

COHRE (Centre on Housing Rights and Eviction). (2008a) 'Housing Rights and the 2010 Football World Cup', *Business as Usual? Housing Rights and 'Slum Eradication' in Durban, South Africa*. Geneva: COHRE.

Concialdi, P. (2008, 4 March) 'Les mauvais calculs de l'INSEE', *Baromètre des Inégalités et de la Pauvreté*. Available at: www.bip40.org/autour-du-bip40/pauvrete/chiffres/mauvais-calculs (accessed 11 July 2016).

Crawford, M. (1991) 'Can Architects Be Socially Responsible?', D. Ghirardo (ed.), *Out of Site: A Social Criticism of Architecture*. Seattle, WA: Bay Press, pp. 27–45.

Crilley, D. (1993) 'Architecture as Advertising: Constructing the Image of Redevelopment', G. Kearns and C. Philo (eds), *Selling Places: The City as Cultural Capital: Past and Present*. Oxford: Pergamon Press, pp. 232–252.

Evans, G. (2003) 'Hard-Branding the Cultural city: From Prado to Prada', *International Journal of Urban and Regional Research*. Vol. 17, pp. 417–440.

Flusty, S. (2001) 'The Banality of Interdiction: Surveillance, Control and the Displacement of Diversity', *International Journal of Urban and Regional Research*. Vol. 25, No. 3, pp. 658–664.

Gaffney, C. (2010) 'Mega-events and Socio-spatial Dynamics in Rio de Janeiro, 1919–2016', *Journal of Latin American Geography*. Vol. 9, No. 1, pp. 7–29.

Garnier, J.-P. (2008) 'Scénographies pour un simulacre: l'espace public réenchanté', *Espaces et sociétés: le consommateur ambulant*. Vol. 134, pp. 67–81.

Ghirardo, D.Y. (1991) 'Introduction', *Out of Site: A Social Criticism of Architecture*. Seattle, WA: Bay Press, pp. 9–16.

Goffman, E. (1976) *Gender Advertisements*. New York: Harper & Row.

Gottdiener, M. (2001) *The Theming of America: American Dreams, Media Fantasies and Themed Environments*. Boulder, Co: Westview.

Gravari-Barbas, M. (2013) *Aménager la ville par la culture et le tourisme*. Paris: Le Moniteur.

Hannigan, J. (1998) *Fantasy City: Pleasure and Profit in the Postmodern Metropolis*. London: Routledge.

Hannigan, J. (2003) 'Symposium on Branding, the Entertainment Economy and Urban Place Building: Introduction', *International Journal of Urban and Regional Research*. Vol. 27, No. 2, pp. 352–360.

Harvey, D. (2004) 'The "New" Imperialism: Accumulation by Dispossession', *The Socialist Register*. Vol. 40, pp. 63–87.

Holcomb, B. (2001) 'Place Marketing: Using Media to Promote Cities', L.J. Vale and S.B. Bass Warner Jr. (eds), *Imaging the City: Continuing Struggles and New Directions*. New Brunswick, NJ: Center for Urban Policy Research, pp. 33–55.

Joubert, P. (2007, 12 January) 'The Greenpoint Gamble', *Mail & Guardian*.

Julier, G. (2005) 'Urban Designscapes and the Production of Aesthetic Consent', *Urban Studies*. Vol. 42, pp. 869–887.

Kaika, M. (2005) *City of Flows: Modernity, Nature, and the City*. London: Routledge.

Karavatzis, M. and Ashworth, G. (2005) 'City Branding: An Effective Assertion of Identity or a Transitory Marketing Trick?', *Tijdschrift voor Economische en Social Geografie*. Vol. 96, No. 5, pp. 506–514.

Kidd, D. and Barker-Plummer, B. (2009) '"Neither Silent nor Invisible": Anti-Poverty Communication in the San Francisco Bay Area', *Development in Practice.* Vol. 19, No. 4–5, pp. 479–490.

Krupar, S. and Al, S. (2012) 'Notes on the Society of the Brand', S.C.C. Greig Crysler, *The SAGE Handbook of Architectural Theory.* London: SAGE, pp. 247–263.

Leach, N. (1999) *The Anaesthetics of Architecture.* Cambridge, MA: MIT Press.

Lim, L. (2003, 31 October) 'China Detains Demolition Gang', *BBC News.* Available at: http://news.bbc.co.uk/2/hi/asia-pacific/3229583.stm (accessed 11 July 2016).

MacAloon, J. (1984) 'Olympic Games and the Theory of Spectacle in Modern Societies', *Rite, Drama, Festival, Spectacle.* Philadelphia, PA: Institute of Human Issues.

McChesney, R. (2004) *The Problem of the Media: U.S. Communication Politics in the Twenty-First Century.* New York: Monthly Review Press.

Meyer, M. (2009) *The Last Days of Old Beijing: Life in the Vanishing Backstreets of a City Transformed.* New York: Walker & Company.

Miles, M. and Miles, S. (2004) *Consuming Cities.* New York: Palgrave Macmillan.

Mitchell, D. (1995) 'The End of Public Space? People's Park, Definitions of the Public, and Democracy', *Annals of the Association of American Geographers.* Vol. 85, No. 1, pp. 108–133.

Mitchell, D. (2003) *The Right to the City: Social Justice and the Fight for Public Space.* New York: The Guilford Press.

Oliveira, N. (2011) 'Força-de-lei: rupturas e realinhamentos institucionais na busca do "sonho olímpico" carioca', *14th National ANPUR Conference.* Rio de Janeiro.

Oliveira, N. (2013) *O Poder Dos Jogos e Os Jogos De Poder: Os Interesses Em Campo na Produção De Uma Cidade Para O Espetáculo Esportivo.* Doctoral Dissertation in Urban and Regional Planning, Federal University of Rio de Janeiro.

Pocha, J.S. (2004, 9 July) 'Demolitions Straining Families in China', *Boston Globe*, A6.

Rabinow, P. (1989) *French Modern: Norms and Forms of the Social Environment.* Cambridge, MA: MIT Press.

Rancière, J. (2006) *The Politics of Aesthetics.* London: Continuum.

Ritzer, G. (1999) *Enchanting a Disenchanted World: Revolutionizing the Means of Consumption.* Thousand Oaks, CA: Pine Forge Press.

Schumpeter, J. (1942) *Capitalism, Socialism, and Democracy.* New York: Harper & Row.

Smith, N. (1996) *The New Urban Frontier: Gentrification and the Revanchist City.* London: Routledge.

Soja, E. (2000) *Postmetropolis: Critical Study of Cities and Regions.* Oxford: Blackwell.

Sylvestre, G. and de Oliveira, N. (2012) 'The Revanchist Logic of Mega-Events: Community Displacement in Rio de Janeiro's West End', *Visual Studies.* Vol. 27, No. 2, pp. 204–210.

Urry, J. (2002) *The Tourist Gaze*, 2nd edition. London: SAGE.

Vainer, C. (2016, August) 'Calamidade Rio 2016', *Jornal das economistas.* Vol. 325, pp. 5–6.

Vale, L.J. (1992) *Architecture, Power, and National Identity.* New Haven, CT: Yale University Press.

Vale, L.J. and Bass Warner, S. (2001) *Imaging the City: Continuing Struggles and New Directions.* New Brunswick: Rutgers University Center for Urban Policy Research.

Vale, L.J. and Gray, A. (2013, April) 'The Displacement Decathlon: Olympian Struggles for Affordable Housing from Atlanta to Rio de Janeiro'. *Places.*

Wacquant, L.J.D. (2007) 'Territorial Stigmatization in the Age of Advanced Marginality', *Thesis Eleven.* Vol. 91, pp. 66–77.

Wright, G. (1991) *The Politics of Design in French Colonial Urbanism.* Chicago, IL: University of Chicago Press.

4 Social image construction in the mega-event city

Civilization, discipline and control

An important aspect of events-led urban image construction that is too often overlooked in the literature is the way high-visibility global-scale events foster state interventions to reform and control social behaviour. The hosting of mega-events does not only act as a catalyst for the physical transformation and beautification of the urban landscape, but also plays a central role in altering the body and the mind of the city's inhabitants. A third dimension of image construction explored in this book is concerned with the conscious and planned management of human activity and the control, regulation and normalization of the city's social environment. Hosting mega-events pressures host cities to reinvent their image through social beautification initiatives that seek to improve the 'quality' of their citizenry to fit global expectations of civility. These social engineering programmes and civilization campaigns aim to inculcate modern norms of public behaviour to produce a tame and docile citizenry.

In order to facilitate their public outreach, such attempts to regulate human activity and to normalize behaviour rest upon diverse instruments of governmentality. Some are discursive, intent on reforming the mind of the people by inculcating new ideals and values; others focus on the body and seek to promote social reform through active participation in embodied practices. More coercive means of enforcing public order and social control are also used, with the tightening of security and limits on freedom of movement and access.

The chapter begins by introducing the notion of the civilization process including its historical purpose as social lubricant and a tool of differentiation. It is followed by a discussion of the role played by social reform programmes in the hosting of mega-events, and of the main actors behind their implementation and their motives. The third part of the chapter analyses empirical examples of social image-construction programmes in both Beijing and Rio de Janeiro. The chapter closes with a reflexion on the social impacts of such initiatives.

Civilization, governmentality and social exclusion

As a major agent of urban change, the hosting of mega-events plays a central part in intensifying the civilization process that has long accompanied modernization and globalization. Norbert Elias defines the historical normalization of behaviour in Europe as the *civilization process*, which he views as an intrinsic part of the modernization and urbanization of society (Elias 2000). For him, the development of social control mechanisms, the rationalization and regulation of social conduct and the imposition of contexts of obedience to the law are closely tied to the modernization of society.

Michel Foucault similarly describes the modern's state use of disciplinary practices to implement the universalizing norms of modern society and to subject bodies to punitive regimes that seek to unify, pacify and control their behaviour (Foucault 1976). Following nineteenth-century social reformers, who conceived of the social as an object of regulation, modern states used social training, public education and other disciplinary measures to reform bodies, maintain social order and produce efficient, well-behaved and productive individuals (Foucault 1975). Contemporary civilizing programmes are clearly inscribed in the logic of what Foucault calls governmentality, or the diverse strategies and technologies of government, control and intelligence that states use to render society governable. He wrote of the organized practices – mentalities, rationalities and techniques – used by governments to produce the best-suited citizen to fulfil state policies. Social beautification programmes, for instance, function through the production of a discourse that defines proper social norms and acceptable demeanour. This discourse is later internalized by individuals who end up governing themselves in a way that eases the need for direct government intervention (Foucault 1975).

Civility has long been known to serve as a social lubricant, meant to harmonize social relations, minimize frictions and facilitate peaceful coexistence. For Foucault (1975), although the enforcement of social norms were historically justified by questions of security, health and hygiene, it was also motivated by a concern for status, appearances and social differentiation. Social distinction was fundamental in the development of 'civilized' norms, and civilizing projects were closely linked to the emergence of modern social hierarchies. The civilization process is thus predicated upon social inequality and competition for status, and follows a logic of social exclusion.[1] Civilizing projects are defined by a fundamental inequality between civilizing agents and the people upon which they act, and have long justified the domination of population groups perceived as needing to be reformed. Notions of civility are inextricably linked to the constitution of citizenship and the right to participate in society. The evaluation of social behaviour marks people as appropriately or insufficiently civilized, establishes eligibility for inclusion in, or exclusion from, an idealized body politics, and ultimately defines citizenship (Friedman 2004).

Mega-events and the civilization process

Mega-events have long played a role in the spread of a civilizing ideal and the globalization of modern cultural norms. As mass celebrations of progress and modernity, early World's Fairs were driven by an implicit civilizing impulse and often acted as sites for the acculturation of the masses into industrialized culture

(Young 2009; Rydell and Gwynn 1994). The modern Olympic movement also strove to inculcate new morals, values and norms of behaviour upon their hosts, visitors and participants (Toohey and Veal 2001; Brownell 1995). These civilization programmes would later be branded of cultural imperialism as host cities imposed imported norms upon local reality and urged their residents to play up to international standards (Choi 2004).[2]

The vast mediatization of mega-events and their rising role in city marketing and national boosterism have now placed citizen behaviour at the forefront of urban image-construction endeavours, prompting the adoption of diverse social reform initiatives. These events' tremendous symbolic power legitimizes disciplining programmes that would otherwise be perceived as oppressive. While the role of international federations like FIFA and the IOC in the management of social behaviour is generally indirect and diffuse, it is clear that their low tolerance for civic disturbances and their insistence upon public image, order and security exert enormous pressures on local organizing committees and host governments to take the issue seriously.[3] The contracts signed between federations and host cities contain carefully worded provisions and covert demands regarding disciplinary protocol and expectations, even regarding public comportment. For example, in its Bid Book, FIFA requires a 'carnavalesque behaviour' from the local population and a 'festive urban atmosphere, free from political manifestations' (Kolamo 2015). Inside corporate-controlled stadia and sponsor-branded enclaves, sports federation stipulations are even more stringent, going as far as restricting what people wear, eat and how they behave. Eager to provide an impeccable social environment for the event, image-conscious civic leaders deploy a host of strategies to get their population to comply (Bennett 1991; Choi 2004).

Before civilizing the bodies of their citizens, modifying their habits, altering their comportment and monitoring their movement, city governments first act upon their minds, and inculcate new values and ideologies that will help to build consensus and facilitate compliance. In order to build strong public support and ensure participation, they must devise ways to seduce the population, to get people to adhere to the mega-event mythology and to partake in the excitement. As Stavrides (2014) notes, people must first be 'inspired' in order to 'participate'. They must feel empowered by the pursuit of a great collective project, get a sense of validation from membership in such an endeavour and gain personal gratification from the belief that great legacies and shared benefits can be obtained from hosting such an event (Rojek 2013). This is why official propaganda around mega-events appeals to local pride, national unity and the common good, with a rhetoric that makes wide use of the collective 'we'. Organizing committees present the event as a major national accomplishment, an important step towards a higher status in the global urban hierarchy and a mark of recognition of the nation's collective worth and progress. Pro-event discourse often appeals to the notion of 'dream', brandished as a shared desire and a noble ideal that can only be realized if all join in and contribute to the cause.

Other discursive means to reform a city's human landscape in preparation for the hosting of mega-events seek to alter people's character by promoting values such as respectability, honesty and fair play, turning good behaviour, social order and hygiene into morality issues. Methods generally rely upon the multiplication of public interest messages in the city's public space and the local media. They range from gentle reminders about proper hygiene, respect for the environment and abiding by anti-smoking regulations, to more direct admonishments regarding proper social etiquette, interaction with foreign guests and adequate conduct in public transportation, all the way to harsher rhetoric against public intoxication, petty crime and other forms of anti-social behaviour. These messages are generally infused with a disciplinary rhetoric that is reminiscent of early modern reformist discourse, and persuasion techniques range from appeals to collaboration to punitive fines (Broudehoux 2007).

International sporting federations also carry out their own social reform initiatives through promotional activities held in the years leading to the event. For example, the IOC requires the deployment of an Olympic cultural programme in the host nation before the Games, to promote tolerance and an open mind-set, to encourage locals to learn foreign languages and to organize international cultural exchanges. They also advocate the adoption of values like self-realization, transcendence, good sportsmanship and fair play. Sporting federations are especially keen on educating crowds on the proper way to behave and celebrate during the event itself. Economic actors, especially event sponsors, with their blanket advertising campaigns, carry out their own ideological campaigns, admonishing people to become good neoliberal subjects, faithful supporters and assiduous consumers.

People's role as active brand makers

A central part of the top-down management of social behaviour associated with the hosting of mega-events is the grooming of event-goers and local residents as co-producers of the event brand. Kolamo and Vuolteenaho (2013) have documented the role of people in the reproduction and diffusion of the event's brand image. Not only are local citizens expected to wear the brand and consume the products of the event and its sponsors, but they are also expected to *be* the brand, to embrace and embody the event's brand identity in their practices and emotional displays before and during the event and to co-create the brand by adopting prescribed behaviours in front of television cameras (Kolamo and Vuolteenaho 2013).

In the demands to host cities and organizers, event franchise owners require the comprehensive support of local residents in the construction of the event spectacle. In the months preceding the event, people are encouraged to participate in series of nationwide education campaigns that promote active involvement in the production of the event. These events exhort people to be emotionally engaged producers of spectacle and to adopt a pre-established criteria of ideal fandom (Whitson and Horne 2006). In the context of the 2010 South Africa World Cup, Kolamo and Vuolteenaho (2013) describe FIFA's attempt to control people's mood as an essential part of a carefully planned branding manoeuvre. South-Africans were instructed on how to perform according to a carefully calibrated carnivalesque behaviour and were educated on the right way to achieve a

FIFA-approved party mood by celebrating in a safe, civilized and respectful manner, with the right costumes, accessories and attitude.

As part of this top-down, industrially manufactured form of mediated urban agency, FIFA also encourages event-goers to be camera-conscious performers. To guarantee maximum visibility for this mega-event in the international mass media, they equip Fan Fest sites with 'photo booths' where football fans are urged to celebrate openly in front of the camera (Kolamo and Vuolteenaho 2013). These sites are designed to act as densely mediated stages, as platforms for the capture of images of festive celebration by broadcast corporations. Social and personal media also contribute to the media saturation of these spaces, which function as sites of self-promotion, where users publicize the event in their social circles around the world on their mobile gadgets.

Kolamo and Vuolteenaho (2013) describe the emotional intensity of fan behaviour in the proximity of camera crews as topopornography, a characterization which predates Gaffney's notion of geoporn discussed in Chapter 2. Drawing upon Bale's definition of topofilia as attachment to place, Van Houtum and Van Dam (2002) had already characterized fan behavior at sporting mega-events as topoporn, or the mediated and commodified form of fan attachment that is replacing previous spatio-emotional forms of attachment to commercial sport. The pornographic dimension of the term refers to the intensive images and acts performed for the gaze of outsiders. For Kolamo and Vuolteenaho (2013), topopornographic football culture harnesses the fans' emotional involvement and exploits their exhibitionist behaviour in front of media cameras as ways to reinforce event branding efforts and to boost the media spectacle.

Discipline and order in the event-city

The transformation of the city's human environment in preparation for mega-events also involves the need to maintain the appearance of order, control and discipline, which is achieved through the use of extensive security mechanisms and theatrical display of punitive power. To guarantee the peaceful celebration of the event, local leaders and event organizers must comply with International Sporting Federations' stipulations for the delivery of a safe and secure environment, free from violence, political agitation or major incidents, with minimum schedule disruption. They must also warrant the zealous safeguarding of the intellectual property rights of private corporations. As a result, mega-events are increasingly infused by the spectacle of public order and security, and justify the superimposition of a new disciplinary landscape upon the city.

Although actual vulnerability is difficult to assess, the vast use of military metaphors and of a specialized martial discourse by security consultants has helped convince local authorities to take drastic actions that have been denounced as oppressive, intrusive and excessive (Fussey *et al.* 2011). Among them is the adoption of extraordinary legal regimes that allow the suspension of many civic rights, and the imposition of limits on personal liberties, including freedom of movement and freedom of speech. The unique circumstances posed by mega-events also justify the state's use of juridico-political means to justify more coercive methods of population control, including repression, internment and expulsion. They foster the implementation of a policing model that draws heavily on zero-tolerance orthodoxies and exceptional forms of penalty, and facilitate the implementation of preventive measures against potential crime and what appears to be excessive policing, with the proliferation of police patrols and the massive presence of local law enforcement officers, private security guards and military police (Kennelly and Watts 2011). Mega-events also help implement an extensive surveillance apparatus that is invasive and makes all citizens the object of suspicion. Obviously, many norms of policing and social control adopted in preparation for mega-events stem from an image-construction imperative rather than from real, measurable threats. By conflating disorder and indiscipline with crime, cities impose stringent regulations to discourage the use and occupation of public space, and ban and criminalize activities that do not cohere with the desired image they seek to project.

The poor as objects of civilization and criminalization

The main targets of such programmes are population groups who are perceived as liabilities in the construction of a positive urban image or who threaten the smooth realization of the event. Social image-construction interventions are aimed at specific classes of people who have themselves become markers of disorder and insecurity, including vagrants, prostitutes, street children, panhandlers, drug users, the homeless and certain classes of youth. It has become common practice for Olympic host cities to introduce restrictive legislation specifically directed at particular population groups (COHRE 2008). Examples include a 1984 pre-Olympic 'gang sweep' in Los Angeles, which sent hundreds of young black men to jail, and the confinement of the homeless and mentally ill and deportation of refugees and asylum seekers by the Greek government for the 2004 Athens Games (COHRE 2008).[4] The poor and the marginal are arbitrarily subjected to differential legal treatment, and are overwhelmingly targeted by repressive measures of control and security (Lenskyj 2002; Broudehoux 2007; Zirin 2011). Neoliberal public policies express a growing intolerance of all forms of disorder and so-called 'quality of life' crimes associated with poverty and informality, mega-events have exacerbated this intolerance and promoted the adoption of measures that often exceed what is permitted by law, ranging from anti-homeless and anti-mendicity regulations, to repressive means of social control (Kennelly and Watts 2011).

Mega-events also promote the socio-symbolic exclusion of the poor from urban space through measures that give preferential treatment to the privileged class, in a process that Kolamo and Vuolteenaho (2013) describe as the 'purification' of the cityscape. This notion refers to the relegation of inappropriate forms of bodily presence seen as threatening to the event's brand identity and the profitability of its sponsors. Blaming the poor for violating the urban landscape and illegitimately inhabiting public spaces, authorities imply that such urban territories are the exclusive domains of the wealthy and fashionable (Kennelly and Watts 2011).

Public space is increasingly policed against visual pollution and other forms of nuisance from the poor, and stringent new regulations discourage their use and occupation. Laws against begging, panhandling, sleeping or public urination cleanse public space from undesirable users to make them available for foreign tourists, middle-class families, business people, wealthy residents and other 'rightful' user groups. In many countries, homeless and beggars are bussed out of the city for the duration of the event, as was the case in Olympic Beijing, where thousands of migrant workers, many of whom had built Olympic projects, were sent back to their villages (Broudehoux 2004).

Such infrastructure of exclusion is generally directed at informal sector workers to discourage their presence in the city's open spaces and force them to stay away for the duration of the event. The harassment and displacement of street vendors and other informal economy workers – who rely on public space for their livelihood – and the criminalization of their informal economic activities has become prevalent at mega-events. As a fixed features of urban life in many parts of the world, street vendors represent an important element of a city's cultural landscape and vastly contribute to the unique character and atmosphere of public space. As a result, mega-event image construction does not only make it more difficult for the disadvantaged to earn a living, but also sanitizes the city's environment. It allows the police to selectively target those whose appearance and activities are incongruous with the idealized image of the rebranded city. The label of not belonging to the presentable and socially purified image of model citizens excludes these people from participation in society. It can have an impact on subject formation, affecting the constitution of identity and the construction of self-esteem. These programmes can affect their capacity to fend for themselves, to fight for people's rights and to resist unfair treatment. Furthermore, by pathologizing the economically marginalized, political and economic elites divert attention from their own corruption and amorality by suggesting that criminality is the exclusive realm of the poor.

Beijing's Olympic civilization programme

The case of Beijing 2008 provides a fascinating incursion into the realm of Olympic-driven social image construction. For Beijing Olympic organizers and China's national leaders alike, the Olympic Games represented a great opportunity for societal advancement and for popular acculturation into global cosmopolitan society. The momentum and civic pride attached to hosting the 29th Summer Games helped hasten the pursuit of a civilization campaign initiated in the 1990s that sought to turn Beijing residents into disciplined representatives of twenty-first-century China (Anagnost 1997). These campaigns were marked by a self-conscious desire to upgrade China's world image, which had become a major concern in the face of growing contact with the international community. Preparations to host the Olympics thus included a series of social engineering programmes that sought to show the world that China has not only developed economically, but socially and culturally as well (Broudehoux 2007).

The state's objectives in launching such an extensive Olympic civilization programme were manifold. Authorities strove to produce a more disciplined, orderly and law-abiding urban culture to improve national stability in a period of mounting popular discontent and worsening social tensions resulting from growing social disparities. They also sought to improve China's image as a rising world power by strengthening the image of Beijing as a twenty-first century world metropolis. Turning Beijing residents into convivial, well-mannered modern citizens not only aimed to seduce the thousands of visitors who would tour the city, but it also intended to reassure potential investors, and to help sustain business confidence, with the production of a docile, contented and obedient workforce. A special arm of the Chinese government's propaganda apparatus, working in concert with Olympic organizers, was thus charged with raising the 'civilization level' of the city's 15 million inhabitants to make sure they were on their best behaviour for the event.

In China, the moral education of the people has long been viewed as a function of good government, and the civilization process went hand-in-hand with modernization. Throughout the twentieth century, Chinese elites, intellectuals and officials have pursued a modern civilization ideal, both as an ideological mission and as a national project, advocating *wenming* (civilization) as a national strategy for radical social transformation (Anagnost 1997; Duara 2001). China's masses were subjected to diverse modernization campaigns, motivated by ideological discourses that had their roots in neo-Confucian principles and in Enlightenment ideals of evolutionary progress (Anagnost 1997).

The Olympic Games helped create specific conditions that facilitated the implementation of a new programme and warranted its success with minimal state intervention. In order to facilitate its public outreach, the civilization campaign rested upon three main strategies: the first was mainly ideological, and consisted of the orchestration of an official discourse surrounding the Beijing Olympiads, through the indoctrination of a cultural vision that promoted wilful compliance and self-sacrifice. The second approach implemented social reform through embodied practices, using active participation and mimetic practices to teach people new behaviour and to reshape them into ideal modern citizens. The third approach was coercive, and focused on more traditional means of social control, such as the tightening of policing and surveillance systems and controlling mobility and access.

The main approach used in the pre-Olympic metamorphosis of Beijing residents relied upon the use of mass persuasion techniques and discursive strategies to engineer consensus and incite pliant cooperation, drawing upon nationalism, patriotism, self-sacrifice and voluntarism as means of enticement. Chinese authorities were keen to strike a delicate balance between their desire to host a successful Olympics and their fear of presenting the image of a police state to the world. To maximize their effectiveness as both an image-construction strategy and a means of social control, reforms had to be achieved through wilful participation rather than through coercive means.

In the years leading to the Games, the Beijing population was relentlessly bombarded with public interest messages, using media saturation as a tool of mass communication and indoctrination (Brady 2009). Messages and slogans were seen and heard on billboards throughout the city, at bus stops, in classrooms, public offices, in the print media, on television and on the internet; these were infused with a mix of political and moral discourse, encouraging self-reform and civic pride. A series of handbooks and pamphlets on etiquette, civility and sports ethics were freely distributed throughout the city.

Olympic propaganda was infused with nationalist rhetoric, to the point that the nation and the Games formed an indivisible whole in the collective imagination and that serving one meant serving the other. Citizens were exhorted to help China rise to greatness by changing their demeanour and improving their manners with complete devotion. Embracing the Olympics became more than a civic duty, but a patriotic gesture and a contribution to the advancement of the motherland. By extension, non-compliance to social reforms became anti-patriotic, and people were rewarded for reporting violations and denouncing uncivilized behaviour (Broudehoux 2007). The patriotic framing of the Olympic civilizing programme reinforced the symbolic importance of the event in the collective imagination. By constructing the Olympics as a paramount historical marker, a unique occasion to redress collective injuries and past humiliation, an opportunity to restore national pride and to regain China's deserving status in the world system, local leaders and Olympic organizers succeeded in creating a social consensus around both the event and the reform programmes that would ensure its success. This propaganda campaign engendered unabated devotion to the Olympic cause, to the point that any sacrifice, no matter the social, cultural, economic or ecological costs, became justified. Its success was also measured in the mutual policing that allowed a vast panoptic surveillance apparatus to function with minimal state involvement (Broudehoux 2007).

If much of the civilizing process rested upon propaganda and discourse, its main *modus operandi* was performative, and included a vast public education programme predicated upon embodied practices. It was through active participation in state-sponsored activities that both the body and mind of the population would be transformed, and state-sanctioned norms of behaviour internalized. The way people spoke, dressed, stood in line (Figure 4.1), cheered at events and carried themselves in public were all considered important measures of Olympic success. Anti-social behaviours such as spitting, queue jumping, jaywalking, hawking, swearing and smoking were specifically targeted. Focusing on manners, personal hygiene, civility, morality, sports ethics and respect for law and order, slogans, posters and television messages instructed citizens on the correct use of public toilets, urged them to speak proper Mandarin, to learn English, to smile more and to keep their shirts on in the summer.

In Beijing, embracing the Games therefore became an embodied engagement to transform oneself and embrace Olympic civilization ideals on a daily basis. People were urged to actively participate in the continuous flow of Olympic education activities that relentlessly punctuated the years leading to the Olympics and pervaded everyday life. To facilitate acculturation into civilized norms of behaviour and to increase participation, activities were often of a

Figure 4.1 Volunteers at Beijing airport demonstrate the proper way to queue. In the years leading to the 2008 Olympics, November 11 was celebrated as "National Queuing Day" and volunteers dressed as penguins gently encouraged people to queue in an orderly fashion (photo by the author, 2007).

festive or ludic nature: role play, simulation games and repetitive rehearsals were ubiquitous. They also drew upon people's competitive spirit, in televised quiz shows on Olympic knowledge, popular etiquette contests, English-language competitions and other forms of challenges held in schools, universities and neighbourhoods around the city. One specific area of concern was sport etiquette and sportsmanship. After local fans had displayed anti-social behaviour against foreign teams at several international competitions, efforts focused on keeping overly nationalist partisanship in check. Strict instructions about proper cheering behaviour (including cheering for non-Chinese teams) and appropriate hand gestures were issued.

If repetition accelerated the assimilation of new social norms, the most effective way to encourage proper behaviour was mimetic. Much of the Olympic civilization programme rested upon the production of idealized citizens, elevated as social models to be emulated. Olympic propaganda called upon movie stars like Jackie Chan and Andy Lau, and sport personalities like hurdler Liu Xiang and basketball icon Yao Ming, to personify the ideals of Olympic civilization. They were ubiquitous in Olympic propaganda, both as proud bearers of the Olympic brand and as social models of virtue. Erected as national heroes and icons of civility, these celebrities embodied the best of what China had to give. Olympic volunteers were similarly promoted to the status of iconic social models in Olympic propaganda, and dominated Beijing's pre-Olympic landscape. Images of these ordinary heroes, idealized for their ethics, hard work and desire to make the nation proud were used to uplift the national psyche and to inspire citizens through their loyalty and dedication to the motherland. The civilizing process thus helped constitute the ideal socialist citizen as an iconic sign, contributing to both national and urban image construction. As a corollary, those who failed to comply with this ideal brought into question their very belonging to Chinese society.

If some model citizens embodied the key qualities of civilization and came to stand for the nation as a whole, others who failed to embody this ideal were denied representation as valued members of Chinese society. Absent from Olympic propaganda were Beijing's mass of rural migrant workers, who were the main target of this civilization campaign, and were discursively constructed as a major threat to the image of civilized modernity conceived for the Games. Their crude manners, coarse language and unhygienic habits – often the result of their own destitution, lack of education and exploitation – were taken as proof of their need for reform. There were 3–5 million migrant workers in Beijing in the years before the Olympics, mainly employed in the construction, manufacturing and service industries (Bonneau 2008).[5] Generally identified by the derogative *waidi* or 'outsider', they were routinely accused of tarnishing the city's image, blamed for the capital city's deteriorating civilization level and portrayed in the media as the perpetrators of most violent crimes (Figure 4.2). As a result, countless migrant workers were expelled from the city for the duration of the Olympics (Broudehoux 2010, 2011).

A last focus of Beijing's Olympic civilization programme was public order and security. Although Beijing has long been among the safest cities in the world,

Figure 4.2 Rural migrant (*waidiren*) in pre-Olympic Beijing (photo by the author, 2006).

China wished to eliminate every potential threat to the largest gathering of world leaders the mainland had ever hosted. The notion that the Olympics could make the city an ideal target for international terrorists in search of maximum visibility, combined with exaggerated reports about internal security threats, especially from insurgent groups such as the Falun Gong, Tibetan activists and Uyghur separatists, justified a massive security operation. With a budget of over US$2 billion, double Athens' 2004 security spending, Beijing mobilized a 150,000-strong antiterrorism force that included commandos and other military units equipped with surface-to-air missiles, cutting-edge helicopters and military aircraft. Over 80,000 policemen, security agents, and other peacekeepers provided added security and surveillance (Bonneau 2008).

Security also served as a code word for social beautification initiatives, meant to ensure that undesirable social elements would not ruin image-construction efforts. Months prior to the Games, Beijing authorities launched a preventive anti-crime campaign to ensure that crime rates stayed as low as possible before and during the Olympics, targeting vagrancy, begging, prostitution and other illicit activities in the city. Citizens were subjected to heightened scrutiny, with the use of over 300,000 surveillance cameras (Zhou *et al.* 2008). Sophisticated, innovative surveillance technology enabled the government to keep tabs on private electronic devices, allowing the surveillance apparatus to reach into the privacy of people's homes. Mobile phones and the internet, often portrayed as instruments of liberation in post-Mao China, were thus turned into instruments of control. They also became instruments of civilization, as mass SMS were routinely sent to Beijing residents to remind them to adopt a civilized demeanour (Zhou *et al.* 2008).

Just as physical signs of poverty and backwardness, which could dispel China's newly proclaimed prosperity and modernity, were carefully camouflaged behind walls, shrubbery and coats of paint, many local residents who did not fit the image of the civilized Beijing citizen were also carefully hidden from view. For the duration of Olympic events, Beijing became a closed city, protected by a series of filtering systems that controlled access to its urban fortress. To preserve the image of a city unburdened by poverty, Chinese authorities began enforcing residence permit (*hukou*) regulations, having turned a blind eye to illegal residents for many years. Migrants were subjected to diverse forms of harassment, including mass identification checks, confiscation of the tools of their trade and the destruction of illegal schools and homes. Those found without Beijing residence permits were fined, forcibly expelled from the city or sent to detention centres and re-education work camps. Police sweeps picked up beggars, street children, the homeless and other conspicuous indigents at train stations, pedestrian underpasses, railway bridges and other hideouts, to be placed in relief centres on the city's outskirts, or in custody and repatriation camps, before being exiled to their hometown.

The criminalization of informal activities, with the banning of unlicensed taxis, sidewalk vending, peddling and hawking furthered the victimization of migrant citizens, rendered 'illegal' in the name of order and security. In spite of their great contribution to Olympic image construction, through their labour as construction workers, street sweepers or garbage collectors, most migrants were barred from active participation in the Olympic celebrations, even as simple bystanders. Innumerable informal businesses were closed, and for the duration of the event the contribution of these workers to the city's economy was made blatantly visible by their absence.

Crowd control was another major area of concern. The Chinese Communist Party's long suspicion of all forms of public gathering, especially in the national capital, meant that all forms of popular congregation remained tightly regulated and closely monitored for the duration of the Olympics. Beijing's public spaces were kept under constant surveillance, while access to several key sites, even those with no relation to the Olympic event, such Tiananmen Square, was tightly controlled by police checkpoints equipped with X-ray machines. The Olympic Park and the area surrounding major Olympic venues were protected by a 'cordon sanitaire'. Entry was restricted according to a finely calibrated social ranking, which included people with tickets for specific daily events, athletes and their entourage and holders of special privilege (accredited members of the press and VIPs, among others). As a result, the expansive park remained eerily empty during most of the Olympic weeks (Figure 4.3). Along the perimeter fence that protected the Olympic Park, crowds of curious local residents and foreign tourists who failed to get their hands on elusive tickets could be seen stretching their necks to catch a glimpse of the world-famous Olympic stadium and of the festivities they had come to celebrate.

Also empty during the Olympic Games were the three official Olympic 'protest zones' that had been set aside by the Chinese government for legal demonstrations.

Figure 4.3 Beijing Olympic Green during the 2008 Games (photo Johan Nilsson 2008, with permission).

Chinese citizens were told they would be free to protest, as long as they obtained a permit from the Public Security Bureau. However, the Bureau held the right to reject protests that could potentially 'harm national, social and collective interests or public order'. As a result, all 77 individuals who applied for permits were either persuaded to withdraw their proposals or saw them rejected (Callick 2008; O'Brien 2008). Some of those who submitted applications were subsequently arrested and detained. International human rights NGOs such as Human Rights Watch denounced protest zones as political traps, set to facilitate the arrest of dissidents, and categorized the application process as a tactic to facilitate the suppression of protests rather than giving people greater freedom of expression (HRW 2008). In the end, the three official protest zones remained devoid of activity for the duration of the Games, except for the occasional foreign journalist.

Civilizing Rio de Janeiro

In Rio de Janeiro, social beautification initiatives were not as extensive as in Beijing, but they carried the same governmentalist logic, pursued parallel political agendas and similarly targeted vulnerable population groups. In both cases, social beautification efforts aimed to build the image of an advanced, ordered, world-class city and exclusionary measures were put in place to attenuate the conspicuous presence of the urban poor, the marginal and the 'unmodern'. If in Beijing multiple state initiatives were combined to transform their city's human landscape, in Rio de Janeiro initiatives were concentrated under two multifaceted municipal programmes that were much more pragmatic in their approach and whose ties with the Olympics were looser than in Beijing. The first approach was interventionist and focused on eradicating urban violence, with the spectacular occupation of Rio's criminalized neighbourhoods through a police pacification programme. The other approach amalgamated under a single umbrella programme efforts to fight urban disorder, discipline the citizenry and curb all sort of uncivilized behaviour.

Pacification, surveillance and urban warfare

One of the first government actions undertaken upon receiving news that Rio would host the Olympic Games in 2009 was to crack down on gang violence and illicit drug trading by launching a vast state programme for the 'pacification' of the city's favelas. Preparations for Rio's two mega-events thus included the occupation of key settlements by a specially trained police force and the disarmament and expulsion of traffickers and militias. The first favelas to be pacified and to receive permanent police pacification units (known as UPP) were all located in the city's South Zone, where elite beach neighbourhoods and the main tourism attractions are concentrated (Freeman 2012).

Official rhetoric on pacification reveals a strong state bias against the urban poor. It legitimizes the differential treatment exacted on the city's most vulnerable, implicitly defining informal settlements as enemy territory and declaring what critics have called a war on the poor. For instance, Dias and Eslava (2013: 190) describe the widely mediatized and sensationalized police invasion of the Complexo of Alemão in 2010 as a 'true act of war'. The favela pacification programme is carried out through the 'reconquest' of favela 'territory' by the BOPE (*Batalhão de Operações Policiais Especiais* or Special Operations Battalion), known as one of the best-trained urban fighting forces in the world (Freeman 2012). Before the favela is 'pacified', it must first be 'invaded' using a 'clear and hold' strategy to shock and demilitarize the drug trade (Yutzy 2012). After weapons have been seized and gang affiliates have fled, the UPP takes possession of the favela by symbolically planting a national flag, and settles in a highly visible building.

Residents of these communities find this war and pacification rhetoric highly offensive, experienced as yet another act of psychological violence against them. Having been dominated by drug traffickers and paramilitary militias for years, they view the pacification police as just another occupying force ruling over them and limiting their ability for self-determination (Freeman 2012). Far from signifying the favela's integration into the formal city, the UPP's presence only reinforces its status as an urban enclave and a space of exception, treated and maintained as a separate territorial entity (Yutzy 2012).

For years, favelas had already been subjected to differential modes of policing in comparison with the rest of the city. Following a logic of containment, in the months leading to the hosting of the World Cup and the Olympics, favelas located near event sites and major tourist attractions were circled by heavily militarized buffer zones. In what Zibechi (2010) denounced as a 'militarization of the poor', unprecedented security measures were deployed around the periphery of some of the city's squatter settlements, with the municipal guard, the military police and other institutions of the criminal justice system acting as border patrols to protect privileged urbanites from the presumed danger within. Morro da Providência, a small favela located at the heart of Porto Maravilha, found itself surrounded by a disproportionate number of police units, which, ironically, did not stop drug-related violence reaching a high point a few months before the Olympics.

Rio de Janeiro's city government skilfully used the pretext of mega-events to implement an elaborate surveillance apparatus steeped in Foucauldian biopower and governmentality. According to the BBC, Rocinha, Rio's largest favela, located near the elite São Conrado, was equipped with some of the most expansive CCTV surveillance in the world, with more cameras per inhabitant than London (BBC News 2013). Also keeping watch upon Rio's citizens is Eduardo Paes's notorious 'control room', the mayor's greatest pride and most noted accomplishment in the years leading to the World Cup and Olympic Games. Inaugurated in 2010, this Big Brother, high-technology operation centre surveys the entire urban territory in real time and integrates most of the city's coordination functions, including security and disaster management. Hailed as the model for 'smarter city' development (Singer 2012), it resembles a war room with dozens of giant LED screens scrutinized by analysts. Like a twenty-first-century equivalent of Haussmann's boulevards, this panoptic tool cuts right into the heart of the city to make it at once transparent, measurable and controllable. Its efficiency at the fast localization of problems and their rapid neutralization was demonstrated during the 2014 student demonstrations, with the quick dispatch of riot police to protest sites and the prompt dispersion of protesters.

The acquisition of such expensive high-tech equipment was denounced as proof of the mayor's power-hungry, repressive and heavily policed approach to governance, betraying a vision of the smart city as a punitive city, and a conceptualization of Rio de Janeiro as a police state. Critics suggested that the security system deployed for both mega-events merely partakes in the spectacularization of security, as a theatrical prop built for the psychological wellbeing of athletes, event participants and other visitors, to reassure Olympic officials and foreign investors and to allow organizers to market Rio as a safe 'event destination' (Singer 2012). Others deplore that a similar but reverse form of surveillance has not been made available for the population to examine state activities, especially as allegations of corruption and collusion began surfacing in 2015.

Rio's shock of order

Rio de Janeiro's other approach to the control and discipline of its human environment was also launched in 2009, only weeks after the city was selected as host of the 2016 Olympics. Mayor Eduardo Paes initiated his *Choque de ordem* (Shock of order), which grouped for the first time into a single programme a series of regularization initiatives and social reform campaigns to crack down on urban crime, disorder and informal trade. The programme was largely modelled on the zero-tolerance policy perfected by Rudolf Giuliani in 1990s New York, influenced by the broken-windows theory (Kelling and Wilson 1982), which rests upon the assumption that disorder and crime are connected as part of a causal chain and that small-scale incivilities, if not taken seriously, will proliferate into a downward spiral of increased crime and chaos (McArdle and Erzen 2001). Although Giuliani's punitive measures have been widely denounced as a neoliberal attack on informal workers and the homeless (Smith 1996), Paes remained adamant in his support for this approach, going as far as hiring Giuliani himself as a security consultant for the 2016 Olympic Games.

In its first years of operation, the *Choque de ordem* focused on purging the landscape of informal commerce, upon which so many city dwellers depend for their survival. This led to the privatization of all beachfront bars along the city's famous beaches and their monopolization by the Orla Rio concessionaria. Ambulant vendors on the beach were also regularized, and several beach-goers' favourite homemade snacks were banned for their alleged insalubrity. To limit visual disorder, a uniform design was imposed upon the temporary beach stands or *barracas* that rent chairs and parasols to sunbathers. Rio's *Choque de ordem* relied upon the vast deployment of police forces and the conspicuous visibility of law and order in the city's public spaces. 'Public order' kiosks run by police shock troops were installed on the beaches to discourage petty theft and reassure beach-goers. The city created a special Public Order Office (Secretaria Especial de Ordem Publica) to coordinate the Rio in Order programme, a 2011 expansion of the *Choque de ordem*, whose mandate included the production of 'maps of disorder' for different urban sectors, and the implementation of more than a dozen public order units (Unidades de ordem publica) in key city neighbourhoods, especially heavily used tourist areas that would be patrolled by hundreds of specially trained municipal guards. These public order units were responsible for regulating small incivilities and unauthorized activities, such as public urination, loitering, panhandling, public drunkenness, illegal parking and transit violations, as well as cracking down on prostitution and drug sales. They also report vacant buildings, empty lots, junk and trash, graffiti and abandoned cars.

Apart from its relentless focus on order, the programme was also concerned with social behaviour in the city's public space. Street children, homeless people and informal vendors were harassed by repeated police sweeps in efforts to drive them away to less visible urban sectors. Some interventions were also aimed at middle-class offenders, especially in attempts to curb public intoxication and to promote civilized behaviour. But the tone of these campaigns was strikingly different, trading aggressive repression for light-hearted humour. For example, in 2010 a series of public interest signs were posted around the neighbourhood of Lapa, popular with both locals and tourists for its animated nightlife. The messages on the posters played on a tame and sanitized version of the mythical *malandro*, a bad boy, samba-player-slash-hustler figure with deep roots in Rio's public culture, rehabilitated as a model citizen with an edge. Slogans included: a *malandro* does not piss on the street; a *malandro* does not park illegally; a *malandro* does not fool around.[6]

Figure 4.4 Malandragem é nao fazer xixi na rua (Being a malandro is not peeing on the street). Public interest message in Rio de Janeiro's Lapa district erected as part of the city's pre-Olympic 'shock of order' campaign (photo by the author, 2012).

More radical attempts to transform Rio de Janeiro's human environment in the years leading to the city's two mega-events went as far as influencing public policies on mental health and drug abuse, under the shock of order programme's so-called 'war on drugs'. For over a decade, public policies regarding drug addiction and the homeless in Rio de Janeiro had followed a public health approach rather than a judiciarization of drug sale and consumption (Silva 2014). As a result, the homeless and drug addicts were considered in need of medical care and treated in outpatient community facilities for mental health issues. But 2010 marked the return of repressive methods that included the forced internment of people in situations of homelessness under pretexts of illicit substance abuse and allegations that they posed a threat to society.

While clearly part of the state's strategy to invisibilize the marginal in the city's public spaces, this shift was legitimized by the development of neo-hygienist policies and the spread of a crisis discourse about the threat of an imminent 'crack epidemic' (Boiteux 2013). From 2010, an alarmist, exaggerated, fear-mongering rhetoric that talked of contagion, violence and crime was broadly spread in the media, helping to create an artificial crisis that would justify the adoption of drastic measures and the instigation of the 'war on drugs'. Although no scientific data supported this alleged rise in consumption, this discourse fostered a climate of panic that legitimated the suspension of the rule of law and the state's resort to repressive emergency measures that included forced internment, in direct contradiction with federal health policies regarding drug users (Silva 2014; Belloni *et al.* 2012).

Over the years leading to the two mega-events, massive sweeps were conducted in Rio de Janeiro's public spaces. All over the city, people were picked up from city parks, under freeway overpasses, abandoned buildings, squats and favelas and sent away to shelters and rehabilitation centres run by religious orders. Users were labelled as dangerous subjects capable of criminal and violent acts and were arbitrarily and involuntarily locked up and forced into compulsory abstinence programmes under the pretext of protecting both themselves and society. Although these measures were hitherto regarded as exceptional, last-recourse solutions to be used when all other options had failed, they became a systematic, blanket policy in the pre-event state of exception.

Widely criticized by healthcare professionals as doing little to solve mental health problems, to reduce physical addiction or to address the social roots of homelessness, these measures were clearly devised to keep undesirable people from disrupting the city's image during both mega-events. Specialists fear that the use of such punitive actions and the banalization of internment under a benevolent rhetoric of 'protection' against 'imminent danger' could make such exceptional measures more acceptable in the long term, turning them into standard policy in the post-event years (Belloni et al. 2012).

In a city known as a prime sex tourism destination, prostitution was also the object of careful image monitoring before and during both mega-events. Authorities had to walk a careful line in limiting the over-visibility of the sex trade – a lucrative and legal industry that is part of the range of attractions offered by the city – and dispelling all appearance of leniency towards sexual tourism, which could spoil Brazil's international image. Discreet instances of crackdown on the sex trade could be observed, especially in the South Zone and other 'respectable, middle-class' areas, but rather than a real diminution of business, the impact took more the form of a reconfiguration of local sexscapes and a remapping of local geographies of desire (De Lisio 2016). The Rio-based Observatory on Prostitution claims that the sex trade only suffered a slight drop during the 2014 World Cup (Ruvolo 2014). Hygienization strategies included the closing of key iconic bars and 'restaurants' known to support sexual commerce in the beach neighbourhood of Copacabana. Those include the Help discothèque, closed in 2010, and Balcony in 2014, just before the World Cup, located directly across from the FIFA Fan Fest on Avenida Atlântica, the second largest FIFA-sanctioned spectatorship zone outside Maracanã. In order to justify the crackdown, a crisis discourse was used to trigger a moral panic among the population, especially about child sexual exploitation and international prostitution networks. However, no case of sexual exploitation was reported or filed with the state prosecutor (De Lisio 2016).

Rio's human beautification campaign did not only focus on modernizing people's habits and civilizing their actions, but also sought to turn the city's unruly masses into rational, productive individuals and good neoliberal subjects. Many social reform programmes were undertaken to reshape those unfit citizens into well-adjusted consumers and reliable taxpayers. One particular action focused on turning local school children into entrepreneurial subjects. In 2013, Rio's city government spent more than one million reais (US$500,000) to buy 20,000 copies of a board game, distributed to the city's public schools, where it was to become a compulsory part of the curriculum. Called *Banco Imobiliário Cidade Olímpica*, or Olympic City Monopoly, the game promoted the Paes administration's many Olympic projects. The initiative was denounced as political propaganda and as an attempt to indoctrinate schoolchildren with the ideology that the city public places be treated as mere commodities used to accrue personal wealth and power. As a result of public outcry, the city had to recall over 2,000 issues of the game that had already been distributed (Agência Estadao 2013).

Great efforts also targeted the consumption habits, behaviour, social practices and leisure activities of at-risk youth, taking them off the street and into the classroom. Members of the UPPs have also taken it upon themselves to act as civilizing agents, initiating series of programmes in order to reform behaviour and proposing more socially acceptable activities to local youth to replace practices deemed reprehensible or illegal. Such practices include *baile funk*, a very popular form of rave parties known for their oversexualized dancing (funk carioca, the ancestor of twerking), considered inappropriate and vulgar by the Brazilian elite (Combs 2014). These events, which purportedly portray an image of the city that could offend the sensitivities of mega-events visitors, were especially targeted as part of the systemic campaign to tame the favelas in sight of the 2014 World Cup and the 2016 Summer Olympics. In the years before these events authorities cracked down on *baile funk*, making the practice illegal in many UPP-controlled favelas and pushing Brazil's congress to consider a national ban. Since funk is mainly associated with poor, black favela residents, its criminalization has been denounced by Juca Ferreira, Brazil's former Minister of Culture, as a veiled attack on Afro-Brazilian culture, similar to previous historical condemnations of black cultural practices such as samba and capoeira (Combs 2014).

In Providência, the port area favela mentioned earlier, members of the UPP vowed to rescue the morality of teenage girls and to encourage young women to adopt a more modest demeanour and embrace civilized values. In August 2011 they organized a debutante ball, held in Rio's National History Museum, in collaboration with local private businesses. Fifteen young girls from the favela, selected according to their school performance and their family's participation in community activities, were thus re-ascribed more traditional gender roles and erected as models to be emulated. The captain of the UPP, who came up with the idea, said that this fairy tale experience would reward those members of the community who acted as good models for society. On another occasion, a group of young favela girls was taken to the Municipal Theater to see a Bolchoi ballet, in what appears to be an attempt to inculcate white, elitist cultural tastes and values on black working-class youth.

The *Choque de ordem* also focused on limiting the poor's mobility in the city and filtering their access to certain urban spaces increasingly secured for the exclusive use of the elite. In November 2013, a panic wave caused by rowdy favela youth sent hundreds running down Rio's most affluent beach in total chaos. The state's response to a phenomenon known as 'dragnets' or *arrastões*, was swift. Access to the upscale South Zone by public transportation would be controlled using identity checks on buses departing from the poor North Zone, and barring young, underdressed riders or those without proper documentation from travelling to wealthy beach neighbourhoods (Costa 2013). In addition, a force of more than 600 men was deployed by the military police to supplement civil policemen in protecting the stretch of beach between Leblon and Leme. The episode reinforced the status of the littoral as the exclusive territory of the wealthy, and demonstrated the state's willingness to protect this exclusive character. Such blatant restriction on the freedom of movement of a particular social group, suspected of being potential criminals on the basis of their place of residence, skin colour and poverty, was widely condemned. Critics asked whether a pass system like in apartheid South Africa would be put in place (Moretzsohn 2014). This episode made clear that what was being protected by the state's vast security apparatus, at mega-events sites, South Zone beaches or key urban spaces, was property values, monetary profits and the conditions of capital accumulation.

Conclusion

Mega-events play an important role in the implementation of social image-construction programmes that justify state interventions to alter both the body and the mind of the city's inhabitants and turn them into docile and compliant citizens. Although the processes described in this chapter are not limited to the particular circumstances posed by mega-events and have, in fact, become regular features of neoliberal city governance, global-scale sporting events do make the described phenomena more observable, amplify their reality and exacerbate their impacts.

This chapter demonstrated how efforts to beautify the social environment in preparation for the hosting of mega-events exacerbate power disparities in ways that threaten both democracy and social justice. By introducing social norms that reinforce social distinction, these civilization programmes justify the emergence of new hierarchies at the local level. They allow for the discursive construction of certain members of society as uncivilized and unworthy of citizenship, thereby redefining the terms of belonging to society. Mega-events also facilitate the state's use of juridico-political means to justify coercive methods of population control, including repression, internment and expulsion. By encouraging social exclusion, discrimination and the persecution of certain categories of people who have become markers of disorder and insecurity, they are barring entire segments of the population from active participation in social life. Conversely, these programmes strengthen the power of political and economic elites by turning a blind eye or diverting attention from their own corruption and power abuses.

The chapter thus underlined how the exceptional nature of mega-events helps justify the suspension of many civic rights, and the imposition of limits on personal liberties, including freedom of movement and freedom of speech. By conflating disorder and indiscipline with crime, cities impose stringent regulations to discourage the use and occupation of public space, and to ban and criminalize activities that do not cohere with the desired image that event organizers seek to project. The chapter thus revealed some of the darker aspects of the neoliberal state, more bent on protecting the benefits and interests of its allies and supporters than ensuring the welfare of its own citizens. The exceptional circumstances offered by mega-events help conceal the abusive and discriminatory nature of neoliberal urban policy, making it increasingly acceptable for people to be arrested for the simple crime of being undesirable.

Finally, the chapter clearly demonstrated that event-related social image-construction programmes open the door for the establishment of an increasingly repressive authoritarian state. Local authorities are using the pretext of mega-events to put in place infrastructure of control, discipline and order that are becoming standard technologies of government. One of the most potent legacies of these events remains the establishment of a security regime and the implementation of an elaborate surveillance apparatus that seeks to make the city more transparent and controllable. While many norms of control adopted in preparation for mega-events stem from an image-construction imperative rather than from real, measurable menace, the IOC and FIFA's emphasis on public safety as a paramount host responsibility and exaggerated media reports about security threats justify the growing militarization and securitization of urban space. Mega-events thus facilitate the implementation of a whole array of preventive measures against potential crime, with the proliferation of police patrols and the massive presence of local law enforcement. Over time, ubiquitous police presence and widespread surveillance may desensitize people to the intrusive nature of these security measures, allowing them to appear as a normal part of urban life.

Notes

1 Elias (2000) identifies good manners and etiquette as resources historically used by upper classes to set themselves apart socially and to dominate lower classes, regularly adding new behaviour restrictions to ensure the maintenance of a comfortable distance from the masses. Bourdieu (1984) in his seminal work in *Distinction* makes a similar argument for modern society.
2 Choi (2004) writes of the image construction programmes carried out in South Korea in the late 1990s in the context of the 2002 FIFA World Cup, hosted jointly by South Korea and Japan. Focusing on global etiquette, cultural mannerism and the Anglicization of the urban landscape, these measures were initiated in order to 'raise [the] standards to match that of an advanced nation' and were criticized for Westernizing Korean society by effacing its own cultural standards with an American replacement.
3 The *Olympic Charter*, published by the IOC, explicitly states that 'no kind of demonstration or political, religious or racial propaganda ... be permitted in the Olympic areas' (IOC 2007: 98).
4 Lenskyj (2002, 2008) discusses similar examples in Sydney, Atlanta and Vancouver.
5 At that time the total municipal population was 17.43 million, with eight million in the city proper (Bonneau 2008).
6 Malandragem é não fazer xixi na rua ; não estaciona num lugar proibido ; O malandro não da bobeira.

References

Agência Estadao. (2013, April 29) *Rio recolhe exemplares de Banco Imobiliário com obras de Eduardo Paes*. Available at: http://politica.estadao.com.br/noticias/geral,rio-recolhe-exemplares-de-banco-imobiliario-com-obras-de-eduardo-paes,1026868 (accessed 7 July 2016).
Anagnost, A. (1997) *National Past-times: Narratives, Representation and Power in Modern China.* Durham, NC: Duke University Press.
BBC News (2013, 11 January) 'Rio favela has "more CCTV cameras than London"'. Available at: www.bbc.co.uk/news/world-latin- america-20992062 (accessed 15 September 2016).
Belloni, F.B., de Ávila, H., Costa, L. and Ferreira, R.N. (2012) 'Reflexões acerca da política de drogas no Brasil e protagonismo da Frente Nacional Drogas e Direitos Humanos', *Cuba Salud 2012: Memorias Convención Internacional de Salud Pública.* Havana.
Bennett, T. (1991) 'The Shaping of Things to Come: Expo '88', *Cultural Studies.* Vol. 5, No. 1, pp. 33–51.
Boiteux, L. (2013, January) 'Liberdades individuais, direitos humanos e a internação forçada em massa de usuários de drogas', *Revista brasileira de estudos constitucionais: RBEC.* Vol. 7, No. 25, pp. 53–80.
Bonneau, C. (2008) 'Pékin 2008: La face cachée des JO', *Science & Vie.* Special edition, pp. 34–63.
Bourdieu, P. (1984) *Distinction.* Cambridge, MA: Harvard University Press
Brady, A.M. (2009) 'The Beijing Olympics as a Campaign of Mass Distraction', *The China Quarterly.* Vol. 197, pp. 1–24.
Broudehoux, A.-M. (2004a) *The Making and Selling of Post-Mao Beijing.* London: Routledge.
Broudehoux, A.-M. (2007) 'Spectacular Beijing: The Conspicuous Construction of an Olympic Metropolis', *Journal of Urban Affairs.* Vol. 29, pp. 383–399.
Broudehoux, A.-M. (2010) 'Images of Power: Architectures of the Integrated Spectacle at the Beijing Olympics', *Journal of Architectural Education.* Vol. 63, pp. 52–62.

Broudehoux, A.-M. (2011) 'The Social and Spatial Impacts of Olympic Image Construction: The Case of Beijing 2008', H. Lenskyj and S. Wagg (eds), *A Handbook of Olympic Studies.* London: Palgrave Macmillan, pp. 195–209.

Brownell, S. (1995) *Training the Body for China: Sports in the Moral Order of the People's Republic.* Chicago, IL: University of Chicago Press.

Callick, R. (2008, 23 August) 'On Top of the World in Beijing: After the Games', *Weekend Australian.*

Choi, Y.S. (2004) 'Football and the South Korean Imagination: South Korea and the 2002 World Cup Tournaments', W. Manzenreiter and J. Horne (eds), *Football Goes East: Business, Culture and the People's Game in East Asia.* London: Routledge, pp. 133–147.

COHRE (Centre on Housing Rights and Eviction). (2008a) 'Housing Rights and the 2010 Football World Cup', *Business as Usual? Housing Rights and 'Slum Eradication' in Durban, South Africa.* Geneva: COHRE.

COHRE (Centre on Housing Rights and Eviction). (2008b) *One World, Whose Dream? Housing Rights Violations and the Beijing Olympic Games.* Geneva: COHRE.

Combs, C. (2014) 'Brazil Prepares for the World Cup by Silencing Favela Culture', *World. Mic.* Available at: www.policymic.com/articles/78169/brazil- prepares-for-the-world-cup-by-silencing-favela-culture (accessed 24 October 2016).

Costa, A.C. (2013) 'Ônibus em direção às praias da Zona Sul serão parados pela polícia', *O Globo.* Available at: http://oglobo.globo.com/rio/onibus-em- direcao-as-praias-da-zona-sul-serao-parados-pela-policia-10859175 (accessed 24 October 2016).

De Lisio, A. (2016) 'Event-led urbanism para quem? FIFA/IOC-Sanctioned Entrepreneurialism and Deviant Development', *Annual Conference of the Canadian Association of Latin American and Caribbean Studies.* University of Calgary.

Dias, M.C. and Eslava, L. (2013) 'Horizons of Inclusion: Life Between Laws and Developments in Rio de Janeiro', *University of Miami Inter-American Law Review.* Vol. 44, pp. 177–218.

Duara, P. (2001) 'The Discourse of Civilization and Pan-Asianism', *Journal of World History.* Vol. 12, No. 1, pp. 99–130.

Elias, N. (2000) *The Civilizing Process.* Malden, MA: Blackwell.

Foucault, M. (1975) *Discipline and Punish: The Birth of the Prison.* New York: Random House.

Foucault, M. (1998 [1976]) *The History of Sexuality Vol. 1: The Will to Knowledge.* London: Penguin.

Freeman, J. (2012) 'Neoliberal Accumulation Strategies and the Visible Hand of Police Pacification in Rio de Janeiro', *Revista de Estudos Universitários.* Vol. 38, No. 1, pp. 95–126.

Friedman, S.L. (2004) 'Embodying Civility: Civilizing Processes and Symbolic Citizenship in Southeastern China', *Journal of Asian Studies.* Vol. 63, pp. 687–718.

Fussey, P., Coaffee, J., Armstrong, G. and Hobbs, D. (2011) *Securing and Sustaining the Olympic City: Reconfiguring London for 2012 and Beyond.* London: Ashgate.

HRW (Human Rights Watch). 'China: Police Detain Would-Be Olympic Protesters'. Available at: www.hrw.org/news/2008/08/13/china-police-detain-would-be-olympic-protesters (accessed 12 May 2009).

IOC (2007). *Olympic Charter.* Lausanne: IOC.

Kelling, G.L. and Wilson, J.Q. (1982) 'Broken Windows: The Police and Neighborhood Safety', *The Atlantic.* Available at: www.theatlantic.com/magazine/archive/1982/03/broken-windows/304465 (accessed 24 October 2016).

Kennelly, J. and Watts, P. (2011) 'Sanitizing Public Space in Olympic Host Cities: The Spatial Experiences of Marginalized Youth in 2010 Vancouver and 2012 London', *Sociology.* Vol. 45, No. 5, pp. 765–781.

Kolamo, S. (2015) 'Staging Resistance Through Sports Media Spectacles: The Dynamics of Camera-Conscious Performativity in the Contemporary FIFA World Cups', *Mediated Urban Mega-events (Presentation at ECREA TWG Conference).* Zagreb.

Kolamo, S. and Vuolteenaho, J. (2013) 'The Interplay of Mediascapes and Cityscapes in a Sports Mega-event: The Power Dynamics of Place Branding in the 2010 FIFA World Cup in South Africa', *International Communication Gazette.* Vol. 75, pp. 502–520.

Lenskyj, H.J. (2002) *The Best Olympics Ever? Social Impacts of Sydney 2000.* Albany, NY: State University of New York Press.

Lenskyj, H.J. (2008) *Olympic Industry Resistance: Challenging Olympic Power and Propaganda.* Stanford, CA: Stanford University Press.

McArdle, A. and Erzen, T. (2001) *Zero Tolerance Quality of Life and the New Police Brutality in New York City.* New York: New York University Press.

Moretzsohn, S.D. (2014) 'Leituras Do "Globo" O arrastão e o retorno do "apartheid"', *Observatorio da Impresa.* Vol. 791.

O'Brien, C. (2008, 17 August) 'Protest Zones in Parks Empty; Permit Process Seen as a Trap', *Washington Times.*

Rojek, C. (2013) *Event Power: How Global Events Manage and Manipulate.* London: SAGE.

Ruvolo, J. (2014, 23 June) 'Are Rio's World Cup Sex Worker Raids Real or Just For Show?', *Vice News.* Available at: https://news.vice.com/article/are-rios-world-cup-sex-worker-raids-real-or-just-for-show (accessed 7 July 2016).

Rydell, R.W. and Gwynn, N.E. (1994) *Fair Representations: World's Fairs and the Modern World.* Amsterdam: VU University Press.

Silva, C.R. (2014) 'Da Punição ao Tratamento: rupturas e continuidades na abordagem do uso de drogas', T. Ramminger and M. Silva (eds), *Mais substâncias para o trabalho em saúde com usuários de drogas.* Porto Alegre: Rede Unida, pp. 51–68.

Singer, N. (2012, 3 March) 'Mission Control, Built for Cities: I.B.M. Takes "Smarter Cities" Concept to Rio de Janeiro', *New York Times.* Available at: www.nytimes.com/2012/03/04/business/ibm-takes-smarter-cities-concept-to-rio-de-janeiro.html?_r=0 (accessed 24 October 2016).

Smith, N. (1996) *The New Urban Frontier: Gentrification and the Revanchist City.* London: Routledge.

Stavrides, S. (2014) 'Athens 2004 Olympics: An Urban State of Exception which Became the Rule', Keynote presentation, *Second International Conference on Mega-Events and the City.* Rio de Janeiro.

Toohey, K. and Veal, A.J. (2001) *The Olympic Games: A Social Science Perspective.* Wallingford: CABI.

Van Houtum, H. and Van Dam, F. (2002) 'Topophilia or Topoporno? Patriotic Place Attachment in International Football Derbies', *International Social Science Review.* Vol. 3, pp. 231–248.

Whitson, D. and Horne, J. (2006) 'Underestimated Costs and Overestimated Benefits? Comparing the Outcomes of Sports Mega-Events in Canada and Japan', J. Horne and W. Manzenreiter (eds), *Sports Mega-Events: Social Scientific Analyses of a Global Phenomenon.* Oxford: Blackwell, pp. 73–89.

Young, P. (2009) *Globalization and the Great Exhibition: The Victorian New World Order.* London: Palgrave.

Yutzy, C. (2012) 'Increased State Presence Through the Unidade De Polícia Pacificadora in Santa Marta, Rio De Janeiro: The Creation of the City's Theme Park and Resulting, Social Issues', *Revista de Estudos Universitários.* Vol. 38, No. 1, pp. 127–146.

Zhou, M., Simpson, P. and Ma, J. (2008, 9 August) 'Spectators Kept Away from Games Area', *South China Morning Post.*

Zibechi, R. (2010, 20 January) 'Rio de Janeiro: Control of the Poor Seen as Crucial for the Olympics Americas Program'. Available at: http://sociologias- com.blogspot.ca/2010/01/rio-de-janeiro-control-of-poor-seen-as.html (accessed 24 October 2016).

Zirin, D. (2011, 12 May) 'Brick by BRIC: How Global Sport has Declared War on Brazil's Poor', *The Nation.*

5 Contesting the mega-event spectacle

Resistance to urban image construction

Previous chapters have demonstrated the multiple ways in which cities, especially those hosting mega-events, transform their world image by altering their mental representation, physical aspect and social environment. This chapter investigates how diverse population groups have reacted to diverse image-construction initiatives, and details some of the tactics devised by local citizens to challenge ill-advised decision-makers, to contest discriminatory measures, to undermine top-down image-construction efforts and to hijack the event spectacle. Recriminations generally centre upon housing eviction issues, the destruction of heritage, excessive public spending, public service cuts, the privatization of public land, restricted access to collective resources, corruption, corporate abuse and monopoly and the tightening of the social control apparatus. Modes of resistance vary according to a host of factors, especially geopolitical context and the type and severity of the offence.

This chapter details three categories of resistance to event-related image construction. The first consists of organized strategies of mass resistance and diverse forms of protest. It includes a discussion of the many factors that impede the formation of efficient collective resistance movements and thus limit organized opposition to event-led urban image construction. The second type concerns the micro-political dynamics of contestations and centres on smaller-scale, individually based strategies that include creative forms of resistance and denunciation. The last section examines virtual forms of resistance that use social networks and the worldwide web to circulate information, denounce abusive practices and exert pressure upon event organizers and local governments.

Organized resistance to event-led image construction: collective movements and mass protests

Over recent decades, a growing number of people in cities around the world have mobilized to protest the allocation of public funds to finance high-profile spectacles such as the Olympics, World Fairs and other mega-events and, more generally, to oppose the broader spectacularization of everyday life (Eisinger 2000; Whitelegg 2000; Andranovich *et al.* 2001; Lenskyj 2008). In sight of the growing pervasiveness of the spectacle in contemporary society, critical awareness of the tentacular power of neoliberal capitalism is rising and people around the world are taking to the streets to protest global market-based agendas. Urban movements covering a range of issues, from racial justice to the anarchist movement in North American cities, the European Slow Food and the Slow City movements and burgeoning anti-globalization, anti-capitalist 'Occupy' movements around the world, have heightened awareness to the corporate penetration of everyday life (Carol 2007; Chatterton and Hollands 2003; Pendras 2002).

In the context of mega-event image construction, affected population groups are looking for effective ways to block deleterious projects, to leverage fair compensations and to force local authorities to act in a more transparent and socially responsible way. The dominant and most effective way to counter the mega-event spectacle is through organized forms of resistance and active engagement in collective civic actions, social movements and conventional forms of civil disobedience. They take the form of public demonstrations on city streets, the peaceful occupation of the city's public spaces, or can include more violent, explosive actions that make the global headlines. There is a very small window of opportunity for such media outreach to occur: it usually is most propitious in the months leading to the event, when foreign journalists are on the ground, acclimatizing to the event setting and eager to find stories to sell. It is essential that such actions take place before the event begins, after which the competition monopolizes all attention and broadcasters and international media outlets may be less inclined to criticize the host (Horne and Whannel 2011).

In spite of the democratic deficit surrounding mega-events preparations in Brazil, where civil society organizations and citizens groups were systematically excluded from the general decision-making process, a robust civil society nonetheless emerged in the years before the two leading mega-events and became surprisingly active. This was exceptional, especially given the Brazilian state's growing authoritarianism, the country's recent history of dictatorship and the relative youth of its democratic institutions. Social actors from across the country developed a vast network of 'people's committees' around the World Cup and the Olympics (*Comitê Popular da Copa e das Olimpíadas*), created before the 2007 Pan American Games to organize people against unlawful evictions.[1] Activists, academics and legal aid workers help these citizens groups develop resistance strategies, organize civil disobedience actions and fight relocation and exclusion in the court. Over the years, this coalition coordinated civil society actions across the country and managed to collect an impressive amount of information on processes, expenditures and rights violations. The national network released two reports, in 2011 and 2014, documenting various abuses and irregularities (ANCOP 2011, 2014). Another coalition in Rio de Janeiro is the *Fórum Comunitário do Porto* (Port Community Forum), an alliance of residents, scholars, activists and community leaders created in January 2011 to fight for the rights of residents of Rio's port area.

Other local groups and issue-based associations have joined transnational resistance networks to give visibility to their struggle, at times managing to bring the issue into the international spotlight. For example, in their effort to gain a voice in the debate, street vendors in Brazil have joined StreetNet International, an NGO born in South Africa before the 2010 World Cup, which campaigns for the rights of the urban poor, including shanty town dwellers, migrant and refugee communities and sex workers. In 2011, StreetNet International had commissioned a study of informal traders in the 12 Brazilian host cities of the 2014 World Cup as a preliminary step to establishing its World Class Cities for All Campaign in Brazil, which has since then helped denounce the plight of informal workers and street vendors around the world.

The most widespread form of strategy used by these coalitions remains mass demonstrations. Street protests were common in Brazil in the run-up to the World Cup. In June 2013, over a two-week period that coincided with FIFA's Confederations Cup, Brazil was shaken by social conflicts on a scale rarely seen in recent history. Throughout the country, crowds in the tens of thousands, among which diverse sectors of civil society were represented, called for a radical transformation of Brazilian society and a deep reform of the exercise of political power (Badaró 2013). Recriminations ranged from evictions to rising costs of living and heavy-handed policing programmes to public transportation, education, health, housing and other pressing collective issues. Protests were also the product of widespread frustrations about public exclusion from the multi-billion dollar national World Cup bonanza. So deep was public anger that even the less politically engaged middle classes briefly joined the movement (Vainer 2013).

In Rio de Janeiro, where mobilization was the strongest, protests quickly focused upon Brazil's corrupt political and social system, driven by opportunism, impunity and prejudice. The absurd amount of public funds poured into the hosting of sporting mega-events and the vast fortunes funnelled into a handful of engineering firms to build unnecessary new stadia figured prominently among denunciations. The fact that an event that stood to be FIFA's most lucrative ever was almost entirely financed by the Brazilian state infuriated protestors (Nunes 2014). Protestors further denounced the handover of land forcibly taken from poor communities to private developers. Another object of collective irk was the conceit, arrogance and brutality of ruling coalitions, especially those with vested interests in mega-events, like media agencies, national corporations, real-estate speculators and a host of international businesses with close links to FIFA and the IOC. According to Vainer (2013), it was their greed and blatant disrespect for democratic institutions that convinced hundreds of thousands of hitherto unpoliticized youth to take to the streets.

The work accomplished by the *Comitê Popular da Copa e das Olimpíadas* played a significant part in raising public awareness of the hardships posed by mega-events image construction. It had been very vocal in condemning shady deals in the construction of World Cup stadia, unjustified evictions and controversial demolitions, especially near the Maracanã, all of which entered the public debate and were widely featured in slogans and on posters during the protests (Comitê Popular da Copa e das Olimpíadas 2013, 2015). What came out of the crisis was an incredibly rich form of resistance that used highly strategic and evocative territories as sites for the expression of discontent: it was around major stadia, in front of emblematic infrastructure and near establishments of power that people came to voice their grievances. The slogans they chanted also made clear that Brazilians had not been duped by the mega-event spectacle, and would no longer tolerate seeing their cities being sold to private corporations.

Acts of resistance often borrow from the realm of the spectacle, in their theatricality, dramatic wording and exaggerated imagery. Many forms of contestation to mega-events have taken such festive dimensions, especially in the form of participant-driven events to provide areas of *genuine festivity* as a counter-reaction to established, organizer-driven and highly formalized events. This notion draws from Debord and his colleagues, who distinguished between *event festivity* and *genuine festivity*, which is the kind of festivity that is not driven by the interests of capital but by human creativity and sociability. In Rio, a city with a century-old carnival tradition and a taste for the dramatic and theatrical, many protests were highly carnivalesque in mood, and drew their strength from carnival's subversive power (DaMatta 1991). Literally using spectacle to fight spectacle, urban youth turned to deception and disguise to denounce the masquerade of capitalist greed that had travestied their city and its most basic values (Rosner 2013). Many participants wore masks and costumes, dressing up as superheroes or as Anonymous' Guy Fawkes. They turned protests into artful performances of urban citizenship, using the city as a stage to reconquer contested urban territories and to reconfigure city spaces. The state's reply to the string of protests was a well-choreographed show of force, with the spectacular deployment of armed troops that turned the joyous street festival into a war zone, right in front of the cameras of the global media, which almost unanimously condemned the repression.

Another festive form of collective resistance to the state of exception imposed by the hosting of mega-event consists of informal and apparently innocuous gatherings that bring attention to a particular cause and are convened on the web and through social media. Their innovative, non-confrontational approach, and highly inclusive, friendly outlook play the double role of boosting the morale of participants and attracting sympathy and solidarity to their cause. Even if they are not always directly related to mega-events image construction, many take advantage of the global spotlight linked to the mega-event spectacle to make their voices heard (Figure 5.1).

For example, in early 2014 young people of colour from all over Rio de Janeiro converged on upscale shopping malls on weekends for a 'little outing' or *rolezinho*, to denounce the exclusionary measures that are increasingly limiting access to urban spaces for marginalized people. Often victimized by private security guards who see them as potential criminals rather than potential consumers, these youth asserted their right of access by 'taking a little walk', attracting hundreds, and sometimes thousands of participants to elite shopping centres. News of the quick and sometimes violent expulsion of these peaceful teens travelled the world just a few months before the World Cup and confirmed Rio's growing reputation as a highly segregated city.

Similarly, on several weekends in 2014 and 2015, a series of picnics convened on Facebook encouraged people from the poor North Zone to congregate on the

Figure 5.1 June 2013 protest in Rio de Janeiro. The board reads: 'We want FIFA-grade subways, ferries and hospitals' (photo by Pablo Vergara 2013, with permission).

elite beach of Ipanema for a festive, family-friendly day out to denounce widespread injustice and discrimination. Ironically called *faroferos*, these events adopted a deprecatory moniker commonly used by elite *carioca* to deride unsophisticated beach-goers who bring their own lunch (*farofa* is grilled manioc flour). These events were held to protest the police expulsion of underprivileged, black youth from public buses connecting the periphery to the littoral on weekends, on suspicion of criminal intent. These families symbolically reclaimed their right to the city's beaches, too often monopolized by the white, rich elite.

A third example of playful acts of collective resistance organized in Rio de Janeiro to bring together diverse communities affected by World Cup-related projects and to denounce the exclusionary nature of the event was the *Copa dos excluidos* (Cup of the Excluded). Held in the summer of 2014, this informal football tournament was organized by the *Comitê Popular da Copa*. Families came together around drinks, food and football, in a convivial and festive day-long act of resistance whose harmless, light-hearted and highly symbolic nature could only attract public sympathy for their cause.

Obstacles to organized resistance

However, several factors have hindered effective mobilization efforts in cities hosting sporting mega-events and are limiting the reach of organized forms of mass protest. Overt and confrontational resistance to the neoliberal reconfiguration of the city and opposition to the violent dislocation of the poor have been weakened by the consensual power of these events, their strong symbolic appeal and their stature as spectacular global media magnets (Broudehoux 2013). Rojek (2013) convincingly argues that the communicative and emotional powers of mega-events, which often help revive the romance of evanescent moments of communitas, act like the *panem et circenses* of the Roman Republic to divert the masses from real political involvement. Events, he claims, are conceived to provide temporary emotional displays of resistance and civic engagement, which ultimately prevent deep structural transformations in contemporary society.

For example, in Beijing, despite a staggering record in terms of forced evictions, labour exploitation and rights violations, the Olympic image-construction programme generated little organized opposition, even when compared with other authoritarian host cities like Seoul. At the time, public expressions of discontent were increasingly heard throughout China from the millions who had lost homes, jobs, healthcare and pensions. Civic actions to fight redevelopment, including diverse forms of civil disobedience movements such as mass sit-ins, traffic blockades and street demonstrations, were on the rise (Zhang 2004; Marquand 2004). While land disputes, the widening income gap, falling social services, nepotism, corruption and self-serving alliances between Party leaders and businessmen had become commonplace, overt, collective and organized mobilization against Olympic projects remained a rare occurrence in the Chinese capital, with a few isolated cases which, in spite of their non-political nature, were swiftly repressed (Magnier 2005; Pocha 2005).

The dearth of public opposition observed in pre-Olympic Beijing is not entirely surprising, especially given the city's particular geopolitical circumstances. The repressive political climate that had prevailed since the 1989 student massacre at Tiananmen was still felt in the years leading to the Games, and restricted freedom of expression, assembly and association limited opportunities for organized resistance. Relentless appeals for patriotism in state propaganda in the years leading to the Games people discouraged people from seeking redress for rights abuses. Only those who felt that a fundamental right had been violated beyond the tolerable dared to contest unfair treatment, especially regarding evictions. The ideological instrumentalization of the Olympic Games and their patriotic framing in official propaganda contributed a considerable amount of economic, political and psychological leverage to Chinese authorities and helped curb challenges to Olympic image construction. Appeals to nationalist sentiment, which guaranteed an overwhelming support for the Games while framing any form of open criticism and organized opposition as a betrayal, helped undermine the legitimacy of diverse forms of protest (COHRE 2007).

In both Beijing and Rio de Janeiro, a major impediment to the development of organized resistance movements against mass eviction was the opaque and complex nature of the relocation process. Authorities managed to limit collective action and to accelerate project realization by keeping citizens in the dark regarding project implementation details. Local resistance was weakened by this lack of transparency, especially regarding the heavily bureaucratic and individualized relocation process.

It often took weeks for people whose house had been marked for demolition to learn about the conditions of their displacement.[2]

Because they are organized under broad umbrella causes, large-scale protests often fail to attract attention to individual or localized situations. Individual causes get lost among the multiplicity of issues defended by these coalitions, which may weaken adhesion to these movements. The formation of locally based solidarity movements is also hindered by fragmentation of interests among people, even from the same community, and by the fact that urban interventions do not have a uniform impact upon different households. For example, in Rio, short-term residents and newcomers to the favela, who are mostly tenants, are more likely to accept cash compensation for their lost home and move on to rent a place elsewhere. For long-term dwellers, especially homeowners, with strong community ties and deep emotional attachment to place, the situation is more dramatic. Demolition does not only signify the loss of a valuable, lifelong investment, but also represents the severance of important social networks and the uprooting from a familiar and convenient living environment, with easy access to essential services, sources of employment and education opportunities.

The state control of the media and various forms of censorship are other impediments to organized resistance. Limited access to the media and to internet communication also undermine the capacity of the poor to organize efficiently and to participate in the democratic process. Media outlets with close connections to both state and corporate interests play a major part in containing dissent, by limiting negative reporting on event preparations, censoring discussions of the adverse impacts of these events and banning coverage of eviction disputes, relocation controversies and other rights violations. This problem was particularly acute in Beijing, where people's ability to have their voices heard was hindered by their lack of access to the media. China's official press and broadcast media remain tightly controlled and are subjected to internal forms of censorship that avoid controversial and socially provocative content. As a sensitive issue perceived as a threat to national stability, resistance to Olympic-related urban redevelopment was considered a forbidden topic for journalists. The official press went so far as to carry out denigration campaigns against opponents to Beijing's urban image construction, denounced for their selfish efforts to safeguard their own vested interests. Widespread repression against outspoken journalists, cyber-dissidents and rights advocates also intimidated potential protesters and encouraged self-policing. In Rio de Janeiro, the *O Globo* conglomerate, which controls much of the Brazilian media and has close ties to the current administration, also manipulated public opinion about those opposing mega-events, and was overtly hostile to their cause, misconstruing their struggle in an attempt to divide residents, de-legitimize their demands and weaken support for their cause.

Despite the vast range of forces that conspire to deflect or stifle opposition and criticism, mega-events still provide possibilities for resistance. Even in circumstances that can be highly repressive or when other factors dampen mass mobilization and weaken their impact, people refuse to remain passive victims of event-led image construction and to give up the struggle to assert their rights. In recent decades, the mega-event spectacle has triggered the development of diverse and creative forms of resistance in host cities around the world, at times sparking protests and awakening a political awareness that had long been dormant.

Micro-political dynamics of contestation: individualized and symbolic resistance

The difficulty and complexity of organized and collective forms of opposition means that much resistance to event-led image-construction projects is individually pursued. Although they lack the force and visibility of more concerted actions, individualized actions are often the first recourse of those who stand to lose the little they have managed to accumulate in their difficult lives. Regardless of geopolitical context, the most common measure of opposition to unlawful home evictions is 'stand-off', a passive form of resistance carried out by recalcitrant residents who simply refuse to vacate their homes.

In China, because of the state's monopoly over collective mobilization, popular resistance to the Olympics was mostly unorganized, uncoordinated and family-based. The most widespread mode of resistance to Beijing's Olympic redevelopment was carried out by *dingzihu* or 'nailed-in households', who resisted eviction by refusing to leave their homes (Zhang 2004). Residents spent months, sometimes years, living in precarious conditions, often without basic services such as electricity and running water, and in constant fear that their house would be torn down if left unoccupied. In spite of the physical and psychological violence endured at the hands of demolition crews and the insufferable wait and insecurity, people held on to the hope that this passive resistance strategy could afford them some leverage in the negotiation process for fair compensation.

Other victims of the event spectacle took more desperate measures to have their voices heard. The psychological trauma of finding themselves uprooted, powerless and disenfranchised took its toll on some Beijing residents, for whom the prospect of being forcibly evicted was so terrifying that they were ready to risk their lives (Lai and Lee 2006; Du Plessis 2005). In certain cases, after fruitless attempts to obtain fair settlement or when eviction could no longer be averted, suicide was used as an ultimate protest strategy to draw attention to their cause. People took their own lives in very spectacular displays of desperation, often through self-immolation in busy public places (Broudehoux 2004).

Aside from more conventional forms of civil disobedience, individuals have also deployed a broad range of alternative ways to challenge and expose the dark side of event-led urban image-construction practices. They have turned to less visible, covert strategies of dissent, using symbolic modes of resistance to voice dissatisfaction, elude domination, seek redress and denounce oppressive situations. These more furtive, micro-scale, approaches resemble the 'weapons of the weak' described by James C. Scott (1985), as everyday acts of subversion and ordinary forms of resistance devised by the powerless to challenge hegemony, destabilize their oppressor or simply to vent their anger. These strategies are also greatly inspired by tactics of *détournement* promoted by the French Situationists in the 1960s in their response to the society of spectacle.

Détournement is a collage-like technique that takes pre-existing materials (texts, slogans, advertising) and reassembles them into a new context, with a message that challenges the status quo (Debord 1967). In his *Commentaries on the Society of Spectacle* (1988), Guy Debord warned of the spectacle's capacity for demobilization. When used as a form of mystification to obscure the effects of capitalism's deprivations, the spectacle can have a depolitizing effect, helping control and pacify detractors in order to facilitate capital accumulation. But Debord also made clear that the spectacle is not all-powerful and that its hegemony can be usurped and subverted, often through simple, everyday acts of *détournement*, which alter the message carried by the spectacle to put forward dissident ideas and pervert the event's power of enchantment.

In the context of sporting mega-events, many of these micro-political contestation practices are developed by artists who borrow from the realm of the spectacle in their denunciation. Tactical deployments of counter-spectacle rely on a media-savvy hijacking of texts and images and exploit legal and linguistic grey zones to appropriate, rework, even sabotage image construction, thereby usurping stereotypes, contesting exclusion and subverting misrepresentations. Their followers also resort to mimicry, mimetism and imitation to replicate what they denounce, and thus make more visible the absurdity of initial claims. Their tactics are often improvised and inventive, and can be opportunist in the sense of adapting to existing circumstances.

Discursive means of resistance

The most universal and widespread medium for the communication of discontent is the uttered word, resorting to popular practices of linguistic resistance and verbal expressions of dissent (Pred 1992). Through both wit and irony, opponents develop multiple forms of oral recalcitrance and linguistic reworkings to unsettle authority and skirt domination. Clever ditties, irreverent word games and other narrative strategies are used to subvert slogans, mimic official lingo and transform dominant discourse into absurdist, derogatory or cunning flips of the tongue. Travelling through the underground grapevine, they spread like wild fire through word of mouth, internet blogging and text-messaging. Bakhtin (1984) referred to irreverent idiomatic reworkings as grotesque realism, which provides an absurdist parody of elitist good taste and a baroque laughter at the expense of power. While betraying a keen sense of humour, these speech acts, performative forms of defiance and symbolic means of discontent carry important ideological underpinnings. Butler (1997) insists on the subversive potential of parody, which, once disruptive, becomes domesticated and recirculated to destabilize the primacy of hegemonic meanings.

Such verbal acts of resistance are not concerted actions, but are covertly devised and spread through word of mouth and everyday exchanges in alleyway conversations, in bars and cafés or in the blogosphere. They gain preeminence through their reiteration, especially by the media and their recirculation on the web. Their true impact in undermining official representation and subverting the hegemony of the spectacle may remain limited, but they play an important entitling role, to embolden individuals to take action, especially where organized resistance are restricted.

In pre-Olympic Beijing, disgruntled citizens made good use of the poetic potential of the Chinese language, whose multiple homonyms and tonalities are highly conducive to the development of linguistic forms of resistance. For centuries, Chinese people have used similar narrative strategies, mixing ambiguity and *double entendre* to remodel official discourse and unsettle domination. Satirical couplets and popular 'rhythmic sayings' (*shunkouliu*) that abound within China's underground grapevine have long served as covert forms of state criticism (Zhou and Link 2001). Because they have no known author, cannot be put into print, into broadcast or recited openly in public, these blunt, playful rhymes remain free of censorship (Broudehoux 2009).

In Beijing, many such linguistic reworkings targeted Olympic-related mega-projects. Like all public architecture and monuments of power, Beijing's Olympic projects were dressed up with rhetorical artifice and elaborate narratives long before they were built. Mainly self-serving and embodying the aspirations of their designers and patrons, such discourse encoded a particular meaning onto the architectural object in order to dictate its reading. Drawing upon myth, allegory, and visual metaphor to impart positive connotations, this narrative was reiterated in the media, where it nurtured popular interpretation.

One of the most widespread means of signalling dissatisfaction with Beijing's Olympic makeover was through the use of colourful nicknames to discredit these new spectacular monuments. Even before their completion, Beijing's grandiose projects had acquired crude monikers that mixed irony and metonymy to unmask government pretence and ridicule design conceit. In such reworking, Beijing's new National Theatre, officially described as a pearl by its designer and sponsors, became a piece of donkey dung, as well as a host of derisive variations on the egg theme. Countless satirical caricatures of the new headquarters of China's official television network, CCTV, as a pair of giant underpants also circulated widely around the web. The daily insecurities suffered by Beijing residents, as their city was literally being remade under their feet, were made palpable in their irreverence. The deceptively prosaic quality of these resistance strategies and their apparent apolitical nature allowed for the safe delivery of a subversive message under the cover of anonymity, without fear of repression. Those who resorted to these weapons of the weak were often close neighbours of Olympic projects, who lost a portion of their neighbourhood, suffered the demolition of their homes or simply witnessed the exploitation of workers during construction. The simple presence of these buildings in the landscape was a constant reminder of their limited control over their destiny, and of their exclusion from the benefits enjoyed by some members of the new China.

In Rio de Janeiro, people also resorted to linguistic means to voice their anger and resentment. Time and again, local residents used the expression *para ingles ver* (also reframed as *para gringo ver* – for the gringo to see) to dismiss beautification projects linked to upcoming mega-events. From spectacular new elevators to the favelas, to the police pacifying units (UPPs) and the construction of acoustic walls along the freeway, the expression was used to express disillusion and voice doubts about the functionality and durability of these 'image projects', likely to be abandoned in the aftermath of the Olympics. Other expressions like *maquiagem* (meaning both makeup or window dressing) were widely used to disqualify state beautification initiatives through skin-deep camouflage interventions. These denunciations were not merely expressions of cynicism for the mishandling of public funds by corrupt economic and political elites; they also allowed marginalized actors to reclaim a sense of power and control by proudly stating that they were not fooled by such potemkin displays.

During the June 2013 protests, demonstrators employed a creative narrative strategy that unsettled authority by mimicking the aestheticized discourse of state politicians. At once witty, humorous and theatrical in tone, slogans creatively merged social demands, mega-event criticism and contempt of Rio's city-branding initiatives, symbolically challenging the consensus that had hitherto prevailed: 'We want FIFA-standard public schools', 'Call me a stadium and invest in me!', 'How many schools are worth one Maracanã?' (Rosner 2013). During the 2014 World Cup, the Brazilian blogosphere was replete with similar creative strategies of resistance that circulated widely and were ultimately picked up by the foreign media. They included several audio and video clips, such as those produced by Rio-based music band Anarco Funk, who cleverly reworked classic samba and bossa nova songs to criticize Olympic-related mega-projects, denounce population displacement and contest the masking of poverty (Soifer 2013). For example, the band turned Jorge Ben's 1972 success 'Fio Maravilha' into a derision of Porto Maravilha, the controversial port revitalization project, 'marvellous for the bourgeois' (*maravilha pra burgues*).

In Rio de Janeiro, the many squatting communities that had invaded some of the port area's many empty building since 2000 after Lula had promised to transform abandoned federal buildings into social housing have also used historical borrowing and linguistic resistance strategies to legitimize their existence. They have framed their plight in terms that symbolically associate their cause to some of the city's notorious historical struggles and identify with black activism, insurrection and heroism. Like many informal settlements around the world, they have named their community after great political or historical leaders, borrowing the names of Afro-Brazilian figures, including leaders of popular rebellions, abolitionist martyrs and other persecuted heroes like Manoel Congo and Zumbi dos Palmares. Associating their cause with the city's long-running race struggle has made their demise a politically sensitive issue. The use of a martial language and references to the struggles of the past in their demands allows them to situate their cause in a continuum of universal battle for equality and justice. But these symbolic means have not warranted their survival. One of the first actions undertaken after the launch of Porto Maravilha in 2009 was the heart-breaking eviction of the Zumbi dos Palmares squat, just as its residents were about to gain legal ownership of the federal building they occupied after years of painstaking negotiations.

Walls that speak

Covert opposition to event-related exclusion also takes a written form, using one of the oldest of supports of mass communication: the wall. In many host cities, resistance to mega-events has taken the form of a war of words waged on the walls of neighbourhoods awaiting demolition. The anonymity of such a mode of communication allows people to powerfully articulate what they would not be able to say in person, and to publicly enunciate what many are silently thinking. Such practices are not only found in the tactical utilization of urban space by graffiti artists, but also in other forms of street art that Borghini *et al.* (2010) call *subvertising*.

In London 2012, one such subvertising resistance strategy was *brandalism*, a global guerrilla movement for reclaiming visual space from the brand intrusion of corporate interests (Goodson 2012). As a contraction between branding and vandalism, brandalism expresses revolt against the corporate control of the visual realm. Following the guerrilla art traditions of the twentieth century and taking inspiration from Agitprop, Situationist and Street Art movements, brandalism seeks to challenge the authority and legitimacy of commercial images within public space and contemporary culture. Based on the conviction that the street is a site of communication that belongs to local residents and communities, it rebels against the media and advertising moguls who pollute and corrupt democratic public space (Smith and Groom 2015). Brandalism is a form of *détournement* that calls on artists to transform advertising billboards with original artworks, whether street art, graffiti, illustration or photo montages, that rework the meaning of the original advert. In Olympic London, brandalism seized the opportunity of the global spotlight to denounce the corporate takeover of city spaces by Olympic sponsors and the constitution of brand exclusion zones.

In 2008 Beijing, the city's walls also bore the evidence of a battle of words fought between local authorities and the population. Where the state painted slogans urging residents to comply with eviction orders to serve the great Olympic cause (Figure 5.2), residents fought back with their own taglines denouncing the unfair eviction process (Figure 5.3). Official slogans were encoded with the imperative tone of state propaganda and shamelessly brandished the Olympic spirit in their appeal for compliance. Residents' rebuttal to such thinly veiled intimidation tactics appealed to basic universal values such as honesty and truth, while safely avoiding political criticism or allusions to the Olympics. Taking the moral high ground allowed citizens to preserve their dignity and retain their integrity while undermining the false claims of their adversaries (Broudehoux 2009).

In Rio de Janeiro, graffiti artists and muralists were extremely prolific in denouncing event-led abuses. Throughout the city, giant paintings depicted the poor's exclusion from the mega-event festival and exposed the greed and corruption of government and FIFA leaders.[3] Rarely aggressive in tone, the murals were poetic and evocative, for example featuring a skinny, tearful child with a football on his dinner plate (Figure 5.4), or satirical, representing businessmen playing football with a moneybag. Graffiti generally bore a more accusatory tone and repeated *ad nauseam* the same slogans throughout the city: FIFA go home! World Cup for Whom?

Figure 5.2 The ominous character 'chai' (demolish) identifies houses to be demolished (photo by Johan Nilsson 2008, with permission).

Figure 5.3 A graffiti artist in Beijing denounces demolition. As part of his Dialogue project, artist Zhang Dali, also known as AK-47, painted enigmatic self-portraits on buildings marked for demolition before the Olympics, in order to awaken popular consciousness to the city's heartless destruction (photo by the author, 2002).

Figure 5.4 Mural denouncing wasteful spending on the 2014 FIFA World Cup in Rio de Janeiro (photo by the author, 2014).

The walls of vulnerable communities, especially favelas, have also become privileged sites for artistic expressions of dissent. In 2008, internationally renowned French artist J.R. used the favela of Providência as a canvas for his photographic project, *Women are Heroes*, which celebrated the strength of underprivileged mothers around the world. A few years later, Mauricio Hora, a photographer and lifetime resident of Providência, used a similar approach to save houses from destruction for the construction of a controversial cable car (*plano inclinado*) leading to the uppermost section of the favela, built as part of the Porto Maravilha urban improvements. Giant photographs of local residents were pasted on the façade of the homes marked for demolition. In the same favela, Portuguese artist Alessandro Farto, alias Vhils, chiselled away plaster on partially demolished homes to create vivid oversized portraits of displaced members of the community.

Resistance 2.0: the rise of web-based resistance movements

Nancy Fraser (1990) has underlined the importance, for marginalized or under-represented groups with limited access to the dominant public spheres (commercial media, local government meetings, academia), to come together and create alternative spaces, which she calls *subaltern counter-public spheres*. In order to carve a space in the existing and increasingly closed commercial media, these groups have turned their attention to producing their own media, where they control the narrative. They circulate counter-discourses which enunciate oppositional interpretations of their needs, interests, and identity. These alternative spheres are sustained by diverse communicative practices that include autonomous newspapers and websites, community networks and other media strategies (Fraser 1990).

In the context of growing media concentration, the internet has opened up possibilities for those with limited access to mainstream platforms and provides new expressions of local autonomy. The web has become an important tactical tool for resistance movements and a crucial weapon in the battle against the event spectacle. As an incredibly cheap, accessible and democratic means of mass communication, the internet is used as an instrument of recruitment and outreach, as a place for discussion and organization and as a vector of diffusion. In a digital world where every phone is a camera and images can be posted or tweeted instantly, individuals are better equipped to reverse the panoptic gaze towards power abusers, and to denounce injustice. Social media have become privileged sites to disseminate information and exchange strategies, and constitute a public forum that helps break the isolation of individual victims. They facilitate outreach, give a voice to those without media access and become a breeding ground for reflexive action and opposition. Web-based platforms can exert pressure upon local authorities, event sponsors, organizers and International Sports Federations to make mega-events more inclusive and transparent, while remaining difficult to control and silence (Broudehoux 2009).

In Beijing, victims of Olympic redevelopment often turned to the internet to leverage the power of the multitude while circumventing interdictions to congregate. They joined web-based interest groups, especially those with an innocuous and apolitical focus, to share their stories, find a support community and give visibility to their cause. Often organized as NGOs, many of these groups gathered around a historical preservation agenda and used the web as a platform to raise awareness, recruit volunteers, coordinate activities and expose their views to the widest possible audience. Their websites recorded Beijing's rapid transformation, assembling visual archives and virtual museums to document the old city's vanishing landscape.[4] Individuals who turned to these pages to share images and information about housing evictions and demolition found on these platforms a form of compensation for the lack of coverage of redevelopment issues in the official media. By keeping the debate alive and fuelling people's resolve and refusal to be silenced, they constituted alternative sites of collective resistance.

In Brazil, a vast and widely successful web-based campaign against the World Cup emerged in 2013, during the June protests that rocked the Confederations Cup. Known by its bold slogan, *Não Vai Ter Copa* (There Will Be No Cup), the movement reached millions around the globe thanks to the wide reach of social media. You could find *Não Vai Ter Copa* groups on Facebook, and proponents used the hashtag #NaoVaiTerCopa on Twitter, often in conjunction with another popular slogan, #CopaPraQuem (Cup For Whom). *Não Vai Ter Copa* was also adopted by the hacker group Anonymous, which used the phrase in the hacking of several government sites and social media accounts in Brazil.

This social media campaign allowed the June 2013 protest movement to reach beyond Brazil's borders. The movement had itself been catalysed by social media and spread across the country using these networks. The web campaign informed the world that the most expensive edition in the history of FIFA's tournament would be held at the cost of widespread corruption, rampant property speculation, police brutality, lack of political accountability and the failure to complete even 50 per cent of its promised infrastructure projects. Although it remains difficult to measure its full impact, the campaign certainly affected the image of the World Cup and helped turn it into a toxic brand, somewhat curbing the extent to which the sporting event could be exploited commercially and politically. It dampened Brazilians' enthusiasm for the event and turned what should have been a festive year into a year of protest and denunciations. It also clearly stated that the World Cup was not going to be another of those public displays of 'cordiality' where Brazilians set aside grievances and put on a show of national unity.

Brazil's government attempted to discredit the campaign and to revamp the image of the event by launching its own counter-slogan with the hashtag #VaiTerCopa, (There Will Be a Cup). But the state's harsh denunciation of anti-World Cup sentiment as international jealousy, national defeatism, leftist agitation and right-wing destabilization only poured oil on the fire and antagonized protesters. The scathing, authoritarian tone of the rebuke proved counterproductive, forcing the state to replace its motto with the more neutral #CopadasCopas (The Cup of Cups), widely used on president Dilma's Twitter feed and Facebook pages. It also circulated on other government social media profiles to share positive messages about the event and to claim that the tournament would benefit all Brazilians. As 2014 went by and the World Cup took place, other copycat slogans emerged to contest other issues, including *Não Vai Ter Tarifa* (There Will Be No Fare Hike – in relation to public transportation) and *Não Vai Ter Final* (There Will Be No Final). These campaigns expressed a sentiment shared by many Brazilians: that their collective hopes for a long-awaited tournament, meant to bring football back to its symbolic home, had been dashed by greed, waste and corruption. For many, there was, indeed, no real World Cup, and the way the final ultimately played out for Brazil confirmed this failure in a spectacular way.

Discussion: measuring the impact of symbolic resistance

This chapter described popular responses to event-led urban image construction in the form of collective resistance movements, smaller-scale, symbolic forms of contestations, minor acts of subversion and web-based strategies to elude the event spectacle, weaken its hegemony and demand fair compensation. These varied actions demonstrate that a large portion of the local population is not duped by the mega-events spectacle and is willing to find creative ways to fight dispossession, contest exclusionary policies and protect the common interest in the face of greed, corruption and power abuses. Popular protests also helped unmask the false promise of collective benefits yielded by the hosting of mega-events and made visible the destructive aspects of the image-construction programmes they foster. By bringing attention to many of the shortcomings of these events for their host population, these movements have not only rendered deep structural inequality manifest, but have also exposed the collective mistrust in public institutions that politicians and mainstream media had actively concealed.

The chapter further demonstrated that urban images are not just the product of top-down processes, but are also shaped by bottom-up, self-organizing, citizen-activist movements. It showed that in their struggle against exclusionary image-construction practices, those excluded have also been able to carve out their own public spheres, to build an alternative urban vision and to develop an enabling and empowering urbanization process (Swyngedouw and Kaika 2000) in response to corporate efforts to transform their city.

There is little evidence to suggest that any of these modes of resistance can effect major changes in terms of state policy and project implementation. The sheer economic and political power of the organizers, sponsors and rights holders of such events severely restricts the scope for bottom-up action, and many resistance strategies appear suboptimal, with limited measurable impacts. Yet, in spite of their limitations, recent amendments to official FIFA and IOC regulations and efforts to rein-in forced evictions, to improve compensation, to control corruption in housing allocation and to increase the supply of affordable homes in China and Brazil, and other host cities around the world, suggest that grievances are being heard and that decision-makers are taking notice. By publicly voicing their complaints, occupying the city's public spaces and showing solidarity for diverse causes, protesters are slowly forcing those responsible for these events to rethink their positions and to seek more sustainable solutions.

Regardless of their minimal immediate impact, these diverse strategies represent important coping mechanisms and afford a certain sense of control to the powerless and disenfranchised, helping them develop an emboldening sense of entitlement. By allowing them to voice frustrations and to criticize by proxy the regime who condoned such image-construction initiatives, resistance strategies allow people to question established social structures, to destabilize neoliberal hegemony, and to open the door to more radical actions. Even the most innocuous forms of resistance can register a cumulative effect, especially when used as a complement to other strategies, and slowly build a greater impact. Partaking in these protest movements helps create an imagined community of resistance, a collectivity of interests that can empower the powerless, lay the groundwork for more concrete political actions and potentially lead to more efficient and better organized forms of opposition. They also enable the expression of critical and dissenting views in the public realm, which can help open-up spaces within which new collectivities may be forged and political agendas refined. The broad public circulation of these subversive messages may also mobilize potential followers and garner popular support, thereby contributing to the formation of a stronger civil society that will protect democratic institutions and basic human rights.

If the impact of these weapons of the weak remains incidental, they do represent small moral victories which allow members of society to maintain the pride and dignity they are so often denied. The chapter suggests that abusive urban image-construction initiatives can prompt the active participation of hitherto apolitical population groups and push individuals to take a host of measures to fight for their rights. No matter what intimidation tactics authorities deploy in the future, it appears that the political landscape of mega-event planning is changing and may never be the same. People are also finding clever new ways to appropriate the spectacle for their own purposes, using parody, satire, masquerade and emerging technologies to successfully regain a voice on the urban stage. The emergence of new modes of communication has helped create a novel, alternative form of public sphere, predicated upon participatory exchanges that transcend localities and allow for more inclusive representation. At a time when the dominant media are abandoning their public responsibilities, grassroots groups and civil society organizations are finding alternative means to gain public visibility and voice. By refusing to be silenced, by taking to the streets in protest, by talking to the global media or partaking in events like *rolezinhos* or *farofaço*, they are reclaiming their right to participate in society, to represent themselves on their own terms and to claim their rightful place in their city's image.

Notes

1 This organization was originally created before the 2007 Pan American Games, as the *Comitê Popular do Pan* (People's Committee for the Pan American Games) (see Mascarenhas *et al.* 2011).
2 Individual households eventually received a convocation to the municipal housing bureau, where they were informed of their compensation options, either a lump sum or of a replacement unit. Those choosing the latter option must usually find temporary lodgings until their new unit is delivered, which can take several months, and receive a modest rent stipend.
3 Many examples can be seen here:www.jornaldiademanews.com.br/exposicao-de-artes-veja-copa-dos-excluidos-na-visao-de-artistas-no-rio-de-janeiro.
4 These include activist Ou Ning's Dazhalan project (www.dazhalan-project.org) or the website www.alternativearchives.com which can be found in the Internet Archive at web.archive.org.

References

ANCOP (Articulaçao National dos Comitês Populares da Copa). (2011) *Dossiê Megaeventos e Violações de Direitos Humanos no Brasil: Dossiê da articulação nacional dos comitês populares da copa*. Rio de Janeiro: ETTERN/Fundação Heinrich Böll.
ANCOP (Articulaçao National dos Comitês Populares da Copa). (2014) *Dossiê Megaeventos e Violações de Direitos Humanos no Brasil*. Rio de Janeiro: ETTERN/ Fundação Heinrich Böll.
Andranovich, G.J., Burbank, M.J. and Heying, C.H. (2001) 'Olympic Cities: Lessons Learned from Mega-Event Politics', *Journal of Urban Affairs*. Vol. 23, pp. 113–131.
Badaró, M.B. (2013) 'A multidão nas ruas: construir a saída para a crise política' [The multitude on the streets: building an exit for a political crisis]. Unpublished text. History department, Federal Fluminense University.
Bakhtin, M. (1984) *Rabelais and his World*. Trans. by Helene Iswolsky. Bloomington, IN: Indiana University Press.
Borghini, S., Visconti, L., Anderson, L. and Sherry, J. (2010) 'Symbiotic Postures of Commercial Advertising and Street Art', *Journal of Advertising*. Vol. 39, No. 3, pp. 113–126.
Broudehoux, A.-M. (2004) *The Making and Selling of Post-Mao Beijing*. London: Routledge.

Broudehoux, A.-M. (2009) 'Seeds of Dissent: The Politics of Resistance to Beijing's Olympic Redevelopment', M. Butcher and S. Velayutham (eds), *Dissent and Cultural Resistance in Asia's Cities*. London: Routledge, pp. 14–32.

Broudehoux, A.-M. (2013) 'Sporting Mega-Events and Urban Regeneration: Planning in a State of Emergency', M.E. Leary and J. McCarthy, *The Routledge Companion to Urban Regeneration*. London: Routledge, pp. 558–568.

Butler, J. (1997) *Excitable Speech: A Politics of the Performative*. New York: Routledge.

Carol, P. (2007) *Slow Food Nation: Why Our Food Should be Good, Clean, and Fair*. New York: Rizzoli.

Chatterton, P. and Hollands, R. (2003) *Urban Nightscapes, Youth Cultures, Pleasure Spaces and Corporate Power*. London: Routledge.

COHRE (Centre on Housing Rights and Eviction). (2007) *Fair Play for Housing Rights: Mega-Events*. Geneva: COHRE.

Comitê Popular da Copa e Olimpíadas do Rio de Janeiro. (2013, May) 'Megaeventos e Violações dos Direitos Humanos no Rio de Janeiro'. Available at: https://comitepopulario.files.wordpress.com/2013/05/dossie_comitepopularcoparj_2013.pdf (accessed 7 July 2016).

Comitê Popular da Copa e Olimpíadas do Rio de Janeiro. (2015, November) 'Megaeventos e Violações dos Direitos Humanos no Rio de Janeiro'. Available at: http://rio.portalpopulardacopa.org.br/?page_id=2972 (accessed 7 July 2016).

DaMatta, R. (1991) *Carnivals, Rogues, and Heroes: An Interpretation of the Brazilian Dilemma*. Notre Dame, IN: University of Notre Dame Press.

Debord, G. (1967) *La société du spectacle*. Paris: Folio.

Debord, G. (1988) *Commentaires sur la société du spectacle*. Paris: Gérard Lebovici.

Du Plessis, J. (2005) 'The Growing Problem of Forced Evictions and the Crucial Importance of Community-Based, Locally Appropriate Alternatives', *Environment and Urbanization*. Vol. 17, pp. 123–134.

Eisinger, P. (2000) 'The Politics of Bread and Circuses: Building the City for the Visitor Class', *Urban Affairs Review*. Vol. 35, No. 3, pp. 316–333.

Fraser, N. (1990) 'Rethinking the Public Sphere: A Contribution to the Critique of Actually Existing Democracy', *Social Text*. Vol. 25–26, pp. 56–80.

Goodson, S. (2012, August 8) 'Brandalism at the London Olympics', Forbes. Available at: www.forbes.com/sites/marketshare/2012/08/08/brandalism-at-the-london-olympics/#23f20703c37d (accessed 24 October 2016).

Horne, J. and Whannel, G. (2011) 'The "Caged Torch Procession": Celebrities, Protesters and the 2008 Olympic Torch Relay in London, Paris and San Francisco', K. Latham and D. Martinez (eds), *Sport in Society: Documenting the Beijing Olympics*. New York: Routledge, pp. 16–26.

Lai, G. and Lee, R.P.L. (2006) 'Market Reforms and Psychological Distress in Urban Beijing', *International Sociology*, Vol. 21, No. 4, pp. 551–579.

Lenskyj, H.J. (2008) *Olympic Industry Resistance: Challenging Olympic Power and Propaganda*. Stanford, CA: Stanford University Press.

Magnier, M. (2005, 25 April) 'Letting Passions Burn May Backfire on China', Los Angeles Times. Available at: http://articles.latimes.com/2005/apr/25/world/fg-chinarage25 (accessed 8 July 2016).

Marquand, R. (2004, 30 November) 'China "gray lists" its intellectuals', *The Christian Science Monitor*.

Mascarenhas, G., Bienenstein, G. and Sánchez, F. (2011) *O Jogo Continua. Megaeventos e Cidades*. Rio de Janeiro: Press of the State University of Rio de Janeiro (EDUERJ).

Nunes, R. (2014, 30 May) 'There Will Have Been No World Cup', *Aljazeera*. Available at: www.aljazeera.com/indepth/opinion/2014/05/brazil-world-cup-protests-201452910299437439.html (accessed 12 July 2016).

Pendras, M. (2002) 'From Local Consciousness to Global Change: Asserting Power at the Local Scale', *International Journal of Urban and Regional Research*. Vol. 26, No. 4, pp. 823–833.

Pocha, J.S. (2005, 15 June) 'China's Inequities Energize New Left: Failures of Reform Buoy New Thinking', *SFGate*. Available at: www.sfgate.com/opinion/article/China-s-inequities-energize-New-Left-Failures-2626893.php (accessed 8 July 2016).

Pred, A. (1992) 'Capitalisms, Crises, and Cultures II: Notes on Local Transformation and Everyday Cultural Struggles', A. Pred and M. Watts (eds), *Reworking Modernity: Capitalisms and Symbolic Discontent*. New Brunswick, NJ: Rutgers, pp. 106–117.

Rojek, C. (2013) *Event Power: How Global Events Manage and Manipulate*. London: SAGE.

Rosner, N. (2013, 7 July) 'Tinker Research Reports, Summer 2013: Masking Urban Marginality', Center for Latin American Studies. Available at: http://clas.berkeley.edu/research/problematizing-socio-spatial-development-margins-rio-de-janeiro (accessed 11 July 2016).

Scott, J.C. (1985) *Weapons of the Weak: Everyday Forms of Peasant Resistance*. New Haven, CT: Yale University Press.

Smith, A. and Groom, J. (2015) 'Brandalism and Subvertising: Hoisting Brands with their Own Petard?', *Journal of Intellectual Property Law & Practice*. Vol. 10, No. 1, pp. 29–34.

Soifer, R. (2013) 'Lyrical Resistance: Urban Reform, Social Memory, and the Imagination of Public Space in Rio de Janeiro'. *Annual Meeting of the American Association of Geographers*. Los Angeles.

Swyngedouw, E. and Kaika, M. (2000) 'The Environment of the City or ... the Urbanisation of Nature', G. Bridge and S. Watson (eds), *A Companion to the City*. Oxford: Blackwell, pp. 567–580.

Vainer, C.B. (2013) 'Megaeventos, meganegócios, megaprotestos'. Available at: www.ettern.ippur.ufrj.br/ultimas-noticias/196/mega-eventos-mega-negocios (accessed 22 July 2013).

Whitelegg, D. (2000) 'Going for Gold: Atlanta's Bid for Fame', *International Journal of Urban and Regional Research*. Vol. 24, pp. 801–817.

Zhang, L. (2004) 'Forced from Home: Property Rights, Civic Activism, and the Politics of Relocation in China', *Urban Anthropology & Studies of Cultural Systems & World Economic Development*. Vol. 33, No. 2–4, pp. 247–281.

Zhou, K. and Link, P. (2001) 'Shunkouliu: Popular Satirical Sayings and Popular Thought', P. Link, R. Madsen and P. Pickowicz (eds), *Popular China*. Lanham, MD: Rowman and Littlefield, pp. 89–110.

6 The human impacts of urban image construction
Revanchism and the neoliberal war on the poor

The object of this book was to investigate the way mega-events impact urban image construction, both as opportunities to impress a new reality upon the existing city and as an alibi to radically rewrite urban policy. Previous chapters have examined diverse strategies used to transform the mental, physical and social dimensions of the city's image, and detailed counter-strategies deployed to contest, derail and usurp the exclusionary character of event-led urban image-construction initiatives. This chapter attempts to further explicate the processes at play and to draw preliminary conclusions by replacing such highly divisive image-construction endeavours, carried out under the specific circumstances posed by the hosting of highly mediatized mega-events, within the broader context of contemporary critical urban theory.

This book has time and again demonstrated how image-construction efforts produce and reproduce inequality, consolidate exclusion and penalize the most vulnerable members of society, in ways that are increasingly brutal and heartless. These attacks on the poor are also overt and blatant product of planned and concerted state actions. In trying to make sense of what could be characterized as the dark side of urban image construction and in order to understand the long-term, multifarious and alienating impacts of such initiatives upon cities and their inhabitants, recent research on the neoliberal city offers an enlightening perspective, particularly Neil Smith's critical work on gentrification and what he came to call the *revanchist city* (1996). Smith (2002) uses the notion of revanchism to denounce the neoliberal tendency to blame urban blight on marginalized populations in order to justify the implementation of aggressive and discriminatory policies directed against them. He borrows the term from the late nineteenth-century Paris Commune, a short-lived radical socialist and revolutionary government violently crushed by a group of right wing nationalist elites intent on restoring public order and reinstating bourgeois society. It was through 'a noxious blend of hatred and viciousness', Smith writes (1996: 227), that these self-labelled 'revanchists' exacted revenge upon all those who had 'usurped' their vision of French society, with a retaliation strategy tinged by moralism and militarism.

Smith's contemporary notion of revanchism is intimately entwined with gentrification strategies and with neoliberal urban transformations. Revanchism's ultimate goal, he claims, is to unlock land values and protect the conditions of capital accumulation. His views resonate with Harvey's notion of *accumulation by dispossession* (2004), which claims that capital expansion is facilitated by the state's brutal reconquest of territories and assets, generally from the hands of the poor. Smith first drew upon the notion of revanchism to describe 1990s New York City and mayor Giuliani's radical urban transformations. For Smith, the economic recession of the 1980s and 1990s had triggered unprecedented anger among the white middle class, who turned on the poor and the marginal as scapegoats for the failure of liberal policies.

For Smith, revanchism was born of the sharp reactionary political break that followed the disintegration of liberal urban policy. It is marked by a powerful anti-welfare ideology and a departure from redistributive policies, anti-poverty legislation and the public provision of services towards a re-commodification of collective consumption (MacLeod 2002). Following Mike Davis' (1990) description of the neoliberal shift *from social welfare to social warfare*, Smith underlines the violence and brutality of revanchist policies, often characterized as a war of the rich against the poor. He sees the neoliberal city as a punitive city, where a self-righteous bourgeoisie intent on defending its privilege and driven by an ontological desire for class revenge attempts to regain control of urban space. Revanchism is thus characterized by a take-back mentality that promotes the violent dispossession of a population thought to have stolen the city from its rightful users. Smith (1996) sums up the revanchist city as a dual city of wealth and poverty, where the victors are increasingly defensive of their privilege and increasingly vicious in defending it.

Revanchism thus testifies to the emergence of a new moral order marked by a growing de-responsibilization and de-solidarization towards the collective. Writing in the context of homelessness and neoliberal urban policy, Don Mitchell (2003) talks of compassion fatigue, which, in a climate of moral indifference to social inequality, has led to widespread erosion of public sympathy for the poor, and a total lack of remorse and empathy. For Mitchell (2003), the post-welfare state era is one in which the benign neglect of the poor has been replaced by a malignant form of neglect. Underlying this new moral order is a deep distrust of democracy, of the idea of equality among citizens and of equal right to the city and its public spaces. In this context, revanchism appears to be driven by a sense of rightfulness, entitlement and superiority on the part of economic elites and by an abject hostility towards difference. It promotes a brutal reconfiguration of citizenship, with a new social hierarchical system based on wealth accumulation and capacity to consume. This vision resonates with Swyngedouw's (2010) characterization of the neoliberal city as decidedly undemocratic, seeking to erase democratic advances and to reinstate rightful inequality in order to let the rich and powerful rule unimpeded. Such democratic deficit would help consolidate a new authoritarian state form, which places the value of property above the value of people and is more concerned with protecting markets than in protecting its citizens.

Evidence presented in this book suggests that the production of a new urban landscape in preparation to host some of the world's most mediatized events may exacerbate the latent revanchist tendencies of current neoliberal urban policies by helping secure the advances of private power-holders over common interests. Mega-events play a palliative function to help create the perfect conditions to bypass democratic processes and to adopt urban policies that serve elite and corporate interests. Their great symbolic appeal provides the necessary context for local leaders to reclaim some of the ground that had been lost to welfare policies and democratization, and to pass new legislation to restore the balance of power towards private interests. Mega-events are also used to exact retribution for a perceived loss of privilege and to regain control of certain urban territories. UN Special Rapporteur on adequate housing Raquel Rolnik (2014) claims that mega-events are part of a global neoliberal political agenda to prevent deep structural transformations in contemporary society while concealing power imbalances and social inequality. She argues that it is no accident that global-scale events have come to embody neoliberal thinking, since they took off during the neoliberal revolution of the 1980s and rose in number and importance during the following two decades. In what follows, further examples from Beijing and Rio de Janeiro illustrate the revanchist character of many event-related image-construction programmes.

Revanchism with Chinese characteristics: the human costs of the Beijing Games

In spite of the unique political economic context in which the 2008 Olympics took place, in the midst of China's important transition from planned to market economy, Beijing's Olympic transformation can be said to embody many aspects of Smith's revanchist theory, especially those developed in a 2002 article where he redefines gentrification as a global urban strategy, closely connected into the circuits of global capital. In this text, Smith argues that massive neoliberal urban reorganization is now affecting metropolises of Asia, Latin America and parts of Africa more dramatically, where old forms of capitalism and the Keynesian welfare state were never significantly installed and where the state now acts more as an agent of the market than as a regulator.

Many examples cited in this book illustrate the important role played by the Olympic Games in transforming post-socialist Beijing in ways that clearly benefited power-holders and their economic allies, and disadvantaged the less fortunate. Thanks to the state's ability to confiscate land in the name of the public interest, local party and government officials used their power to exploit provisions in the Chinese legislation concerning evictions and land acquisition. By acquiring most of the land on which Olympic projects were built well below market value, they made a fortune leasing this land to private developers (Fang and Zhang 2003). Much of the new wealth generated by Beijing's image-construction programme thus came at the direct expense of the poor. The national image of prosperity that was showcased during the Games was built on the back of the economically deprived, who were doubly taxed: first by the diversion of public funds from welfare programmes, and then by their direct exploitation as construction workers or evictees. The realization of Olympic mega-projects relied on the labour of a vast, pliant and disposable labour force made up mainly of migrant workers who enjoyed few rights in the city. Even though they already subsidized Olympic projects through their underpaid labour, they often suffered pay arrears of up to a year in back wages, or work-related injuries without any form of compensation (Toy 2006). The extent of their suffering and exploitation is well documented (Broudehoux 2004). In the months leading to the Summer Games, violence against superiors, destruction of property and mass protests by migrant workers became widespread. Several unpaid construction workers committed suicides by jumping off buildings in a desperate attempt to draw attention to their plight (Toy 2006).

While the Beijing Olympics were praised as some of the most successful in history and brought spectacular benefits to their political and economic sponsors, Olympic image construction had a direct impact on the livelihood of economically and socially marginalized groups in Beijing, accelerating a process of downward mobility that had existed since the reforms of the late 1970s. COHRE (2007) estimates that one out of five people displaced by Olympic projects were impoverished as a result of their relocation and suffered a significant deterioration in their living conditions and life opportunities. Displaced Beijing residents faced increased costs of living due to relocation to the city's outlying suburbs, away from schools, jobs and basic services. Olympic redevelopment also greatly reduced the affordable housing stock and caused property prices around Olympic projects to rise dramatically, making it less affordable for people to live near the city centre. In the absence of public transportation, many had to cope with increased transportation costs and commuting time to be able to earn a decent living. Relocation apartments also carry important hidden charges, such as management fees, and unsubsidised utility charges that often exceed people's capacity to pay.

One should be reminded that the 2008 Olympics were held by a state that still officially called itself socialist and that Beijing's transformation was led and supervised by state authorities. Its negative impacts were largely foreseeable and cannot be dismissed as accidental by-products of market-led redevelopment, which may suggest that they were both planned and intentional. Sadly, Olympic redevelopment not only lowered some people's standards of living, but also made them more vulnerable to abuse and exploitation. The destruction of several inner-city neighbourhoods and the massive displacement of the underprivileged affected the forms of sociability that used to unite different segments of society, weakened community ties and impaired social cohesion, making it difficult to rebuild social networks for mutual assistance. The important social dislocation that has resulted from people's dispersal to outlying suburbs thus diminished people's capacity to organize and to fight for their rights.

Olympic transformations also had a lasting impact on Beijing's urban structure, deeply affecting its socio-spatial configuration and fostering income-based segregation. The concentration of investments in certain sectors of the city exacerbated pre-existing spatial inequalities and sharpened the spatial divide between the city's new rich and its emerging new poor. The social solidarity of the socialist years was replaced by a jealous desire to protect newly acquired wealth against those perceived as backward, hostile and dangerous, with a total absence of class guilt (Broudehoux 2009).

Expectedly, those who paid for the Games through self-sacrifice, underfunded social services and evictions were not to reap the benefits. Despite being partly funded by the public sector (40–60 per cent), most Olympic facilities built on the ashes of demolished neighbourhoods were privatized after the Games and turned into commercial ventures, especially private health clubs, and leisure and entertainment spaces for the affluent. The Swim Centre became an entertainment palace, complete with wave pool, artificial beach, fitness club, skating rink, cinema, restaurants and shops. The Olympic Horse Racetrack was turned into a golf course, while the Olympic Village was converted into an upscale residential district with privatized amenities including a convention centre and an international school.

In spite of the strong patriotic overtone of the event, the Olympics marked an important turning point in the perceptions of the Chinese state among the poor; a sustained feeling of injustice began to erode much of the popular allegiance the Party retained among the underprivileged. For many, abusive state policies in the preparation for the Olympics represented a breach in a social contract that had linked China's masses and the Communist Party since the 1949 revolution. People grieved for not just the loss of livelihood and residence, but also for the violation of a fundamental citizenship right. Yet, the spectacular rise of the Olympic metropolis remained quite successful in diverting public attention from the human tragedies that took place in its shadow. Within less than a decade, the hosting of Beijing's mega-event helped transform a sleepy socialist capital city into a world-class metropolis, and the city's new image came to be recognized worldwide as proof of China's rise as a new global power.

But, like Dorian Gray's portrait, this shiny new façade of success conceals the city's darker side, as a place of selfish opportunism and broken promises. Its megalomaniacal architecture mirrors its new, increasingly individualist society, where a predatory elite of private entrepreneurs, technocrats and Party members preys on a disenfranchised and vulnerable populace. Olympic Beijing is a city that glitters on the surface but is hollow at the core, a city that gladly sold its soul for a mirage of prosperity and illusionary grandeur.

Revanchism in black and white: Rio de Janeiro as a schizophrenic metropolis

While class warfare was also part of Rio de Janeiro's pre-event transformation, the city's own brand of revanchism was uniquely marked by its racial character. Neil Smith's analysis of 1990s New York describes a gentrification process that was explicitly classist but also implicitly racist, justified by a colour-blind neoliberal free market ideology that resulted in the displacement of poor blacks and immigrants by a wealthier and whiter class (Smith 2002; Hetzler *et al.* 2006). Smith (1998) writes that revanchism constructs and reproduces social differences, which, in Brazil, much like in the United States, are largely based on ethnicity. Brazilian society is organized according to a complex, deeply rooted hierarchical classification based on race, religion and class. What many examples in the previous chapters have hinted at without fully explicating is that in Rio de Janeiro, revanchism was not only waged in socio-economic terms, but that it was also deeply racialized. Although the racial character of social inequality is often negated in Brazil, a great proportion of revanchist policies put in place in the context of mega-event preparation overwhelmingly affected the Afro-Brazilian population and their cultural practices. In Rio de Janeiro, recent mega-events exacerbated the longstanding class war between the white establishment and the dark masses, and helped legitimize and legalize race-based inequality, inscribing it in official policy.

From early colonial times until well into the twenty-first century, white elites have seen Afro-Brazilians as intruders and perceived their ubiquitous presence in Rio de Janeiro's urban spaces as a temporary inconvenience they had to put up with for the sake of development. They never accepted the idea that those who worked in their mines and plantations, cooked their meals, raised their children, guarded their homes and tended their gardens would grow roots and make the city their own. But evidence suggests that colonial Rio de Janeiro was largely a black city (*Cidade Negra*), especially its port area, long known as *Pequena África* (Little Africa) (Farias 2006). Between 1831 and 1888, Rio was the largest slave city of the Americas, and probably the largest black city in the world (Souty 2013). Urban life in colonial and republican Rio was dominated by free and enslaved Africans who occupied the city streets and public squares, working, vending, running errands and socializing. Local elites and authorities were weary of these dangerous classes, which they both feared and depended upon for the development of the economy. What made the situation insufferable for the elite was that Afro-Brazilians were essential for their survival. Not only did they represent a plentiful reserve of domestic labour, but they were also at the centre of the slave-driven capitalist economy, based on mining and agricultural exports.

The great paradox in the historical construction of Rio de Janeiro's urban image lies in the denial of its reality as a black city and the refusal of the white minority to conceive of blacks as permanent members of society, deserving equal rights and opportunities. Much like Oscar Wilde's narcissist protagonist, Rio de Janeiro has long suffered from a schizophrenic personality, marked by the coexistence of two conflicting urban identities: the utopian White City idealized by the ruling Portuguese elite, and the heterotopian Black City, consistently repressed as shameful, illegitimate and provisional. Rio's urban leaders have long negated the existence of this dual identity and coveted the dream of eradicating this Black City with a series of disciplinary methods, civilizing initiatives and urban reforms that condemned the practices and ways of life of their inhabitants.

This paradoxical situation of simultaneous dependency and repulsion resonates with what sociologist Milton Santos (2016) calls *ressentimento branco*, or white resentment. Santos calls for a re-examination and a reversal of the hegemonic, common knowledge discourse on black resentment for the ill treatment suffered at the hands of white society. In reality, he maintains, it is the white population who resents the social ascension of blacks, their access to high-quality education, their appropriation of urban space and their desire to be seen as legitimate and integral members of Brazilian society. Santos (2016) does not deny the existence of black resentment, but views it as inconsequent and ineffective because it lacks direct access to power. White resentment, on the other hand, is very real and effective as it belongs to those who still control political and economic power in Brazil.

In recent years, the rise of neoliberalism and the multiplication of revanchist public policies around the world have allowed this long-contained white resentment to gain legitimacy and to be voiced more openly. Contemporary Brazilian elites deeply despise the 13-year rule of the democratically elected PT (*Partido dos Trabalhabores* or Labour Party), whose redistributive policies, including the celebrated *Bolsa Familia*, have greatly reduced poverty, helping millions of people move into the ranks of the middle class (Anderson 2011). Intent on protecting its centuries-old privilege, the elite came to vastly resent the PT's progressive policies, which recognized several rights for the poor, including labour protections, housing rights and the right to the city, and granted the poor a certain level of entitlement. Although these concessions to the poor have come at little cost to the rich, who have, for their part, enjoyed regressive taxation, market-friendly policies and the ever-growing concentration of landownership, thereby achieving what Perry Anderson (2011) has termed 'progress without conflict' or 'distribution without redistribution', elites still felt the erosion of their dominion over territory and power. The economic crisis of 2014–2015 exacerbated this resentment, which ultimately culminated, in 2016, with what the world's media widely described as a soft coup, orchestrated by the Right against president Dilma Rousseff and other members of the PT. Conservative Michel Temer, who took over Rousseff's role as president, lost no time in assembling an all-white, all-male cabinet, hardly representative of a country with a 53 per cent proportion of blacks and 'pardos'. He immediately dismantled a series of ministries, including those of women, racial equality and human rights, and started taking apart all progressive policies instated by the PT.

To this day, Rio's Black City persists, concentrated in the port area, in the city's many favelas and in the north-western periphery. It continues to be perceived as illegitimate, rebellious, marginal and antithetical to the official, formal, civilized White City (Souty 2014). The strong communal ties, solidarity, and collectivist ideology that characterize this Black City, which result more from necessity than political idealism, stand in sharp contrast to the individualist and capitalist social values that prevail in the White City (Souty 2014).

Porto Maravilha as the new embodiment of Rio de Janeiro's White City project

Throughout the history of Rio de Janeiro, campaigns initiated to improve the city's image have aimed for the utopian realization of an advanced White City by erasing its black, uncivilized and primitive components. From the hygienist Passos reforms of the early twentieth century, to the modernization programmes of the 1940s, to the post-modern, Miami-style suburbanization of the West Zone in the 1970s, authorities sought to repress the city's African identity and to impose urban images and values imported from Europe and North America. In the neoliberal era, as the city prepared to host the world's top mega-events, Rio seized a new opportunity to shake off the remnants of the Black City, especially in the city centre.

Porto Maravilha was thus launched as a last attempt to actualize the dream of the exclusive White City, concentrating its effort on what remained of Little Africa. In recent years, multiple attempts at the whitening of Rio's Port Area have been denounced by intellectuals and activists alike (Daflon 2016; Souty 2013). They are visible, for example, in recent historic preservation efforts, which primarily highlight elements of the landscape closely associated with Europeans and Catholics, and present residents of Portuguese and Spanish descent as the area's legitimate residents. According to this Eurocentric vision, which is part of a territorial de-stigmatization strategy aimed at facilitating real-estate valuation, the African past is minimized and its Afro-Brazilian legacies, including important contributions to Brazilian culture such as carnival, samba and capoeira, are turned into folklore, depoliticized, sanitized and easily repackaged for touristic consumption (Broudehoux 2013).

Even after excavation work carried out in 2010 unearthed rare relics from the slave trade near the old Valongo wharf, where close to one million African slaves landed in the nineteenth century, little was done to pay tribute to this important facet of local history (Romero 2014). Porto Maravilha reluctantly agreed to make part of the ruins visible and the polemical issue of the area's slave past was summarily evacuated by creating an African heritage walk, that identifies a few key sites with basic plaques. The richest traces of the slave past that have been made visible today are the result of local grassroots initiatives. For example, the Instituto do Pretos Novos is the site of a shallow African burial ground known as the Cemetery of the New Blacks, which was turned, with limited state investment, into a memorial, a heritage museum and a research and a cultural centre.

What makes this and other pre-Olympic urban interventions qualify as revanchism is their planned and targeted nature. In his first book on revanchism, Neil Smith (1996: 225) equates gentrification to a 'symbolic extermination and erasure of the urban poor'. In Porto Maravilha, race and poverty are part of a complex territorial stigma that prevents local middle- and upper-class Brazilians regarding this area as a potential investment opportunity and which has slowed residential development in Porto Maravilha. The financial success of the redevelopment project thus depends largely on the expulsion of this population and on the symbolic silencing of the area's disturbing past. In many ways, Porto Maravilha echoes what Arantes (2009) calls *strategic gentrification*, or the planned expulsion of the poor. In Porto Maravilha, gentrification is not the product of an urban renewal process led by the market's invisible hand, but it represented one of the project's primary objectives. Although the displacement of the poor and black from the port results from the coordinated efforts of the state and its private sector allies, it was made to appear as the simple consequence of market pressure, or what Brazilians call 'expulsao branca' (white expulsion). In reality, this expulsion was the direct outcome of the state's massive infrastructure investments, meant to attract high-paying residents and investors.

Elsewhere in Rio de Janeiro, other event-led initiatives called upon revanchist urban policy for their realization, especially regarding the violent eradication of favelas in the urban landscape or their 'pacification' by heavily armed police forces. Here again, local political and economic elites have sought to benefit from unlocked land values, this time using security as a pretext to take back control of strategic sites for the construction of the future Olympic city. In 2013, the *Guardian* described the pacification programme as a planned gentrification designed to displace, both directly and indirectly, the favela's long-time residents (Gibson and Watts 2013). Many aggressive pacification interventions were thus carried out to free-up profitable real estate that had been devalued by drug trafficking. The revaluation of land around pacified favelas would later justify the displacement of their residents and its redevelopment.

The 2009 decision to enclose Rio's informal settlements and their residents against their will with the construction of favela walls (see Chapter 4) also testifies to a shift in attitude towards the urban poor, in favour of a more vindictive posture. In *City of Walls*, Teresa Caldeira (2000) traces the gradual insularization of Brazilian urban space over the end of the twentieth century, which resulted in the creation of fortified elite enclaves and the abandonment of leftover civic spaces to the poor and marginal. The walling of Rio's favelas suggests that it is no longer enough for local elites to withdraw themselves from public life while blaming the poor for the instability and insecurity caused by globalization and neoliberalism. The radical containment of these territories of exclusion betrays a desire on the part of both political and economic elites to strike back, limit the expansion of illegal settlements and reconquer city spaces from the undeserving poor, in order to stimulate profitable urban development. The favela wall is thus at once the product of neoliberal ideology, the expression of revanchist class warfare and the embodiment of deeply rooted prejudices. Above all, the wall symbolizes the utopia of social equality and the myth of racial democracy in Brazilian society. As an offensive and hostile gesture of internment, the wall can only amplify resentment, fuel antagonism and postpone conflict resolution, making the realization of social equality and urban peace ever more utopian (Figure 6.1).

In pre-Olympic Rio de Janeiro, event-related revanchism also took the form of economic dispossession, with appropriation by the business sector of funds that had been allocated to poverty alleviation. Many gentrifying projects, which mainly benefited the real-estate industry, have been financed by funds dedicated to social projects, low-income housing or infrastructure improvement in marginalized communities. For example, the construction of two cable car systems in Rio's favelas in preparation for mega-events, denounced as serving more the tourist class that local communities, were financed with funds from the accelerated development programme, intended for sanitation and housing provision (Broudehoux and Legroux 2013). The costs of displacing residents to make way for Olympic-related projects built in public–private partnerships was covered by the Minha Casa Minha Vida low-cost housing programme. Finally, the controversial Porto Maravilha, source of some of the greatest population displacements in the city, was financed using Brazilian taxpayers' Workers Retirement Fund (Sánchez and Broudehoux 2013).

Figure 6.1 Wall erected in 2010 in the favela of Santa Marta amid much controversy (photo by the author, 2011).

Vila Autódromo: revanchism in the Olympic city of exception

One particularly emblematic embodiment of the revanchism that has become a symbol of the Olympic state of exception in Rio de Janeiro is Vila Autódromo, a well-established, low-income neighbourhood in the city's western periphery. Settled in 1967 as a fishing village between the Jacarepaguá Lagoon and an old car racetrack about 30 km from downtown, this quiet community has been the victim of a decades-long campaign of state-led harassment. The 40-year history of the community was marked by continuous struggles for survival and its persistence in fighting for its rights and claiming its legitimacy made it a symbol of resistance to forced evictions, both in Rio de Janeiro and around the world. Having survived waves of expulsions in the 1960s and 1970s, Vila Autódromo faced serious demolition threats on the eve of the 2007 Pan American Games, despite holding a series of legal assurances against evictions. In 1992 the state governor of Rio de Janeiro had granted the community a 33-year lease for the land, which was extended to a 99 years 'concession of use' land title in 1994. In 2005 the city declared part of the community to be a Special Zone of Social Interest (ZEIS).

In the years leading to the 2016 Olympics, the community was targeted once again, this time more virulently because of its location on the edge of the future Olympic Park, where most sport venues and media services were to be concentrated. Even if the settlement did not lie within the official Olympic Park premises, its unfinished aspect and the stigma attached to its designation as a favela made it an undesirable neighbour for the prestigious event. After Rio de Janeiro won the Olympic bid in October 2009, the city quickly revoked Vila Autódromo's 2005 protected status and embarked on a relentless campaign to eradicate the community. Over the next seven years, a series of ever-shifting rationales, from the construction of an access road, to the realization of an IOC-required safety perimeter and alleged environmental damages to the nearby lagoon were used to justify its demolition. But it was clear that the city's motivations had more to do with its promise to cede this prime waterfront real estate to a private consortium in exchange for the provision of Olympic facilities.[1] The radically different treatment given to another settlement, located on the north-western side of the Olympic Park, supports such allegation. Although it also lies within the security perimeter, this agglomeration of 20 condominium blocks, used as military housing for the Brazilian Air Force, was never threatened by the Olympic Park development.

Vila Autódromo residents were well aware that they were being evicted for the benefit of real-estate interests with close links to the mayor's office. Initial plans for the Olympic Park submitted by British design firm AECOM had proposed the preservation of the entire community. It was after the project was put into the hands of a private consortium, to be redeveloped as a public–private partnership with limited public funding, that the pressure to vacate the land began to be felt. The consortium, comprising Odebrecht, Andrade Gutierrez and Cavalho Hosken, known to be among the top campaign donors to the current city and state administrations, would invest more than R$1 billion in Olympic infrastructure against the right to redevelop the land after the Olympics, and planned to build upscale private housing, shopping malls and hotels. The 2030 Olympic Legacy Plan for the site shows a new urbanism-inspired elite gated community that conforms to Barra da Tijuca's dominant car-dependent, closed-condominium residential model that promotes a high-consumption, luxury lifestyle (Gaffney 2016).

In a 2015 interview given to the BBC, Carlos Cavalho, owner of one of Rio's top real-estate companies and Barra's largest landlord, was very transparent about the necessity for the poor to be displaced from the area. Calling the Olympics 'a blessing from the gods', Cavalho explained that there were plenty of urban areas more appropriate for the poor, but that Barra belonged to those who could afford to live there. His company also built the Olympic athletes' village, to be converted into an exclusive housing complex, presumptuously named Pure Island, where the 3,604 units should sell for up to R$1 million apiece.

With the law on their side, residents of Vila Autódromo remained adamant in their demands to stay and relentlessly fought their case in the courts. Well versed in the art of resistance, the community was surprisingly efficient in its collective organization to fight Olympic-related demolition, attracting support from academics, journalists and several local and national NGOs. It gained visibility by joining city-wide interest groups, especially the *Comitês Populares* mentioned in Chapter 5, which helped them organize protest actions, marches and mass demonstrations both in Barra da Tijuca and in the city centre. Members of the *Comitês* were extremely creative in devising resistance strategies – for example, organizing clever social media opinion campaigns such as the 'urbanize now' celebrity web shorts. The *Comitês* also managed to secure the mailing list of all major media outlets and made a point of keeping them informed of all new developments. To maintain pressure upon authorities, keep media coverage of the struggle alive and lift the morale of the troops, they also periodically held on-site festive gatherings and solidarity events.

The community's struggle attracted the sympathy of a great part of the Brazilian intelligentsia. Residents received assistance from the *Movimento Nacional de Luta Pela Moradia*, a national movement for the protection of housing rights, from the public defender's office and the Order of Brazilian Attorneys. They were also assisted by public intellectuals and academics, who offered their technical or specialized knowledge and broad experience to help organize and strategize their struggle, and articulate their demands. A group of planning and architecture professors at two of Rio's top universities along with some of their students devised a sustainable alternative development plan for the Olympic Park peninsula at the outset of an extensive participatory process. In July 2012, community representatives unveiled Vila Autódromo's first People's Plan (*Plano Popular*), which demonstrated the possibility to retain what remained of the community, upgrading existing buildings, infrastructure and environmental protections at one-third of the cost of relocation. The plan received wide public acclaim, especially abroad, where the Alfred Herrhausen Association, a Deutschbank organization, in partnership with the London School of Economics, granted the plan its 2013 Urban Age Award, accompanied by a generous grant, which gave the resistance movement fresh impetus.

The city was inconsistent in its response to this organized resistance movement, oscillating between conciliatory compensation offers and interventions of unforeseen brutality. Emotionally and mentally exhausted by years of broken promises, having been subjected on a daily basis to undue pressure and coercion tactics on the part of city representatives, some residents began accepting relocation offers. In spite of a court order banning demolitions, houses were torn down as soon as their residents left. Between March and May 2014, over 300 houses scattered throughout the settlement were destroyed or partly gutted, giving the settlement the appearance of a warzone. In May 2014, in what residents termed an act of heartless psychological violence, all trees along the community's main road were cut down. A few months later, a violent altercation with riot police left several residents injured and photographs of bloodied elderly women circulated around the world.

Many actors weighed in on this long and complex battle. The Brazilian media played a major part in manipulating public opinion against the community, discrediting its struggle and limiting its visibility. In December 2015, a visit to Vila Autódromo by United Nations representatives, on their way to the Mariana Dam disaster site in Minas Gerais, went largely unreported in the Brazilian press. Also absent from the mainstream media was any mention of the Urban Age Award granted to the innovative planning proposal. The City also manipulated the media in its attempt to erode the resolve of residents. On several occasions, it was through the media that residents learned of the mayor's intentions and that new rounds of demolition were announced. Although those announcements often proved premature or unfounded, they added to the psychological pressure felt by the community and played a part in convincing some residents to give in and accept relocation. The *O Globo* media conglomerate was especially active in misconstruing the community's struggle as the action of greedy individuals wishing to cheat the system, and systematically sided with state efforts to expel residents.

The stand-off lasted until 2016. The residents' legal status as property owners ensured they were fairly compensated, with the last remaining residents receiving close to market value for their highly desirable lakefront lots. As the Olympics grew near, the village began to look post-apocalyptic, with its hollowed out homes, precarious debris piles and mosquito infested puddles. By May 2016, only 20 of the community's 500 homes remained. In July, the mayor's office finally caved in and acted on its promise to rapidly urbanize what was left of the community, granting security of tenure to the remaining residents. All but one house was torn down (Figure 6.2), people were transferred to emergency prefabricated cabins and they finally moved into their brand new, barely finished cinder-block homes a few days before the August 2016 Olympic Opening Ceremonies.

Figure 6.2 Last house standing, Vila Autódromo, during the 2016 Olympic Games. Graffiti denounce the demolition of this community in the shadow of the Olympic Park (photo by the author, 2016).

Conclusion

In his perceptive 2016 book, George Monbiot claims that the power of neoliberalism lies in its invisibility and anonymity. Thanks to its ability to hide behind the common-sense notions of 'the free market' or 'the system', it is rarely recognized as an ideology, and, in spite of its pervasiveness, it is seldom called by its name. Such unquestioned, blind faith in the power of the free market and its ability to ensure that everyone gets what they deserve in ways that planning could never achieve may explain the rising ascendancy and normalisation of revanchism in contemporary mainstream society. Not only does neoliberalism's power of mystification allow the rich to persuade themselves that they acquired their wealth through merit rather that advantages such as education, inheritance and class, but the poor have also begun to internalize and reproduce this creed, blaming themselves for their failures, even with limited power over their own circumstances. As a result, Monbiot (2016) claims, the past four decades have been characterized by a transfer of wealth from the poor to the rich, resulting in a gradual disempowerment of the poor and middle classes. Mega-events play a central role in veiling the impacts of neoliberal ideology and in maintaining faith in what has been called 'free market fundamentalism'. These weeks-long global spectacles and celebrations of conspicuous consumption help conceal the tragic shortcomings of this system. Like Dorian Gray's deteriorating portrait, they erect stunning façades of success, prosperity and wealth to suggest that, all is well in the best of worlds.

Examples presented in this chapter suggest that, as products of neoliberalist excess, event-led urban image-construction practices are inherently predisposed to violence, and are marked by a growing intolerance for democracy and a profound disregard for equal rights and opportunities. In his 2010 book, Tony Judt underlines neoliberalism's latent authoritarianism, claiming that governments who have lost the moral authority that arises from the delivery of public services, are reduced to 'cajoling, threatening and ultimately coercing people to obey them' (p. 120). While mega-events may not be the main culprit behind the naturalization and growing acceptability of a vindictive attitude towards the poor and powerless in the global mainstream, the examples discussed in this book suggest that these events' glorification of wealth, their promotion of success at all cost and their aestheticization of power and greed may play an important part in the banalization of revanchism. Not only do they promote a worldview that disqualifies the losers – those who do not have the means or connections to rise to the very top – they also encourage their invisibilization and relegation to the bottom of the pile.

Underlying much of the revanchism found in the examples cited in this book is a desire to reinstate old power structures and social hierarchies. In the two cities under study, event-led urban image construction helped undercut the democratic process to allow politicians and their economic allies to advance policies they could never institute under normal political circumstances. In both cases, urban transformations have aimed to frame the limits of democratization and to create a divided and ordered society where people know their place.

In this context, mega-events become a dangerous instrument of domination that allows the ambitious and power-hungry to feed on inequality and injustice and to let loose their wildest fantasies of urban erasure, cleansing the land of the undeserving and unwanted. Meanwhile, urban image construction helps mask the ugly face of greed behind make-believe dreamworlds of schizophrenic denial. No matter how reactionary, anti-democratic and repressive the world vision of these political and economic elites, these events provide them with an alibi that allows them to maintain a respectable front and to protect their privileges. The event-city described in this book is a city of fractures and fictions, which too often denies rather than promotes the professed Olympic values of friendship, equality and respect. It is a city where the rich and powerful are at war against the poor and the weak. A city that separates rather than unites; protects the privileges of the few at the expense of the many; values confrontation rather than friendship; promotes selfish greed and predatory opportunism rather than solidarity, generosity and altruism; fosters neglect and exclusion rather than respect; and upholds power and dominion rather than equality.

Note

1 In August 2009, the city first announced that Vila Autódromo would be demolished to allow the construction of a new Bus Rapid Transit line, as planned in the binding agreement with the IOC. In early 2010 the City talked of the need to establish a safety perimeter around the Olympic Park. Later the same year, Vila Autódromo appeared on a list of 119 favelas that city planners claimed should be removed because of the risk they posed to the environment. In February 2011 a judge used federal legislation that requires a buffer between construction and any body of water to order the demolition of Vila Autódromo homes that were within 25 metres of the lagoon.

References

Anderson, P. (2011) 'Lula's Brazil', *London Review of Books.* Vol. 33, pp. 3–12.
Arantes, O. (2009) 'Uma estratégia fatal A cultura nas novas gestões urbanas', O. Arantes, C. Vainer and E. Maricato (eds). *A cidade do pensamento único: Desmanchando consensos.* Petrópolis: Vozes, pp. 11–74.
Broudehoux, A.-M. (2004) *The Making and Selling of Post-Mao Beijing.* London: Routledge.
Broudehoux, A.-M. (2009) 'Seeds of Dissent: The Politics of Resistance to Beijing's Olympic Redevelopment', M. Butcher and S. Velayutham (eds), *Dissent and Cultural Resistance in Asia's Cities.* London: Routledge, pp. 14–32.
Broudehoux, A.-M. (2013) 'Sporting Mega-Events and Urban Regeneration: Planning in a State of Emergency', M.E. Leary and J. McCarthy, *The Routledge Companion to Urban Regeneration.* London: Routledge, pp. 558–568.
Broudehoux, A.-M. and Legroux, J. (2013) 'L'option téléphérique dans les favelas de Rio de Janeiro: Conflits d'intérêts entre méga-événements, tourisme et besoins locaux', *Téoros.* Vol. 32, No. 2, pp. 16–25.
Caldeira, T. (2000) *City of Walls: Crime, Segregation and Citizenship in Sao Paulo.* Berkeley, CA: University of California Press.
COHRE (Centre on Housing Rights and Eviction). (2007) *Fair Play for Housing Rights: Mega-Events.* Geneva: COHRE.

Daflon, R. (2016, July 22) 'O Porto Maravilha é negro', *Carta Capital.* Available at: www.cartacapital.com.br/sociedade/o-porto-maravilha-e-negro (accessed 25 September 2016).

Davis, M. (1990) *City of Quartz: Excavating the Future in Los Angeles.* London: Verso.

Fang, K. and Zhang, Y. (2003) 'Plan and Market Mismatch: Urban Redevelopment in Beijing During a Period of Transition', *Asia Pacific Viewpoint.* Vol. 44, pp. 149–162.

Farias, J. (2006) *Cidades negras: africanos, crioulos e espaços urbanos no Brasil escravista do século XIX.* São Paulo: Alameda.

Gaffney, C. (2010) 'Mega-events and Socio-spatial Dynamics in Rio de Janeiro, 1919–2016', *Journal of Latin American Geography.* Vol. 9, No. 1, pp. 7–29.

Gibson, O. and Watts, J. (2013, 5 December) 'World Cup: Rio Favelas being "socially cleansed" in runup to sporting events', *Guardian.* Available at: www.theguardian.com/world/2013/dec/05/world-cup-favelas-socially- cleansed-olympics (accessed 24 October 2016).

Harvey, D. (2004) 'The "New" Imperialism: Accumulation by Dispossession', *The Socialist Register.* Vol. 40, pp. 63–87.

Hetzler, O., Medina, V.E. and Overfelt, D. (2006) 'Gentrification, Displacement and New Urbanism: The Next Racial Project', *Sociation Today.* Vol. 4, No. 2.

Judt, T. (2010) *Ill Fares the Land.* New York: Penguin.

MacLeod, Gordon. (2002) 'From Urban Entrepreneurialism to a "Revanchist City"? On the Spatial Injustice of Glasgow's Renaissance', *Antipodes.* Vol. 34, No. 3, pp. 602–624.

Mitchell, D. (2003) *The Right to the City: Social Justice and the Fight for Public Space.* New York: The Guilford Press.

Monbiot, G. (2016) *How Did We Get into this Mess? Politics, Equality, Nature.* London: Verso.

Rolnik, R. (2014) 'Keynote Presentation', *Second International Conference on Mega-Events and the City.* Rio de Janeiro.

Romero, S. (2014) 'Rio's Race to Future Intersects Slave Past', *New York Times.* Available at: http://topics.nytimes.com/top/reference/timestopics/people/r/ simon_romero/index.html (accessed 24 October 2016).

Sánchez, F. and Broudehoux, A.-M. (2013) 'Mega-Events and Urban Regeneration in Rio de Janeiro: Planning in a State of Emergency', *International Journal of Urban Sustainable Development.* Vol. 5, No. 2, pp. 132–163.

Santos, M. (2016, 3 March) 'Como é ser negro no Brasil', *Geledés.* Available at: www.geledes.org.br/como-e-ser-negro-no-brasil-por-milton-santos (accessed 8 July 2016).

Smith, N. (1996) *The New Urban Frontier: Gentrification and the Revanchist City.* London: Routledge.

Smith, N. (1998) 'Giuliani Time: The Revanchist 1990s', *Social Text.* Vol. 57, pp. 1–20.

Smith, N. (2002) 'New Globalism, New Urbanism: Gentrification as Global Urban Strategy', *Antipode.* Vol. 34, pp. 427–450.

Souty, J. (2013) 'Dinâmicas de patrimonialização em contexto de revitalização e de globalização urbana: Notas sobre a região portuária do Rio de Janeiro', *Memória em Rede.* Vol. 3.

Souty, J. (2014) 'O quilombo como metáfora: espaços sociais de resistência na região portuária carioca', P. Birman, S. De Sa Carneiro, C. Machado and M. Pereira Leite (eds), *Dispositivos urbanos e trama dos viventes: ordens e resistências.* Rio de Janeiro: FGV, chapter 11.

Swyngedouw, E. (2010) 'Post-Democratic Cities for *Whom* and for What?'. *Regional Studies Association Annual Conference.* Budapest.

Toy, M.-A. (2006, 30 January) 'New China Rises on the Backs of Unpaid Migrant Workers', *The Age.* Available at: www.theage.com.au/news/world/new-china-rises-on-the-backs-of-unpaid-migrant-workers/2006/01/29/1138469606834.html (accessed 7 July 2016).

Conclusion

Event-led urban image construction, a critical appraisal

As one of the highest expressions of contemporary spectacle, mega-events are fascinating, complex mechanisms for the production of meaning. While they often function in self-serving ways to reify the production and consumption of the event itself, mega-events also play a central role in expanding the narratives and mythologies that lie behind the construction of a city's image. The main objective of this book was to identify, describe and analyse in details the mechanisms used in the artificial construction, projection and manipulation of the image of the city and to reveal the main motives behind this 'economy of appearances' (Tsing 2000). With its openly critical perspective, much of the book explored the role of the mega-event spectacle as a powerful instrument of deception and disguise in the accelerated transformation of the urban environment. It detailed diverse strategies devised to legitimate the radical transformation of host cities, including the city as spectacle and the city of exception.

This book began with the hypothesis that an inquiry into the ways cities build, control and use their image can provide a glimpse into the inner workings of urban society. It posited that the study of the mechanisms involved in the production of an urban image allows a privileged access into the complex, unspoken rules that underlie social relations and exposes the power struggles that shape and define urban organization, especially in highly unequal countries. Even if many of the resulting images are often nothing more than mirages, potemkin façades and fabricated projections, they do reveal rich and multiple insights into the collective desires, aspirations and ambitions of those who have the power to shape and transform the urban landscape. By examining the way decision-makers, event organizers and other influential agents choose to portray the city, what they push to the fore and what they brush aside and conceal, the book sheds light upon the social biases, prejudices and ideologies that govern our society of spectacle.

Images of power and the power of images

Evidence presented in this book suggests that controlling the image of the city is a way for economically and politically powerful elites to control society, to reshape it according to their own devices and to serve their own interests. As great moments of collective euphoria, mega-events represent unequal opportunities for ambitious elites, market agents and their political allies to impose a particular worldview upon society, especially by implementing measures that resonate with their revanchist impulse and accumulative fantasies. Examples cited suggest that mega-events represent unique opportunities to launch highly profitable projects and advance the commercial interests of a small group of well-connected stakeholders. They also reveal the disproportionate power that marketers and public relations firms have in defining urban reality and how it is advertised to the world, in ways that clearly advantage the economic and cultural interests of dominant groups. This work thus exemplified the way power is gradually sliding towards greater executive and judiciary powers which are increasingly professionalized and specialized.

The book explained the role of mega-events in the construction, consolidation and reconfiguration of the neoliberal city and the way they facilitate the adoption of often unpopular, market-oriented urban policies, helping them appear at once urgent, necessary, unavoidable and beneficial for all. Mega-events provide power elites with hegemonic tools by which to promote their political visions and warrant their control over the production and reproduction of urban space. Their uncompromising focus on image, and on securing the benefits promised to International Sporting Federations, broadcasters and global sponsors, have allowed a market logic to determine the way cities are governed and managed, without any regard for transparent democratic accountability.

Another aspect of event-led urban image construction widely discussed in this book is the way these initiatives affect the reconfiguration of power structures, and exacerbate pre-existing power disparities, class prejudices and segregation. Urban image construction often discounts the voices of the poor in favour of multinational corporate sponsors, powerful property developers, international sports organizations and other local and international elite interests, which prioritize financial benefits over meeting basic local needs. Other traditionally powerful economic and political forces, including media industries and their representatives, also exert tremendous control over the physical and discursive transformation of the city. Event-led image construction can thus foster socio-spatial polarization, exacerbate power imbalances and aggravate existing tensions rooted in class, race and gender inequalities, thereby triggering conflicts, especially when they attempt to mask and deny these shortcomings.

The book further suggests that the image of the city promoted by these events heralds the return to an urban reality marked by polarization, unequal access to services and resources, and ultimately what Klein (2007) has called 'democracy avoidance'. Stories from both Beijing and Rio point to the re-emergence of authoritarianism, characterized not by a benevolent paternalism, but by an increasingly vindictive and brutal posture. Many of the image-construction examples cited in this book underline the revanchist character of event-led urban interventions, and suggest that beyond the mere dismantling of a planning vision concerned with the common good, we are witnessing the rise of a regressive mode of city management that fosters the active concealment of structural inequality and the edification of a permanently divided society.

Recognizing mega-events' global positioning as the vanguard of contemporary entrepreneurial planning, the book paid particular attention to the strategies used by event host coalitions and other stakeholders to transform the urban environment. It highlighted the important territorial implications of event-led urban image-construction initiatives and their central role in the reconfiguration of space. It showed how these events are instrumentalized by local political and economic elites to strengthen their hold upon urban territory, helping mask the power relations that have brought the event and its attendant urban and social dynamics into being. The host city status thus assists power-holders in mobilizing the urban landscape to sustain the state-assisted privatization and commodification of the urban realm while exacerbating territorial imbalance and conflicts.

But more than anything, the book has revealed the important role of the state in leading this transformation and in implementing exclusive urban policies and repressive measures that give free rein to their non-elected allies. If, on the one hand, local leaders still use image construction as a political tool to reconfigure the state and secure access to power, legislation and other instruments of rule, governments are also largely instrumentalized, manipulated and exploited as partners in asymmetrical public–private partnerships that shield capitalists from all risk and ultimately weaken democracy.

The concrete and dubious legacies of event-led image construction

Far from being harmless and innocuous, image-construction strategies have very concrete impacts with potentially long-term consequences. While promoting images of community, solidarity and universally shared communities of interest, mega-events are the source of multiple social, economic and psychological hardships for many of the city's most vulnerable citizens. This book detailed multiple aspects of event-led image-construction efforts that directly targeted the poor, including the tightening of state control, the criminalization of the informal and the concealment of the unsightly, which also compromised basic rights and freedoms, including the right to the city and the right to be seen. Among other forms of abuses associated with event-led transformations, the violation of housing rights, especially with the massive expulsion of the poor, is certainly the most pervasive, insidious and well-documented offence, with lasting impacts on those who have invested much time, resources and energy providing for their own housing needs.

One should not underestimate the effects of image-construction strategies upon cities and their inhabitants. Many of the tangible legacies of the mega-events studied in this book have been shown to negatively impact vulnerable population groups. The present research confirmed the important role played by event-led image-construction in the destruction of social and cultural fabric that has taken decades, if not centuries, to develop. But this urban fragmentation, which fosters disconnection and alienation and leaves behind a trail of exclusion and despair, is only part of the multiple dispossessions suffered by the poor. The fact that public funds are redirected away from welfare uses and into the pockets of a handful of oligarchs and are not spent on education, hospitals or social programmes represents a real impediment to the realization of social and economic gains for the urban majority. Often associated with socially regressive urban policies, event-related interventions bring little improvement to the quality of life of those at the bottom of the economic strata.

This book exposed the highly divisive and exclusionary character of many state-led urban image-construction interventions, which often seek to exclude elements of society that are deemed irrelevant to the new economy. By projecting a highly restricted image of the city, which omits the poor, the ugly or the informal, these images and their manipulation by market forces and power-holders can have very real, direct and lasting consequences for the lives of those excluded. The book also suggests that the socio-aesthetic transformation of the city promotes the construction of a consensual image, hostile to conflict and difference, and the silencing of dissident voices. Aestheticized representations of the urban landscape, at once unproblematic and simplified, thus carry a powerful depoliticizing effect.

Just as Debord (1967) had forewarned, the mega-event spectacle continues, more than ever, to act as a social opiate to pacify the masses. By distracting attention from real urban issues, it helps defuse the numerous conflicts linked to the city's transformation, silence discordant voices, deflect criticism and delegitimize opposition. The danger is that exclusionary images of the city constructed and projected in preparation for mega-events become naturalized by local elites as part of normal, desirable reality, and serve as ammunition to promote more exclusive urban policies. Carefully crafted, consensual urban representations can prevent the elaboration of alternative visions, thereby helping legitimate the reproduction of urban policies that silence and make invisible part of the population. By contributing to the crystallization of a partial and reductive representation of society, confirming long-held beliefs in the potential of a city unencumbered by impoverished masses, and allowing for the construction of certain members of society as structurally irrelevant and unworthy of equal rights and opportunities, these consensual images both validate and consolidate exclusive urban ideals, exacerbate class prejudice and perpetuate patterns of stratification.

In spite of its highly critical stance, the book maintains that all hope is not lost, but that a new era in the hosting of mega-events may be on the horizon. Evidence suggests that the imposition of a 'geography of exclusion' (Sibley 1995) such as the one seen in the construction of the event-city does not go unchallenged, and that expressions of political opposition to the hosting of mega-events are on the rise. Growing media interest in social-interest stories, the increasing popularity of critical academic research on global-scale festivals and the rise of a political activism against the hosting of sporting mega-events demonstrate that the status quo may no longer be acceptable. While International Sporting Federations attempt to skirt mounting criticism by selecting host cities located in less democratic countries, this tactic will not be sustainable in the long run. The way mega-events have become more environmentally conscious over the last decade, at least in their discourse, also suggests the possibility for more democratic, socially conscious and ethically responsible mega-events in the future.

As people start to realize that the biggest show on earth is actually the biggest heist on the planet, they may begin grasp the extent to which they have been conned, and come to realize, as sociologist Carlos Vainer (2016) puts it, that they have been fooled by the emperor's new clothes. Still, the city will ultimately get back on its feet and snap out of its stupor; people will not capitulate and passively accept to be discarded, ignored and silenced. They will rise and use their collective might and creativity to devise innovative new strategies and reinvent the city as a more just, fair and equal place for all.

References

Debord, G. (1967) *La société du spectacle.* Paris: Folio.
Klein, N. (2007) *The Shock Doctrine: The Rise of Disaster Capitalism.* Toronto: Alfred A. Knopf.
Sibley, D. (1995) *Geographies of Exclusion.* London: Routledge.
Tsing, A. (2000) 'Inside the Economy of Appearances', *Public Culture.* Vol. 12, No. 1, pp. 115–144.
Vainer, C. (2016, August) 'Calamidade Rio 2016', *Jornal das economistas.* Vol. 325, pp. 5–6.

Index

For Product Safety Concerns and Information please contact our EU
representative GPSR@taylorandfrancis.com
Taylor & Francis Verlag GmbH, Kaufingerstraße 24, 80331 München, Germany

www.ingramcontent.com/pod-product-compliance
Ingram Content Group UK Ltd.
Pitfield, Milton Keynes, MK11 3LW, UK
UKHW020948180425
457613UK00019B/592